Les collections des arts du spectacle et leur traitement

Performing Arts Collections and Their Treatment

Congrès de Rome
SIBMAS
Congress
(2002)

P.I.E. Peter Lang

Bruxelles · Bern · Berlin · Frankfurt am Main · New York · Oxford · Wien

Nicole LECLERCQ, Kristy DAVIS
& Maria Teresa IOVINELLI (dir./eds.)

Les collections des arts du spectacle et leur traitement

Performing Arts Collections and Their Treatment

Congrès de Rome
SIBMAS
Congress
(2002)

Ce volume est publié par / This volume has been published by la Société inter-nationale des bibliothèques et musées des arts du spectacle (SIBMAS) avec le soutien de /with the support of Les Archives & Musée de la Littérature (Bruxelles/ Brussels) et le / and the Centre belge de la SIBMAS.

■ARCHIV
ES & MUS
EE ᴰᴱ ʟᴬ LITT
ERATURE

Nous voudrions remercier pour leur aide à la réalisation des présents actes / We would like to thank the following for their help in making this publication pos-sible: Véronique Meunier, Marc Quaghebeur, Laurent Rossion et Jan Van Goethem.

Couverture / cover: Aldert Mijer, graveur ; Carel Allard (1648-ca. 1709), éditeur. Habit de l'Indienne du ballet du *Triomphe de l'amour*. Gravure aquarellée. Cos-tume pour le ballet de cour *Le Triomphe de l'amour*, musique de Jean-Baptiste Lully, livret de Isaac de Benserade et Philippe Quinault, 1681.

© P.I.E. PETER LANG S.A.
Éditions scientifiques internationales
Brussels / Bruxelles, 2012
1 avenue Maurice, B-1050 Brussels / Bruxelles, Belgium / Belgique
pie@peterlang.com ; www.peterlang.com

ISBN 978-90-5201-818-8
D/2012/5678/35

Printed in Germany / Imprimé en Allemagne

Library of Congress Cataloging-in-Publication Data
International Association of Libraries and Museums of the Performing Arts. Congress (24th : 2002 : Rome, Italy) Les collections des arts du spectacle et leur traitement / Congrès de Rome = Performing arts collections and their treatment / SIBMAS Congress (2002) ; Nicole Leclercq, Kristy Davis & Maria Teresa Iovinelli (dir./eds). pages cm English and French. Papers from the 24th SIBMAS Congress, Rome, September 2-7, 2002. Includes bibliographical references and index. ISBN 978-90-5201-818-8
1. Performing arts libraries--Congresses. 2. Performing arts--Museums--Congresses. 3. Performing arts archives--Congresses. I. Leclercq, Nicole. II. Davis, Kristy. III. Iovinelli, Maria Teresa. IV. Title. V. Title: Performing arts collections and their treatment.
Z675.P45I565 2002   026.7902--dc23   2012013260

CIP available from the British Library, GB.
"Die Deutsche National Bibliothek" lists this publication in the "Deutsche National-bibliografie"; detailed bibliographic data is available on the Internet at <http://dnb.de>.
« Die Deutsche National bibliothek » répertorie cette publication dans la « Deutsche Nationalbibliografie » ; les données bibliographiques détaillées sont disponibles sur le site http://dnb.de.

Table des matières / Table of Contents

Séance inaugurale

Opening Session

Opening Speech

Claudia BALK

President, SIBMAS (Munich – Germany)

It is a great pleasure for me to be able to welcome you here to the 24th Congress of SIBMAS. As you know, this is the first opening of a SIBMAS Congress in my capacity as President and it is a special pleasure for me because I regard Maria Teresa very highly and know what really great trouble she has already taken in the initial conceptual and structural preparation of this Congress. So my initial thanks go to the promoters of this Congress, Maria Teresa Iovinelli and her committed team. My thanks also go to the President of the SIAE, Professor Masi, for hosting and – as I have heard – also sponsoring our Congress here in Rome this year.

Since Maria Teresa will later talk about the subject matter of the Congress, another duty falls to me. At our last ExCom meeting, when amongst other things we discussed the preparation of this Congress, "cara" Maria Teresa kindly game me a clear brief for the opening speech. I should talk about "what SIBMAS is". As we are welcoming a number of participants, particularly from Italy, who could be regarded as "outsiders", or perhaps in a more positive light as "newcomers", this duty, of course, makes sense.

"What SIBMAS is" – I believe that each of us who has come together here has a slightly different idea of this. It is made up from different levels of knowledge, as well as from individual personal experiences and recollections. Visits to Congresses, impressions of lectures, preparations of one's own lectures, cooperation of diverse kind from preparing Congresses to working on the Council and, "last but really not least" personal meetings – "what SIBMAS is" is made up from all these individual impressions.

And of course not only this – there are also objective facts such as the fact that we are meeting here for the 24th Congress of SIBMAS and that this organisation has now existed for 48 years. This means that in two years' time at our next congress in Barcelona we can celebrate the

50th anniversary of its existence. This Saturday at the General Assembly I will be able to report to you in greater detail on initial plans for this pleasant occasion. But in now touching upon the history of SIBMAS I cannot avoid remembering one person who is very closely linked with this history: I mean André Veinstein, who passed away last December. We will be remembering him at the General Assembly at the end of this week.

But to return now to the factual data about SIBMAS: we currently number more than 250 members on all five continents and maintain contacts with various other organisations such as ICOM, FIRT, IFLA, ITI, OISTAT and others. Strengthening these contacts has been a particular matter of concern for me over the last two years, and this Saturday there will also be details to report on this. In any event, I believe that SIBMAS is very well embedded in a very diverse network, which can in turn only be of benefit to every single one of our members.

All of us who work in theatre collections are, from our everyday working life, very well aware of the serious pertinent question concealed behind the simple phrase "what SIBMAS is". For is it not the case that in our job we are time and again asked "What do you do, what do you actually collect?". Often I try to clarify this to outsiders with simple sentences such as "We collect almost everything which is left behind from an evening at the theatre and which is used as preparation for theatre work". In this connection I like to remind people in the same breath that yesterday's evening at the theatre is already theatrical history. Rescuing theatre museums and collections from, what is unfortunately not a seldom, shadowy existence and demonstrating their legitimacy as an indispensable and extremely valuable element of cultural memory – this is a difficult, necessary but appealing task. In this connection there is one concept which I am particularly fond of when publicly trying to explain our work and the necessity of it: Theatre collections are "the memory of the theatre"! All the collections, whose representatives you are, together represent an immense cultural treasure, which is united under the patronage of SIBMAS. How best to deal with these impressive cultural assets, this is the theme of our Congress here, and I hope we have a rich exchange of experiences.

The subject matter and structure of this Congress have been discussed and decided upon by the ExCom of SIBMAS that is by the Executive Committee and the Council, the bodies that are to be elected again this Saturday. Candidates are still being sought for this, and for details I would ask you to please contact our General Secretary, Claire Hudson. The deadline for nominations is 24 hours before the General Assembly. I can only encourage you to participate, since active executive bodies are of the utmost importance for every organisation. Or in other words, the answer to "what SIBMAS is" also comes specifically from its individual members and how they are involved.

Finally, over the next few days I should like to wish all of us useful and stimulating contributions, fruitful discussions and intellectual enjoyment, as well as great pleasure in your personal meetings, which certainly also count amongst the benefits of a Congress. Thank you for your attention.

Mot d'ouverture

Claudia BALK

Présidente de la SIBMAS (Munich – Allemagne)

C'est pour moi un grand plaisir de pouvoir vous accueillir à l'occasion de ce 24ᵉ congrès de la SIBMAS. Mon premier congrès SIBMAS en tant que présidente, vous le savez, me tient spécialement à cœur car j'ai une grande estime pour Maria Teresa et je sais les difficultés qu'elle a eues à surmonter lors de la conception puis de la préparation de cet événement. C'est pourquoi mes premiers remerciements iront aux organisateurs, Maria Teresa Iovinelli et son équipe si dévouée. Des remerciements que j'adresse également au Président de la SIAE, le professeur Masi, puisqu'il nous accueille ici et aujourd'hui à Rome et – me suis-je laissé dire – puisqu'il parraine nos journées.

Étant donné que Maria Teresa présentera plus tard le thème de notre congrès, une tâche m'incombe. En effet, lors de la dernière réunion du ComEx, alors qu'entre autres nous discutions de l'organisation de ce congrès, « cara » Maria Teresa m'a gentiment invitée à parler, pour le discours d'ouverture, du sujet suivant : « Qu'est-ce que la SIBMAS ? » Or, nous accueillons ici de nombreux participants, spécialement d'Italie, que l'on pourrait décrire comme « des personnes extérieures », ou peut-être, pour adoucir les contours de cette expression, comme des « nouveaux venus ». Dès lors, bien sûr, cette tâche est tout à fait opportune.

« Qu'est-ce que la SIBMAS ? »… Je crois bien que chacun de nous a son idée sur la question. Mais une idée qui est néanmoins légèrement différente de celle de son voisin, car elle se bâtit à différents niveaux de connaissance, d'expériences personnelles, de souvenirs intimes… Ainsi, se rendre à un congrès de la SIBMAS, y écouter les communications ou en préparer une, participer de diverses façons à son organisation, travailler au Conseil et, enfin et surtout, y faire des rencontres personnelles… « Qu'est-ce que la SIBMAS », sinon l'ensemble de ces ressentis individuels ?

Mais plus encore : il y a aussi des faits objectifs, comme notre rencontre ici, pour le 24ᵉ congrès de la SIBMAS, ou comme l'existence de cette organisation qui date maintenant de 48 ans. Cela implique que dans deux ans, lors de notre prochaine rencontre à Barcelone, nous célébrerons son 50e anniversaire. Ce samedi à l'assemblée générale, j'en dirai plus sur ce que nous projetons de faire pour cette belle date. Par ailleurs, si l'on s'intéresse à l'histoire même de la SIBMAS, il est impossible de passer outre celui qui lui est si intimement lié : André Veinstein, bien sûr, qui nous a quittés en décembre dernier. Nous honorerons sa mémoire lors de l'assemblée générale à la fin de la semaine.

Mais, pour en revenir aux données factuelles la concernant, la SIBMAS compte actuellement plus de 250 membres sur les cinq continents et entretient des contacts réguliers avec plusieurs organisations telles que l'ICOM, la FIRT, l'IFLA, l'IIT, l'OISTAT, etc. Renforcer ces contacts a été pour moi une constante préoccupation ces deux dernières années – j'en parlerai plus longuement samedi. De toute façon, je pense vraiment que la SIBMAS fait partie d'un réseau extrêmement riche qui, à son tour, peut bénéficier à chacun de nos membres.

Quiconque parmi nous travaille dans le domaine des archives théâtrales sait, dans son travail quotidien, l'importance de cette simple phrase « Qu'est-ce que la SIBMAS ? ». Dans notre travail, on nous demande sans cesse « En fait, de quoi vous occupez-vous, qu'est-ce que vous conservez ? » J'essaie souvent de résumer cela, pour les novices, en quelques phrases simples comme « Nous tentons de recueillir le plus possible de ce qui reste d'une soirée au théâtre ou de ce que l'on emploie pour préparer le travail théâtral ». À ce titre, j'aimerais rappeler que la soirée que nous avons passée hier au théâtre est déjà de l'histoire théâtrale... Sauver les musées et les bibliothèques du théâtre de ce qui est, hélas le plus souvent, une vie dans l'ombre, et montrer leur légitimité en tant qu'éléments indispensables et précieux de notre mémoire culturelle est une mission ardue, vitale... et passionnante. Dans cet ordre d'idée, j'aime beaucoup, quand je tente publiquement d'expliquer notre travail et son intérêt, utiliser ce concept : les archives théâtrales sont « la mémoire du théâtre » ! Réunis tous ensemble, les fonds d'archives, dont vous êtes les garants, représentent un immense trésor culturel, groupés sous le patronage de la SIBMAS. Comment gérer au mieux ces merveilleux biens culturels ? C'est tout le thème qui nous réunit ici, et j'espère que nous pourrons pleinement discuter de toute notre expérience.

Le sujet et la structure de ce congrès ont été discutés et approuvés par le ComEx de la SIBMAS, c'est-à-dire par le Comité exécutif et par le Conseil, les deux organes qui seront réélus ce samedi. Il est toujours possible de se porter candidat à ces fonctions. Pour plus d'informations, je vous prie de bien vouloir contacter Claire Hudson, notre secrétaire générale. Les candidatures sont recevables au plus tard vingt-quatre heures avant l'assemblée générale. Je ne peux que vous encourager à participer, car pour toute organisation, un exécutif actif est essentiel. En d'autres termes, la réponse à la question « Qu'est-ce que la SIBMAS ? » découle également de ceux qui la composent et de la façon qu'ils ont de s'impliquer.

Enfin, j'aimerais vous souhaiter à tous, pour les prochains jours, des communications utiles et stimulantes, des discussions fructueuses, beaucoup de joies intellectuelles, sans oublier des rencontres personnelles agréables, qui contribuent, à n'en pas douter, à l'intérêt d'un congrès. Merci de votre attention.

Introduction

Maria Teresa IOVINELLI

Biblioteca e Museo Teatrale SIAE del Burcardo (Rome – Italy)

I think many of you already know me, as I have been attending SIBMAS congresses since the 18th congress in Lisbon, in 1992. During these ten years, I have been very engaged in SIBMAS' life. I was elected in the Council in 1994, and was Vice-President from 1996 to 2000.

I am very happy to welcome you now in Rome. The theme we have chosen for this 24th Congress, *Performing Arts Collections and Their Treatment*, is very wide: when planning the structure of the congress, we tried to reproduce the way each item in our collections goes, from the decision whether to acquire it or not, to the dissemination of information about our collections outside of our library, archive or museum.

First of all, we will hear about what our collections are, and how they were started. The history of our collections deeply influences the decisions we take every day; every library or museum has a peculiar nature, which is the product of this history. One of our major efforts is trying to redefine the meaning and the scope of our collections, day after day, at the same time for the sake of their history and peculiarities, and in view of the necessary adjustments to our users' needs.

The history of our collections sometimes originates some practical problems connected to their expansion and storage spaces. The Burcardo Library and Theatre Collection – which is housed in a late 15th century building – is a good example of an institution confronted with serious problems of storage spaces. We will hear about some interesting experiences in planning and designing new spaces for performing arts collections, and about the new possibilities offered by the recent technological developments.

When launching the call for papers for this congress, we were aware of the great interest aroused by technological developments among librarians, archivists and museum curators. Yet, we did not expect to receive so many papers related to the issues of digital collections and computerised cataloguing: the sessions devoted to technological issues will be very, very full, and I am looking forward to learning about your experiences in these fields.

This congress is very important for me from a national point of view, too. I am happy to welcome the many representatives of the Italian institutions devoted to the preservation of the memory of the performing arts. I hope at least some of them will join us in our work for SIBMAS, but in any case, this is a good opportunity for the progress of our initiatives aiming to an effective network of the Italian performing arts collections.

I know by experience that the friendly relationships we are able to establish with our colleagues during SIBMAS congresses are very important and fruitful. I hope you will enjoy the various convivial occasions provided by this congress, and I wish you a good stay in Rome. *Benvenuti al 24°Congresso Internazionale della SIBMAS.*

Introduction

Maria Teresa IOVINELLI

Biblioteca e Museo Teatrale SIAE del Burcardo (Rome – Italy)

Beaucoup d'entre vous me connaissent sans doute puisque je prends part aux congrès de la SIBMAS depuis le 18ᵉ congrès à Lisbonne en 1992. Pendant ces dix années, je me suis fortement impliquée dans la vie de la SIBMAS. J'ai été élue au Conseil au 1994 et j'ai été vice-présidente de 1996 à 2000.

Je suis très heureuse de vous accueillir à Rome. Le thème que nous avons choisi pour ce 24ᵉ congrès, *Les Collections des arts du spectacle et leur traitement*, est très vaste : au moment où nous réfléchissions à la structure du congrès, nous avons essayé de retracer le parcours de chacun des objets de nos collections, depuis la décision de l'acquérir ou de ne pas l'acquérir jusqu'à la diffusion des informations concernant nos collections en dehors de nos bibliothèques, archives ou musées.

Nous apprendrons d'abord ce que sont nos collections et comment elles ont commencé. L'histoire de nos collections influence profondément les décisions que nous prenons chaque jour ; chaque bibliothèque ou musée possède sa propre nature, qui est le fruit de cette histoire. Une de nos principales préoccupations est de redéfinir la signification et l'étendue de nos collections, jour après jour, aussi bien par égard pour leur histoire et leurs spécificités que dans la perspective des ajustements nécessaires aux besoins de nos utilisateurs.

L'histoire de nos collections génère parfois des problèmes techniques liés à leur expansion et à leurs espaces de rangement. La Biblioteca e Museo Teatrale SIAE del Burcardo – qui est logée dans un bâtiment de la fin du XVᵉ siècle – est un bon exemple d'une institution confrontée à de sérieux problèmes d'espaces de rangement. Nous entendrons parler de quelques expériences intéressantes de planification et de conception de nouveaux espaces destinés aux collections des arts du spectacle, ainsi que de possibilités nouvelles offertes par les récents développements technologiques.

Au moment de l'appel aux communications pour ce congrès, nous avons pris conscience du grand intérêt que les développements technologiques éveillent parmi les bibliothécaires, archivistes et conservateurs de musées. Nous ne nous attendions pas, néanmoins, à recevoir autant de communications portant sur les collections numériques et les catalogues informatisés : les sessions consacrées aux questions technologiques seront très remplies et je suis impatiente d'en savoir plus au sujet de vos expériences dans ce domaine.

À mes yeux, ce congrès est aussi d'une grande importance du point de vue national. Je suis heureuse de saluer les nombreux représentants d'institutions italiennes consacrées à la préservation de la mémoire des arts du spectacle. J'espère que certains d'entre eux se joindront à notre travail pour la SIBMAS mais dans tous les cas, l'occasion est bonne pour l'avancement de nos initiatives visant à la création d'un réseau efficace des collections italiennes des arts du spectacle.

Je sais par expérience que les relations amicales que nous établissons avec nos collègues pendant les congrès de la SIBMAS sont très importantes et fructueuses. J'espère que vous apprécierez les divers moments de convivialité offerts par ce congrès et je vous souhaite un agréable séjour à Rome. *Benvenuti al 24°Congresso Internazionale della SIBMAS.*

Première partie

Les collections des arts du spectacle : typologies et problèmes

First Part

Performing Arts Collections: Typologies and Problems

En matière d'art du théâtre, quelles archives, pour quelle vie, au sein d'un organisme vivant ou d'un centre d'archivage ?

Vincent RADERMECKER

Archives et Musée de la Littérature (Bruxelles – Belgique)

L'archive théâtrale n'est pas une archive « historique » comme celle d'un homme d'État ou d'un homme d'Église. Elle n'émane jamais directement de l'activité concernée : le jeu du comédien sur le plateau. Celui-ci n'est abordé, reconnu, interrogé... que par des biais. Ce sont ces biais que nous avons voulu mettre au jour, montrant que toute politique d'acquisition est aussi une politique de choix, ainsi qu'une politique de gestion des fonds sur le lieu même de leur production.

L'aspect physique du contact entre public et acteurs, et sa répétitivité, nous semblent rejoindre ce que Hans-Georg Gadamer a évoqué dans *Vérité et méthode* quand il fait de la « finitude » de la vie humaine, la caractéristique fondamentale de toute expérience du savoir et de la beauté, expérience que chaque individu, chaque génération, chaque peuple... renouvelle et revivifie.

Cette « revitalisation » nous paraît liée au phénomène, et de la réappropriation collective – la collectivité s'identifie et se perpétue dans les écrits –, et de l'intimité secrète où se noue tout contact profond. Le spectacle n'est pas, dans sa plus grande exigence, show exhibitionniste, mais présentation, réactualisation d'un contact antérieur, personnalisé, secret. La différence de destin, maléfique pour Thèbes, bénéfique pour Athènes, des cadavres de Polynice et d'Œdipe dans la tragédie des Labdacides, nous semble significative sur ce point, en lien avec la corporéité du métier de l'acteur.

Il importe donc, à l'heure où la mode – et la nécessité – sont au : « tout à tous, par et à travers l'informatique » de réinterroger notre pratique à sa source même, pour, enrichis par ces réflexions, se lancer dans les nouvelles technologies avec assurance et justesse.

De la sorte, cette communication qui se démarque des autres contributions plus axées sur la catalographie et la mise en ligne des collections, aura participé, nous l'espérons, à rendre équilibré et fructueux le 24ᵉ congrès de la SIBMAS.

Les grandes catégories d'archives théâtrales

Les archives théâtrales peuvent être divisées en trois catégories : deux principales et une annexe. Il y a celles que nous nommerons « volontaires », qui sont générées par l'entreprise théâtrale comme toute entreprise en engendre, et celles « involontaires » qui sont produites dans le courant même de la préparation et de la réalisation d'un spectacle. Les premières comprennent les papiers conservés « par devers » les gestionnaires : courrier, documentation, actes juridiques... mais aussi des documents qui le sont « par delà » : affiches, programmes... Les secondes sont le travail d'adaptation sur l'œuvre originale, les brochures annotées des acteurs, la maquette du décor, la bande-son...

Outre ces archives *sui generis* existent des documents « reflets » qui touchent à la vie de l'entreprise, aux spectacles produits ou à la biographie de tel ou tel participant. Ils peuvent émaner de personnes étrangères aux activités – journalistes, historiens... – mais aussi de travailleurs impliqués dans le processus – comptables, acteurs, animateurs... Traditionnellement, ce sont les comptes rendus des journaux et des revues qui forment le gros de ces écrits. Toutefois s'y insèrent aussi un livre de souvenirs, des notes dans un journal, un mémoire, une monographie... Aujourd'hui, la captation audiovisuelle tend à être LE reflet par excellence.

La spécificité de ces documents dans la perspective d'une histoire du théâtre

Les archives générées par le spectacle proprement dit

Débutons par une comparaison qui, comme toute mise en perspective, vaut ce qu'elle vaut. Vous disposez des ingrédients d'une recette du Moyen Âge. Vous savez qu'on mélangeait « à feu doux » deux potirons, trois cailles, du miel et du persil... Sans oublier une demi-carotte. Retrouverez-vous la saveur d'antan ? Non. Votre plat sera une « reconstitution ». La qualité des produits, le modèle des casseroles, le procédé de cuisson... ainsi qu'une manière de manger et de goûter qui a évolué, feront du tout une « expérience ». Sans plus. Ce fossé qui se crée, après des siècles, pour ce qui est des légumes et de la viande, se creuse, quand il s'agit d'éléments humains, bien plus vite. Auriez-vous la maquette des décors et les costumes d'une pièce jouée il y a cent ans, le texte avec l'annotation des intonations, la partition de la musique, disposeriez-vous d'acteurs aux physiques et voix ressemblants, le mélange, si vous le tentez, ne sera qu'un bric-à-brac. Non seulement la chose différera de la réalisation initiale, mais, du fait de son caractère de « reconstitution », le spectacle sera, dans son essence, plus éloigné de son modèle que de toute autre pièce jouée aujourd'hui. C'est que le théâtre existe moins par la qualité et la spécificité de ses éléments que par le mélange – et même quelque chose de plus – qui en est fait[1]. Il est un phénomène qui, par excellence, n'existe que dans un temps et un lieu déterminés.

Soyons cependant attentif – à ce point de notre raisonnement – à ne pas verser dans l'excès contraire pour, emporté par le goût du paradoxe, faire de ce « mélange » quelque chose de magique. N'y a-t-il pas des opéras qui, réalisés dans les conditions d'antan, continuent à charmer ? De même, une recette ancienne ne peut-elle redevenir à la mode, et un spectacle « façon classique » produire lui aussi, d'une certaine manière, un enchantement ? Peut-être d'autant plus que l'on ne s'attend pas à y voir de la « vérité » !

Mais il y a une différence ! Comme la saveur d'une recette de grand-mère vient de ce que nous goûtons un « dépaysement », alors qu'à l'époque elle ne faisait que rassasier, le spectacle « reconstitué » sera goûté parce que les vers en seront peut-être, dans une sorte de court-circuit temporel, plus beaux et plus parlants. Alors qu'au moment de sa création, l'on admirait surtout, qui sait, la puissance vocale de la vedette, son charisme… Bref, une autre « relation » est instaurée. Presque un autre phénomène.

Et, de même que le fait de manger comporte toujours et assouvissement et goût – dans des proportions toujours différentes –, le spectacle comporte lui aussi un aspect connu et un aspect inconnu, un caractère de vérité et un caractère de fausseté. Et cet aspect de fausseté peut – de manière délibérée bien sûr – consister en la mise en relief d'un donné passé, « usé jusqu'à la corde ». Il y a plus. L'art en lui-même évolue

---

[1] « N'est-ce pas grâce au même idéal que la morale de la foule (au théâtre, par exemple) est infiniment supérieure à la morale des unités qui la composent », tiré de Maurice Maeterlinck, « L'inquiétude de notre santé morale » dans *L'Intelligence des fleurs*, Paris, E. Fasquelle, 1907, p. 166. Voir aussi Guy de Maupassant, « Les foules » dans *Chroniques*, t. 2, Paris, Union générale d'éditions, 1980, p. 17-18. : « C'est au théâtre que l'on peut le mieux étudier les foules. Quiconque fréquente un peu les coulisses a entendu bien souvent les acteurs dire : "La salle est bonne, aujourd'hui", ou bien : "Aujourd'hui, la salle est détestable. " (…) Et chaque soir le phénomène recommence. Car chaque salle de spectacle forme une foule, et chaque foule se forme une espèce d'âme instinctive différente par ses joies, ses colères, ses indignations et ses attendrissements, de l'âme qu'avait la foule de la veille et de celle qu'aura la foule du lendemain. »

sans cesse entre l'appropriation d'éléments anciens et la découverte de procédés nouveaux. Ainsi, dans *Minetti* de Thomas Bernhard, l'auteur crée une structure dramaturgique nouvelle avec des personnages qui dialoguent de manière inhabituelle. Mais – contrepoint nécessaire –, toute l'œuvre s'appuie sur le souvenir qu'ont les spectateurs du théâtre classique, et spécialement de Shakespeare dans deux de ses chefs-d'œuvre, *Le Roi Lear* et *La Tempête*. La nouveauté, au théâtre, est, d'une certaine manière, condamnée à n'exister que sur le « cadavre » du passé.

L'on voit où nous voulons en venir. Le passé irriguant le présent, la conservation d'éléments déjà utilisés dans le processus de réalisation sera, en art dramatique, un levain pour l'avenir.

Cette réutilisation s'opère de différentes manières. Le metteur en scène réutilisera la bande musicale d'une de ses mises en scène antérieures ou une idée de décor, des types de déplacements... Il peut aussi s'inspirer d'autres mises en scène, soit pour s'en démarquer, soit pour s'en rapprocher.

D'autres réappropriations sont plus complexes et plus fécondes. Une partie des cours sténographiés de Louis Jouvet faisant répéter *Dom Juan* de Molière ont été réutilisés pour l'écriture d'*Elvire Jouvet 40*[2]. La jeune comédienne d'alors étant juive, et le cours ayant été donné début 1940, l'auteur a ressenti que l'histoire rejoignait le théâtre, imposant une interrogation urgente qui forme le cours de la nouvelle réalisation.

Mais l'archive « involontaire », n'est-elle pas aussi simple miroir de l'activité passée. Et, si oui, de quelle manière ?

Pour mieux cerner cette spécificité, ayons recours à une autre comparaison. L'art militaire marie deux éléments principaux : la force morale des participants et l'art de la tactique joint à l'état de l'armement. Ces deux éléments, s'ils paraissent parfois associés à une culture, une tradition, un peuple... ne le sont pas tout à fait. Prime le but, la victoire : destruction ou défense... Aussi est-il possible d'étudier les tactiques d'Hannibal sans être carthaginois. De même, la notion d'Empire – le modèle de l'Empire romain par exemple – sera reprise aussi bien par Napoléon que par Hitler.

Quand il s'agira d'illustrer l'art dramatique, les « reconstitutions » – qui sont aussi le fait des musées de cire pour des individus particuliers – ne seront plus de mise. Mieux vaut utiliser des maquettes de

---

[2] *Elvire Jouvet 40. Sept leçons de L. J. à Claudia sur la seconde scène d'Elvire du* Dom Juan *de Molière tirées de « Molière et la comédie classique » de Louis Jouvet,* Paris, Solin, 1992.

décor, des manuscrits d'adaptation, des notes de mise en scène…, toutes choses à vision globale et réalisées en cours de processus.

D'un côté donc, une activité qui use « dans l'absolu » d'éléments efficaces et opérationnels liés qu'ils sont à une volonté de s'approprier une réalité et de devancer ce qui, même en imagination, demeure difficilement envisageable, est illustrée *a posteriori* par des objets particuliers et « théâtralisés ». De l'autre, une coquille d'activité ne se justifiant qu'en particulier – le temps d'une représentation, pour des spectateurs x –, et basée sur la réutilisation ludique, sera illustrée, pour mémoire, par des documents essentiellement « panoramiques » et témoignant du processus en question.

Outils pour de nouvelles créations, miroir du passé, l'archive « involontaire » cumule encore une autre fonction : celle d'agent de processus identificatoires.

Un document sera d'autant mieux conservé, dupliqué,… que le spectacle a été, pour une raison ou une autre, surchargé de réalité ou surinvesti artistiquement. Pour prendre un exemple « belge », l'on conservera la maquette des décors de l'opéra *La Muette de Portici* qui, en 1830, enflamma la fibre patriotique d'une Belgique dont la devise « L'Union fait la force » résonnait haut et clair. L'on prendra aussi soin – jusqu'à les éditer – de l'adaptation de *Macbeth* par Maeterlinck, ou des indications de mise en scène d'un Stanislavski pour *Othello*, ou d'un Jacques Copeau pour telle pièce de Molière.

Qu'en déduire ?

Fondé sur la métaphore qui décrit la réalité – et non sur la volonté de façonner, s'approprier ou apprivoiser celle-ci – le théâtre génère, dans la catégorie que nous avons appelée « involontaires », des archives utiles et inutiles, tant à la mémoire du passé qu'aux créations futures. Il s'ensuit une qualité spécifique de ces « témoins » : maquette, bande-son, plan de mise en place des acteurs, partition avec intonations d'un texte… Ni tout à fait morts, ni tout à fait vivants, ces éléments ne sont ni des archives dans l'acception courante du terme, simple témoignage du passé, ni des éléments artistiques au sens plein. Ils tiennent des deux, cristallisant l'« âme » d'une collectivité.

Malgré cette ambivalence, ces documents demeurent le parent pauvre de l'archivage. Les institutions les conservent peu. Les créateurs et propriétaires les délaissent, les considérant tantôt comme un matériau, tantôt comme un vestige. Les archivistes, eux, ne leur réservent que rarement la place qu'ils méritent parce qu'ils sont aussi difficiles à trouver qu'à conserver.

Ce choix ou cet état de fait n'est – vu avec un peu de recul –, ni idéal pour une juste mémoire des réalisations scéniques, ni adéquat pour d'éventuelles contributions aux créations.

Il conviendrait de se demander s'il ne faut pas accroître la recherche de ces documents, en favoriser la conservation, et réfléchir à leur mise en valeur. Éventuellement en les mettant en parallèle ou en les confrontant avec les deux autres catégories d'archives que nous abordons maintenant.

Les documents d'entreprise

À première vue, la conservation et l'utilisation des documents que nous avons appelés « volontaires » semblent plus simples. Émis pour résoudre des problèmes spécifiques, ces archives témoignent des étapes de la réalisation. Leur mise bout à bout reconstitue, plus ou moins fidèlement, l'image, si pas des spectacles, du moins de leurs conditions d'élaboration : contacts pris, motivations, difficultés rencontrées...

Si tel est le cas pour la plupart des théâtres, parfois les choses se compliquent. Ainsi, lorsque l'entreprise est liée à une personnalité, situation courante au XXe siècle. Documents privés et documents officiels, vie personnelle et vie publique se mêlent alors au point qu'il devient difficile de les distinguer. Surtout quand, comme au milieu du siècle passé, la conjoncture a permis jusqu'à un certain point le développement d'expériences théâtrales sans l'aide de subventions officielles.

Peu de documents attestent dans ce cas des relations entre l'animateur et ses collaborateurs. Et, de même que l'archive du spectacle a une tendance centrifuge se focalisant sur le carrément artistique ou le carrément événementiel, le danger vient ici d'une tendance centripète, l'archive étant encline à refléter plutôt le trajet artistique d'une personne que d'une équipe.

Un de nos fonds lié à des « chœurs parlés » mis sur pied par une élève de Jacques Copeau, professeur au Conservatoire de Bruxelles, Madeleine Renaud-Thévenet – Stocq de son vrai nom –, ainsi que les archives d'une autre figure emblématique du théâtre belge de l'entre-deux guerre, Albert Lepage, offrent de telles caractéristiques. Dans ces exemples, cette particularité est poussée à l'extrême. Elle peut n'être que partielle comme dans le cas du « Jeune Théâtre » belge. Là, subventions, relations avec l'ONSS (Office national de Sécurité sociale), actes juridiques... sont mêlés à des documents parfois extrêmement personnels, tant privés qu'artistiques, émanant de la personnalité phare.

Il est encore un leurre qui menace les documents « volontaires » destinés au public. On a tendance à voir dans les affiches, les programmes... un reflet fidèle. Or, spécialement dans le cas de l'affiche, il s'agit d'être vigilant. Car, en dehors de tout lien avec la qualité des spectacles, l'affiche peut être « parasitée » – tout en restant un témoignage –, soit par l'habileté du designer, soit par la volonté de la compagnie de faire événement.

De même, on ne peut compter pour médiocres tous les spectacles réalisés sous une affiche « standard », uniquement dactylographiées, comme ce fut longtemps l'usage dans nos théâtres, et mettre au pinacle les premiers spectacles « off » dotés de moyens publicitaires. L'affiche « neutre » est, d'une certaine manière, plus fidèle, faisant appel à la mémoire des habitués. L'affiche « artistique », si elle embellit nos collections, est, en tant que document « doublon » au spectacle, sujette à caution.

Plus généralement, il importe de se souvenir, pour une politique d'acquisition, que l'artifice est au cœur de l'art dramatique et irrigue, non seulement les réalisations, mais la gestion et même les contacts d'un théâtre. L'on peut même postuler que, plus l'artifice a contaminé la vie « privée » du théâtre, plus la valeur réelle des productions devient suspecte. Or, l'archive « pétrie d'artifice » est plus riche, plus accrocheuse, qu'un document neutre mais parlant. Il suffit de voir comment sont fêtés certains jubilés. S'en souvenir pour l'acquisition et la présentation des documents, est judicieux. Qui, s'il ne connaissait Baudelaire que par sa correspondance, imaginerait son génie ? Instinctivement, peut-on dire, nous confondons comportement artistique et réalisation artistique. De là notre insistance : l'archiviste de théâtre étant sevré – contrairement à celui qui travaille sur les beaux-arts... – du produit artistique, il convient de ne pas transposer les critères de sélection d'un domaine à un autre.

Pour conclure

Moins directement en prise avec l'activité artistique, les archives privées et/ou d'entreprises sont plus susceptibles d'illustrer cette activité fondée en un lieu et en un temps. Mais il convient de ne pas faire primer la qualité propre des pièces – lettre d'un écrivain célèbre, affiche à l'iconographie ou au graphisme séduisant, programme intellectuellement fouillé... – sur l'analyse de la cohérence et de l'intensité du tout en tant qu'activité collective.

Les archives qui témoignent
a posteriori *de l'activité et des spectacles*

Nous ne parlerons pas ici des écrits habituellement rédigés sur base d'archives. Envisageons trois types de documents « reflet » : la presse, la mémoire orale et les captations audiovisuelles.

Si elle est diversifiée et assidue – malheureusement, c'est de moins en moins le cas – la presse est une source de premier plan. Mais malgré son « effet miroir », elle ne témoigne que des premières représentations. On peut presque dire que, plus un spectacle est potentiellement vivant, plus l'accouchement est long et difficile. Un spectacle exceptionnel n'arrive à maturité qu'après une période de tâtonnements, certains metteurs en scène prévoyant même des représentations « pour du beurre », entre amis, en province... *A contrario*, un spectacle peut éblouir, le temps d'une représentation, pour décevoir ensuite. Le théâtre, en fait, n'est qu'en tant qu'il répète. Et, de même que les cycles de vie ne tirent leur vitalité que d'eux-mêmes – et non d'une ressemblance aux cycles précédents – de même la « chaque fois nouvelle » représentation d'un spectacle ne tient son efficacité que si le mélange des divers ingrédients s'opère toujours de nouveau, selon des processus éprouvés.

Il faut dès lors comparer – ou acquérir – presse de la création et presse des reprises et tournées ; presse des quotidiens et presse des magazines.

Comme la presse n'offre qu'une image fragmentaire, il est bon de la compléter par des interviews, de la mémoire orale... émanant d'acteurs artistiques de l'entreprise : auteurs, metteurs en scène, acteurs, spectateurs... ou de personnes extérieures au processus : secrétaire, comptable, contrôleur des comptes... Ces témoignages tantôt collent à l'événement : enquête auprès des spectateurs après le spectacle... tantôt sont réalisés *a posteriori* : interview à l'occasion d'un jubilé... Plus les témoins seront diversifiés, plus leur confrontation sera intéressante.

Qu'en est-il des captations audiovisuelles ? La déformation est ici à la mesure de l'attrait et de l'intérêt. Les différents éléments et êtres que la représentation lie en un même temps et lieu, le sont dans un processus à base et à finalité fictionnelles. Cette fiction est entravée – mais aussi stimulée – dans son accomplissement par la matérialité des corps et du décor. D'où le sentiment d'un manque, même après une représentation réussie. Cette nostalgie « de la fiction non totalement réalisée », il est tentant d'en surprendre et suspendre les traits dans une image en deux dimensions, en l'occurrence la captation audiovisuelle. Mais la fiction n'est pas la virtualité. Son processus – même dans le cerveau de l'écrivain – est plus complexe et se nourrit des obstacles qu'il rencontre autant que de l'inspiration proprement dite. On représente sur scène non ce qui est arrivé, mais quelque chose qui, à base ludique, entretient l'échauffement d'un mystère dont la force poétique reste entière car liée à un mélange particulier de corporéité et de spiritualité. Ce mélange et ses effets puisent leurs racines dans des peurs, des défis et des instincts, comme l'a démontré Johan Huizinga dans son *Homo Ludens*. Les danses initiatiques, les chants sacrés, les duels et les joutes en sont des formes larvées.

L'image vidéo témoigne donc de l'acte artistique, mais ne le remplace pas.

On y voit les choix d'adaptation, de qualité de la distribution, l'option du décor (dépouillé ou baroque, technicisé ou artisanal...) ; on y suit les évolutions des personnages ; on y découvre la scénographie... Chaque année, un important budget est consacré, aux Archives et Musée de la Littérature, aux captations audiovisuelles qui, réalisées dans des conditions les plus neutres possibles, témoignent des représentations marquantes d'œuvres francophones belges. La vidéo rend donc compte, si pas de l'effet de ce face à face, du moins des spécificités du message et des moyens mis en œuvre.

Les implications de ces constats dans la politique d'acquisition des archives

Quel centre d'archivage peut se vanter d'une politique d'acquisition consciente, planifiée, et menée étape par étape ? Peu de livres traitent de ce sujet. Comment dégager une ligne de conduite ?

L'archive n'existe que par sa rareté, comme l'histoire par ses silences. De même que ce n'est pas à l'histoire à décider de ses silences, ce n'est pas à l'archiviste de décider des acquisitions.

Mais l'archive théâtrale est-elle un dinosaure ? Le chasseur de dinosaures doit découvrir et traiter le mieux possible. Mais celui qui travaille sur des documents vieux de quelques dizaines d'années, parfois moins, ne fait pas que recueillir : il suppute la valeur de documents à acquérir pour les générations à venir. Aussi l'état dans lequel ils leur parviendront car les supports vieillissent différemment : la photo couleur se dégrade plus vite que la photo noir et blanc ; les cassettes audiovisuelles plus rapidement que les DVD, les CD-ROM...

Bref, l'accumulation est un danger, d'autant que notre monde, avec sa technicité, encourage le cumul.

L'archiviste aura donc un rôle auprès des entreprises théâtrales elles-mêmes : à la politique d'acquisition, il convient d'adjoindre ce que nous nommerons une politique de gestion.

La politique de gestion

Un premier moyen, facile et efficace, de conscientiser les théâtres, centres culturels..., possesseurs d'archives, est de répertorier. L'informatique – nous avons l'exemple du *Répertoire des arts du spectacle* en France –, facilite l'échange d'informations et permet aux chercheurs, artistes... de savoir où, quand, comment consulter tel ou tel document « caché ». Sachant leurs collections répertoriées et, sous certaines conditions, consultables, les institutions sont d'autant plus motivées à mieux conserver. Le danger gît toutefois dans une tendance consécutive au classement à outrance[3]. Il convient de rendre directeurs et documentalistes conscients de la nécessité de dissocier les documents « en série » à classer chronologiquement, alphabétiquement... et les documents « thématiques » où l'ordre émane du travail en lui-même et qui sont à compiler.

Un autre souhait serait de faire en sorte que les normes « juridiques » d'archivage ne deviennent pas des normes effectives. Si, par exemple, l'on ne doit légalement conserver que la comptabilité des cinq dernières années, pourquoi ne pas la garder malgré tout une année sur trois ou sur quatre, de manière à permettre des études statistiques ?

Une autre initiative que l'archiviste spécialisé encouragerait avec bonheur est d'élargir l'éventail des objets ou documents préservés. En faisant prendre conscience que la richesse ne tient pas seulement à la valeur intrinsèque des pièces, mais à leur diversité et aux rapports possibles à réaliser *a posteriori*. Ainsi, certaines archives habituellement délaissées : brochures de comédiens, adaptations annotées, maquettes de décor, costumes... seraient heureusement collationnées. Du moins pour certaines réalisations.

Autre source ayant trait au cœur de l'activité théâtrale – le jeu du comédien –, les notes des metteurs en scène aux comédiens ou les cahiers de régie sont, aujourd'hui que le théâtre « interprète » les œuvres, des documents incontournables pour une histoire future. Cela au même titre que les brouillons des auteurs. Pour donner une image de la richesse et de la profondeur des réalisations actuelles, il ne suffit plus d'allier la correspondance entre auteur et théâtre à quelques mémoires ou souvenirs d'acteurs célèbres.

Ceci pour l'aspect « qualité ». Mais il y a aussi l'aspect « série » des représentations. L'on pourrait à ce niveau suggérer aux directions du théâtre de faire enregistrer par la régie – un formulaire suffit – quelques

---

[3] En parlant avec des documentalistes attachés à différents théâtres belges, il est apparu, dans une réunion de la SIBMAS Belgique à la Maison de la Bellone, que la préoccupation principale des employés était souvent le rangement et la mise à disposition rapide pour d'éventuels consultants. Le souci premier de l'historien d'art est, lui, de retrouver les documents « en l'état », surtout pas surclassés. Car le document parle autant par lui-même que par son contenu. Le rangement maniaque inquiète l'historien qui préfère une simple identification et datation des lots. Le journaliste, lui, préfère une documentation rapidement identifiable, comme peut-être la direction du théâtre si elle organise un jubilé, une rétrospective... Il semble qu'un juste milieu soit à trouver.

variations journalières : nombre de spectateurs, qualité de l'interprétation, réaction du public, événements particuliers à signaler, personnalités présentes à mentionner. Le metteur en scène y ajouterait quelques mots sur la qualité de la représentation du jour. Réalisées sur le long terme, ces notes représenteraient une riche source d'analyse et de réflexion. D'autant plus, évidemment, qu'est intéressante la production en cours.

Bref, de même que la dramaturgie ne se focalise plus sur les vedettes mais sur l'imbrication de personnages aux origines et destinées multiples, tout fonds d'archives s'humanise en diversifiant les points de vue et les types de documents. Une étude comparative est alors rendue possible d'ensemble à ensemble.

Sensibiliser les théâtres à la longévité de certains supports numérisés en lien avec l'informatique, est également utile, comme d'harmoniser les procédures d'accès aux collections *in situ*. Notre informaticien a installé un logiciel et une base de données de même configuration que les nôtres dans un théâtre proche, le Rideau de Bruxelles. Le travail du chercheur en est facilité, tout comme l'échange d'informations d'institution à institution.

La politique d'acquisition

« L'acquisition est d'abord une sélection » mentionne un manuel destiné à l'acquisition dans les bibliothèques publiques[4], qui détermine trois publics, l'actuel – celui qui fréquente la bibliothèque –, le potentiel – celui qui pourrait la fréquenter – et le futur qui « existe surtout dans l'imaginaire de la collectivité qui se projette dans le futur. Il est en fait héritier de la mémoire de cette collectivité, au niveau de développement de cette collectivité [...] »[5].

C'est ce troisième public que visent les fonds patrimoniaux[6]. Les réflexions qui suivent sont autant de pistes pour aider à une « sélection » des archives théâtrales.

Des sources d'origines diverses

Trois types d'archive sont, nous semble-t-il, identifiables selon leur origine : les archives privées, les archives d'entreprise et les archives ministérielles, les deux premières pouvant parfois se confondre.

---

[4] Bernard Calenge, *Les Politiques d'acquisition. Constituer une collection dans une bibliothèque*, Paris, Éditions du Cercle de la librairie, 1994, p. 25.

[5] *Ibidem*, p. 38.

[6] *Ibidem*, p. 83.

L'archive privée est chargée de plus d'affectivité et de créativité. D'une certaine facticité aussi : on tend à se donner et à donner une image de soi. Acquise, elle permet un jeu d'échos entre partenaires, correspondants, lieux de travail... Les motivations, la genèse des projets s'en trouvent éclairées.

Les archives d'entreprise sont plus sérielles. Moins lisibles, plus secs, plus objectifs aussi, ces documents prennent en compte tous les participants des projets et réalisations. Des aspects pratiques – financiers et organisationnels – y apparaissent : budget à équilibrer, équipe à rassembler, éléments matériels à concevoir et à réaliser ou à se procurer par don ou achat...

Considérées comme rébarbatives, les archives ministérielles traiteront des aspects juridiques et contractuels de la structure ou de la personne étudiée. On apprend par exemple dans nos fonds comment René Kalisky a longtemps « mendié » une aide à l'écriture. Comme certains théâtres en sont arrivés à des conflits presque passionnels avec tel ou tel homme politique qui leur semblait indifférent ou impuissant face à leurs problèmes financiers...

Mises en interaction, ces trois types d'archives forment une constellation qui éclaire le ciel artistique d'une période. Aux Archives et Musée de la Littérature à Bruxelles, nous possédons ainsi les archives d'un scénographe, Arik Joukoswski, architecte de nombreux centres culturels construits dans les années 1970-1980. Nous détenons le fonds d'un théâtre auquel il a collaboré : le Théâtre de l'Esprit frappeur, ainsi que les fonds d'autres ensembles de la même époque : le Théâtre du Parvis, le Théâtre de l'Alliance... Nous disposons également des archives de comédiens ou comédiennes : André Burton, Suzy Falk... qui participèrent à ces aventures. Une série d'archives ministérielles concerne la période en question.

Le mélange de différents types de document

Chaque type d'art du spectacle possède ses documents « privilégiés ». En ce qui concerne l'opéra, on est enclin à collationner et à préserver les maquettes des décors du fait que les livrets et partitions sont souvent édités. Les costumes y sont aussi parfois récupérés et réutilisés. Le conservateur d'un musée du cirque s'attachera, lui, aux objets, car ils permettent la reconstitution des gestes qui présidaient aux manipulations. L'archiviste de théâtre collationnera en priorité les écrits et les supports audiovisuels.

Ces choix ont leur fondement, mais ils figent l'archivage.

Devant l'impossibilité matérielle de tout conserver, comme de trancher : « je garde », « je jette », peut-être une commission composée d'historiens du spectacle et d'artistes pourrait-elle sélectionner et se donner les moyens d'acquérir telle ou telle maquette, la brochure d'un tel metteur en scène ou tel acteur, quelques accessoires et costumes si l'événement le requiert... Les fonds qui en résulteraient seraient représentatifs et intéressants.

Séparer archivage et documentation

Les documents classés par ordre alphabétique de noms de personnes ou de noms de théâtre sont plus facilement et plus rapidement accessibles que les fonds structurels conservés, eux, en l'état, pour des consultations plus longues, plus attentives et plus précises.

Éventuellement répartis dans des centres spécialisés distincts, ces deux types de classement contenteront journaliste et chercheur. Bien les différencier éviterait les manipulations inutiles ainsi que la contamination de types de tri, classement et valorisation différentes.

Nouveaux supports en relation avec la qualité de l'archivage

A priori, dupliquer une archive n'est pas déterminant pour l'archivage. Sa mission est avant tout de conserver et de restaurer. Grâce à l'informatique, et vu la longévité limitée de certains documents, il est toutefois indispensable d'enregistrer ou de photographier l'information sur des supports durables. De nouvelles possibilités s'ouvrent en ce domaine[7].

Ces manipulations ont un impact et sur la manière dont on prend connaissance des documents, et sur l'archivage. D'autant que la tendance est au renouvellement constant des supports, de manière à perfectionner l'accessibilité et la convivialité des réseaux. En conséquence, l'approche du particulier au général se généralise. La fragmentation s'immisce dans nos pratiques.

Cette évolution est accentuée par un autre phénomène. De manière naturelle, l'information tend à se résumer en trois formes : citations, images et nombres. Le phénomène est frappant pour qui se penche sur les civilisations anciennes. Certains historiens ont enrobé inconsidérément de chair ces bribes et ces comptabilisations. Si notre époque se méfie des pseudo-reconstitutions, elle tend à transformer l'environnement en extraits, images et chiffres.

---

[7]   Voir à ce propos, entre autres : Almuth Grésillon, *Éléments de critique génétique. Lire les manuscrits modernes*, Paris, Presses universitaires de France, 1994.

L'archive théâtrale n'étant pas un témoignage direct de l'activité dont elle témoigne, la tentation est forte de retravailler les sources. Sans remettre en question les progrès merveilleux de l'interaction, ne faut-il pas se ressouvenir, surtout dans un domaine humain comme le théâtre, que la source – et elle oblitère autant qu'elle révèle – demeure le point de départ de tout contact vrai, et qu'une difficulté d'accès fait « partie du jeu ».

Quel pôle centralisateur pour quel type d'archive ?

On écrit l'histoire d'une vie ; un livre est écrit ; un spectacle s'écrit.

Chacun de ces trois pôles mériterait un archivage selon que l'archive y est miroir d'existence, conservation d'actes artistiques ou témoignage d'interprétation. Tout centre d'archivage peut donc se donner une spécificité et/ou user de la complexité du phénomène, mêlant grande et petite histoire, art et réalité.

À Bruxelles, des archives théâtrales se retrouvent dans des lieux à vocation « historique » comme aux Archives de la Ville de Bruxelles ou au Centre d'études et de documentation Guerre et Société. Ceci, en plus des fonds détenus par les théâtres et par les institutions qui leur sont liées, ainsi que par les centres spécialisés.

Une réalisation majeure serait, pour notre Communauté française de Belgique, à l'instar ou dans le sillage du *Répertoire des arts du spectacle* en France, d'éditer un ouvrage (ou une base de données) renseignant sur le contenu des collections, les choix opérés, la manière dont le tout est conservé, accessible… Fortes de tels renseignements, les acquisitions de chaque organisme gagneraient en homogénéité.

Un peu sèche, colorée, enfonçant des portes ouvertes, notre présentation ne donne pas des « impératifs ». Elle éclaire la spécificité de l'archive théâtrale et délimite quelques objectifs d'une politique d'acquisition, objectifs que les nécessités journalières et les innovations technologiques fragilisent.

Comme l'eau sert à boire, à refléter ou à rafraîchir, l'archive théâtrale est tantôt le reflet d'une pratique, tantôt un ingrédient pour une création nouvelle, tantôt le levain d'une culture.

A contrario d'autres sources archivistiques, elle demeure longtemps dans le circuit de la « vie », patrimoine de l'institution mère ou consultable dans des centres. Elle ne se solidifie pas comme la lave d'un volcan. D'où les compromis entre réutilisation avec transformations et « solidification en l'état ».

Cet écartèlement n'est toutefois pas effrayant ou stérile. Comme l'a évoqué Hans-Georg Gadamer, le processus vivant est nécessaire :

> Ce phénomène se vérifie par exemple dans le théâtre moderne, là où une tradition résulte d'une mise en scène, d'une création de rôle ou de la pratique d'une exécution musicale. On n'a pas ici affaire à une juxtaposition arbitraire d'interprétations, à une simple variété de conceptions ; il se dégage plutôt de l'imitation et de la modification inventive de certains modèles, une tradition avec laquelle tout nouvel essai devra se confronter.[8]

---

[8] Hans-Georg Gadamer, *Vérité et méthode. Les Grandes lignes d'une herméneutique philosophique*, Paris, Seuil, « L'ordre philosophique », 1976, p. 45.

The Institute for Letters, Theatre and Melodrama of the Cini Foundation

Maria Ida BIGGI

Fondazione Giorgio Cini (Venice - Italy)

Count Vittorio Cini set up the Cini Foundation in 1951 in memory of his son Giorgio, who tragically died in an air crash. During more than fifty years of activity, on the island of San Giorgio Maggiore, opposite Saint Mark's, many collections and donations have arrived, several of them with connections to the performing arts.

The Cini Foundation comprises a series of research Institutes. One of them, founded in 1957 by Vittore Branca and Piero Nardi, is called *Istituto per le Lettere, il Teatro e la Musica* (Institute for Letters, Theatre and Melodrama). Under the direction of Giuseppe Ortolani many collections relating to the performing arts were acquired or donated.

Many Institutes are now concerned with these arguments: one of them, established in 1985 and directed by Professor Giovanni Morelli is dedicated to musical studies. Others, like the Italian Antonio Vivaldi Institute, which is entirely devoted to the Venetian musician, or the Ottorino Respighi Institute, are more specific. Over the last two decades, the Institute for Music has acquired many archives regarding important artistic personalities in 20th century Italian music: Arrigo Boito, Gian Francesco Malipiero, Alfredo Casella, Nino Rota, Aurél Milloss, Camillo Togni, Egidina Sartori and Olga Rudge. This Institute has also produced many publications about them.

However, I want to focus attention on the Institute for Letters, Theatre and Melodrama. This Institute contains a library, open to the public, of more than 20,000 books and 300 periodicals concerning music, theatre and dance. Many books are old and rare: collections of theatrical operas, works and treatises on dramaturgy with a specific section dedicated to the Veneto. Of great interest is the entire library of Gian Francesco Malipiero who was a passionate bibliophile and owned a lot of 16th century publications and early books in general. Some of those were books sources of inspiration for his eclectic librettos. There is also the recent acquisition of the Gallia Library with more than 1,100 books on Wagner and his work.

The most important endowment is, without any doubt, the collection of Ulderico Rolandi, a Roman doctor who died in 1951. Rolandi was a collector, critic and eminent scholar who, during his life, created this big opera libretto collection. It comprises more of 37,500 pieces and 5,000 scores. In reality, it is one of the biggest collections in the world concerning Italian opera – not only opera in Italy, but also Italian opera in other countries – Mozart, Handel, Haydn, Meyerbeer, all wrote Italian operas. Some of the librettos are very rare; the earliest date starts from the second half of the 16th century while others are almost contemporary. The 19th century librettos represent some 44% of the entire collection. They comprise both which are no longer in the repertory and those in an enormous section dedicated to the first performances of the most important composers such as Rossini, Bellini, Donizetti, Verdi, etc in Europe and all over the world. This collection is also very interesting for studying the history of dance since it contains some 2,000 independent prints of dance librettos. To these must be added the great number of dances indicated inside the opera librettos.

Around the opera librettos, Rolandi built a specialised library for opera studies, and in this, it is possible to find repertoires, treatises, monographs, theatrical texts and a rich series of literary editions of great librettists, as well as theatrical chronology, musical scores, theatre bill and a miscellany of portraits of singers, composers, musicians, and librettists.

The Fondazione Cini promoted a computerised catalogue which was to have led to the publication of a paper catalogue with the Istituto dell'Enciclopedia Italiana; however, it has now been replaced by an on-line cataloguing project, guided by a scientific committee composed of Anna Laura Bellina, Bruno Brizzi, Luigi Ferrara and Anna Maria Pensa, all pupils of professor Gianfranco Folena who originated the enterprise. This project allowed for the publication of the electronic files in a Website endowed with instruments which permitted interrogations of the database both with selection queries on indexed fields (names, places, types) and free research of descriptive fields (title-page, examinations, dramatic personage and performers, character types, etc) with a full-text research motor with advanced functions (wild cards, Boolean operator, relationship of nearness and distance, etc).

Alongside the Rolandi Collection is the Theatrical Iconographic Archive created some 30 years ago by Maria Teresa Muaro. It contains visual materials comprising the staging of opera: scenography, stage design, costumes, photos, book illustrations, title-pages and prints of theatrical subjects from early to modern times. In the Collection it is possible to find a section on theatrical architecture with plans and interior and exterior views and a particular focus on the Venetian area. The entries regarding each imagine, bring together all possible information about the object and the theatrical representation to which it refers. Presently, there are 16,000 slides, but now we are adding 5,000 more. Like the Rolandi project, the catalogue will be put on line, and then we have to add the photographic material from the Eleonora Duse and Aurell Milloss collections.

It is now possible to make a search on the iconographic material using the Archimusica programme used for the Acom project; however, it is not possible to have the image on video.

The Iconographic Archives, also contains the original material of the Cini Foundation art collection of original drawings and prints: these are stage design sketches of the Bologna School with the Certani Collection and they are signed by Ferdinando and Francesco Bibiena and collaborators; together with many by Antonio Basoli and his school. Others sketches are from the Milan School, that came from the Daniele Donghi Collection, which were made by his father, Felice Donghi, a stage designer at the Scala Theatre during the 19th century. In the latter collection it is possible to find important drawings by Alessandro Sanquirico, Pietro Gonzaga, Francesco Fontanesi and other stage designers of this era.

Of particular interest is the album signed by Anton Maria Zanetti the Elder, in which it is possible to find a total of 350 caricatures of the variegated world of the 18th century Venetian stage. Here leading actors and singers in the world of music are often recognised by a manuscript annotation: examples are the Giuseppe Farinelli or Sebastiano Ricci.

Among the collections is a very important corpus relating to the actress Eleonora Duse. It was donated to the Cini Foundation in the 1960 and 70's and it contains different, but complementary, documents of varying origins which together form a collection permitting deeper analysis of the artistic figure of the actress.

Her granddaughter, Sister Mary of Saint Mark, Eleonora Ilaria Bullogh, the daughter of Duse's only daughter, donated the most important part of the collection. It arrived in Venice during the 1968: it contains letters, books, scripts, dresses, personal objects and furniture. Some 570 letters were written by Eleonora to different correspondents, many in the last years of her life. It is possible to find the names of famous writers or theatrical people such as Giovanni Papini, Grazia Deleda, Natalia Gontcharova, Yvette Gilbert, Angelo Conti, Gabriele D'Annunzio, Marco Praga, Ermete Zacconi or Morris Gest. Many letters, perhaps about a thousand, were addressed to her by people such as Giuseppe Primoli, Ida Rubinstein, Luigi Pirandello and others. Many letters directed to the Duse's daughter Enrichetta after the actress death and up to 1954; there are also letters by various authors to different addressees.

The corpus consists of the correspondence between actress and daughter and it contains more than 80 letters; and most interestingly are Enrichetta's notebooks.

Some 40 scripts contain autograph production notes and documents of theatrical life: contracts and indications for costume and stage designers. Sister Mary's donations include some hundreds of original photographs that represent the actress from her youth to her last days in the United States.

It is possible to find some rare examples of 19th century prints showing the actress in costume or portraits made in the studios of important artists like Edward Steichen, Mario Nunes Vais and Giuseppe Primoli. The archive was further enriched by the donation of Olga Signorelli. Together this material provided the basis for the CD-ROM prepared for the Duse exhibition organised in Venice last year. More than 700 photographs are catalogued on the CD-ROM; a very simple system enables the material to be used for the purposes of performance didactics.

Nineteen dresses owned by the actress form an integral part of the collection. These dresses were her private property, but she sometimes used them on the stage. Other collections relating to Duse are the Carandini-Albertini Collection, which contains the correspondence between the actress and Arrigo Boito, and the Agostini Collection, which has 130 letters addressed to the Casali family, 113 of them written by Eleonora Duse during the years between 1884 and 1922; the Cervi Collection contains a mere 6 letters from Duse to Annunzio Cervi, an official during World War I.

The Nardi Collection brings together different kinds of material, including 40 letters from Duse to Giuseppe Giacosa. This and the Olga Signorelli Collection contain material assembled by the author while writing Duse's biography. The Signorelli Collection contains over 500 letters written by Duse to various correspondents and about 350 to her friend Emma Garzes of Florence, wife of the actor Francesco Garzes. As of yet, none of these materials have been catalogued.

Last but not least is the donation of Aurél Milloss (1906-1988) to the Cini Foundation. Its is a precious collection of some 3,000 books, including important 17th and 18th century treatises, original photos, theatre programmes, magazines and periodicals documenting the art of dance during the 20th century.

A summary cataloguing project of the 5,000 photos of the dance performances in the collection is now under way with the *Photoshop Infofile* program.

The Herla Project: Inventorying Gonzaga's Italian and European Documentation on Performance

Simona BRUNETTI

Fondazione Mantova Capitale dello Spettacolo (Mantua - Italy)

This paper aims to point out the leading criteria, the methodological and practical questions, leading to the elaboration of the Herla database (Fig. 1) of the Mantova Capitale Europea dello Spettacolo Foundation[1]. The Herla archive doesn't include a pre-existing collection, but is the result of a specific document research project still in progress. The Foundation has been operating within the municipal and provincial cultural projects of Mantua since January 1999, and a group of researchers have been setting up a store of data, bibliographical information and sources aiming at the creation of a Research Centre on Renaissance and Baroque Theatre, or, to be specific, on the origin and development of the *Commedia dell'Arte*.

The Herla Project is carried out by a team of experts, co-ordinated by Professor Umberto Artioli (Professor of Storia del teatro e dello spettacolo at Padua University), and entails collecting the documentation related to the spectacular events supported by the Gonzagas at the height of their maximum splendour (1480-1630), and recording it in one comprehensive electronic database. During this period the Dukes of Mantua stood out from other reigning houses because of the special attention devoted to theatrical spectacles. Engaging many important and worthy artists, they employed theatres to organise unforgettable events, which were meant to spread and entrench their political power. Among the most significant results of this effective policy we can mention the celebrations arranged in 1608, on the occasion of the marriage between Prince Francesco Gonzaga and Infanta Margaret of Savoy; or the triumphal scenery prepared for many sovereigns at their entrance to the city.

---

[1] www.capitalespettacolo.it.

Moreover, so many companies of Comici dell'Arte served under their patronage throughout Europe, that from 1585 to 1630 Mantua became the capital of the *Commedia dell'Arte*. Tristano Martinelli (1557-1630), the actor who first played Arlecchino in Parisian fee-paying theatres during the theatrical season 1584-1585, was Mantuan as well. Changing his name to one coming from ancient and popular French tales, he stained the typical grey Zanni costume with the bright colours of medieval jesters and turned the mask into that of a devil.

The story of "Herla King" is one of the several versions of the legend, and finds its roots in the Nordic saga of the "wild hunt"; the character who leads a "hellish band of souls" – is condemned to furiously pursue howling wild beasts during certain stormy nights. *Arlecchino* seems to derive its name from this source; evidence of this can be found in the lumps that were on the black mask of the origin – a residue of devilish horns. Our database is called Herla to pay homage to this tradition.

The topic of the research is considered in its widest sense: not only is theatre examined in its literal sense (Court theatre, *Commedia dell'Arte*, Opera, Jewish theatre), but also all the events which required stage setting – starting from sumptuous nuptial banquets, in which actors, dancers and musicians took part, up to triumphal entries, funeral celebrations, carnival masquerades, and tournaments. These are not necessarily spectacular events: often some relatively unimportant names, such as those of the intermediaries between the Gonzaga family and some actors or musicians turn out to be important links to reconstruct spectacle artists' activity. As far as the chronological limit of the whole project is concerned, the research work has recently been focused on the decades between the end of the 16th and the beginning of the 17th century (1570-1630), pointing out the spectacle-related relationship and exchanges between the Gonzaga and the Imperial Court.

The multiplicity of the cases investigated is due to the remarkable variety of the sources examined: printed volumes of acted dramas; chronicles coming from envoys from other Courts; payments to craftsmen who made the scenarios; legal deeds useful to reconstruct artists' biographies; but above all a plentiful correspondence (between Court and comedians but also signed by academicians, writers, architects, musicians or sovereigns from other countries) offering information about spectacular events in a wider sense. This kind of material, representing a conspicuous part of the entire world-wide documentation on Renaissance and Baroque spectacles is scattered all over Europe: Paris, London, Madrid, Vienna, Munich, Innsbruck, Lion, Lisbon, Brussels, Antwerp and all the Italian cities related with Mantuan Court at that time.

A fundamental part of the job lies in setting out the database and establishing methodological criteria. To begin with, in order to settle some practical and operational rules, we've made a preliminary exploration at Mantua State Archive, collecting about a hundred document samples representing a useful variety of typologies or contemplating as wide a range of spectacular cases as possible. This work allowed creating an ideal cataloguing model, with a few essential variables, to record the document as a whole. After verifying that none of the main existing databases had the optimum characteristics needed, we decided to create an *ad hoc* electronic archive. Next to traditional fields we chose to supply each card with a *struttura* and some *categorie*.

The *struttura* tells in detail which kind of evidence we are recording. This item is strictly linked with our call number, the so-called *segnatura definitiva*, which is made of two parts, a letter and a number. The letter refers to the document typology specified in the field *struttura*. So far we've used six letters:

A – *atti, decreti e simili* (legal deeds, decrees and similar acts)

C – *corrispondenza* (correspondence)

I – *iconografia* (iconography)

L – *altro tipo di materiale* (other materials such as plays or chronicles)

P – *pagamenti* (payments)

S – *edizioni a stampa* (printed books). A file with this letter is pretty different from the others, because it only records the characteristics of the volume in print and not its content, which will be entered in other files.

Elenco Strutture

1. Corrispondenza

1.1 Firmata da comici

1.2 Firmata dai Gonzaga

1.3 Firmata da altri

1.3.1 Teatrali

1.3.2 Extra teatrali

1.4 Non firmata / non identificata

2. Pagamenti

2.1 Artigiani

2.1.1 Pittori

2.1.2 Scultori

2.1.3 Intagliatori

2.1.4 Decoratori

2.1.5 Falegnami

2.1.6 Lanternai

2.1.7 Muratori

2.1.8 Fabbri

2.1.9 Architetti e apparatori

2.2 Oggetti di scena

2.2.1 Strumenti musicali

2.2.2 Maschere

2.2.3 Costumi

2.2.4 Legname

2.2.5 Tessuti

2.2.6 Cristalli

2.2.7 Lumi e torce

2.2.8 Gioielli ed ornamenti

2.3 Altro (profumi, vernici, facchini, ecc.)

2.4 Attori

2.4.1 Comici

2.4.2 Danzatori

2.4.3 Musici

On the other hand, the field *categorie* describes the document through a grid of terms expressly conceived for this project, and allows the researcher to associate data not available by traditional searches. Our *categorie* links in a thematic route fleeting fragments of evidence, at first sight, doesn't always seem related.

Elenco Categorie

1. Attori

1.1   *Comici*

1.2   *Danzatori*

1.3   *Musicisti*

1.4   *Cantanti*

1.5   *Buffoni e intrattenitori*

1.6   *Nani*

1.7   *Cerretani, saltimbanchi, acrobati, giocolieri*

1.8   *Altri interpreti*

2. Itinerari attori

2.1   *Città*

2.2   *Mezzi e vie di percorso*

2.3   *Spese*

2.4   *Permessi*

3. Relazioni degli attori

3.1   *Relazioni teatrali*

3.1.1 Composizione e formazione delle ompagnie

3.1.2 Rapporti tra compagnie

3.1.3 Rapporti tra attori e rivalità

3.1.4 Avvento dell'attrice

3.2   *Relazioni sociali*

3.2.1 Committenza

3.2.2 Protezione e richiesta di favori

3.2.3 Incarichi e privilegi

3.2.4 Donativi e onorificenze

3.2.5 Suppliche

3.2.6 Vicende economiche, giudiziarie e atti legali

4. Allestimenti di spettacoli

4.1   *Scenografia e spazio teatrale*

4.1.1 Pittura

4.1.2 Disegno

4.1.3 Prospettiva

4.1.4 Scultura

4.1.5 Architettura

4.1.6 Illuminotecnica

4.1.7 Costumi e oggetti di scena

4.1.8 Macchine sceniche

4.1.9 Altro (artigiani: fabbri, falegnami, ecc.)

4.1.10 Apparatori

4.2   Luoghi di spettacolo

4.2.1 Stanze

4.2.2 Sale di corte

4.2.3 Piazza / strada / giardino

4.2.4 Teatri

4.2.5 Spazi acquatici

4.2.6 Sagrato e chiese

4.2.7 Strutture effimere

4.3   Questioni connesse alla produzione dello spettacolo

4.3.1 Alloggio attori

4.3.2 Intermediari

4.3.3 Compensi e guadagni

4.3.4 Altro

4.3.5 Censura

5 Apparati cerimoniali

5.1   Ingressi e visite

5.2   Banchetti

5.3   Processioni e cortei

5.4   Funerali

5.5   Matrimoni

5.6   Trionfi

5.7   Cerimonie, riti e occasioni festive

5.8   Incoronazioni e simili

6. Tipologie spettacolari

6.1   *Commedia dell'Arte*

6.2   *Commedia*

6.3   *Pastorale (Favola) e Boschereccia*

6.4   *Tragedia*

6.5   *Intermedi*

6.6   *Balletto*

6.7   *Melodramma*

6.8   *Armeggerie*

6.8.1 Barriera

6.8.2 Quintana

6.8.3 Giostra

6.8.4 Torneo

6.8.5 Altro

6.9   *Rappresentazioni con musica*

6.10 *Spettacoli acquatici*

6.10.1 Naumachia

6.10.2 Piscatoria

6.10.3 Altro

6.11 *Fuochi d'artificio*

6.12 *Rappresentazioni a soggetto sacro*

7. Musica

7.1   *Musica per danze*

7.2   *Musica vocale profana*

7.3   *Musica vocale sacra*

7.4   *Musica strumentale*

7.5   *Composizioni musicali*

8. Danza

8.1   *Moresca*

8.2   *Mattacina*

8.3   *Saltarello*

8.4   *Altre danze*

9. Spettatori e cronache

10. Drammaturgia e altro materiale letterario
10.1   Commissioni, testi, commedie
10.2   Scrittori
10.3   Copisti
10.4   Canovacci
10.5   Prologhi
10.6   Materiale letterario degli attori
10.7   Trattatistica

11. Editoria
11.1   Teatro
11.2   Musica
11.3   Danza
11.4   Altro

12. Teatro Ebraico

13. Accademie

14. Ruoli teatrali
14.1   Commedia dell'Arte
14.2   Melodramma
14.3   Altro

15. Iconografia spettacolare
15.1   Ritrattistica
15.2   Commedia dell'Arte
15.3   Feste, Cerimonie, altri generi spettacolari
15.4   altro

Once we reached the final form of the database, we started to consider all the records kept in Italian and European archives that fell within our range. So far we have checked libraries and archives in Bologna, Brescia, Cremona, Florence, Ferrara, Milan, Modena, Padua, Parma, Rome, Turin, the Vatican, Venice, Verona, Munich, Paris, and Vienna. Yet it's necessary to stress how many difficulties this phase of our work shows.

To find documents kept in places outside Mantua, we mostly make use of bibliographical catalogues and critical essays, which are helpful to trace the classification of well-known sources and also to go further and obtain unpublished materials. However, it's not always possible to find precise archival classifications even of well-known records; in many cases second-hand quotations may be important critical references but not at all useful tools to find where the original documents actually are. In foreign countries the research becomes more difficult and sometimes definitely hard. For instance, according to critics, the best reference concerning all the documentation on *Comici dell'Arte* kept in Paris is still Baschet's essay, dating back to 19th century[2].

The project began in 1999 with three people working on it and after three years we've started calling in researchers to collaborate with our work and collect materials outside Mantua. The difficulty in finding ideal partners is due mostly to our requirements: the collaborator should have a basic knowledge of archival research, should be able to read manuscripts (16th and 17th century) and should be familiar with the history of theatre of that period.

Let's get into the details of the Herla database in its final shape. Herla is the database in which the evidence is recorded with a strictly archival description, a brief abstract, some keywords and a sequence of categories useful to simplify the research. Our cataloguing is referred only to the part of the document dealing with the History of Performance. The record shown in the frames (Herla C914) is a letter sent in 1606 by the actor Pier Maria Cecchini, also known as *Frittellino*, to someone belonging to the Court of Mantua.

Data Entry: the layout is divided into four sections

1) *Generale* (Fig. 2) – Fields included in this area are *titolo* (a title, made of *incipit*, sender and receiver of the document), *struttura*, *categorie, abstract per uso interno* (restricted to the archivists).

2) *Chiavi* (Fig. 3) – This section contains the public *abstract* of the document, dealing with the research, and five keywords fields:

---

[2] See Baschet, *Les Comédiens italiens à la cour de France sous Charles IX, Henri III, Henri IV et Louis XIII*, Paris, Plon, 1882.

parole chiave (keywords), *comici* (comedians), *persone notevoli* (noteworthy persons), *luoghi* (quoted places), *opere citate* (literary, musical and dramatic works quoted, but also tournaments subjects and scenarios).

3) *Collocazione* (Fig. 4) – This area includes strictly archival fields: *luogo* (place from which the document comes from), *data di inizio e data di fine* (the precise date of the document or a likely period of time), *segnatura definitiva* (call number), *note* (notes), *definizione* (definitions such as letter, decree and payment), *supporto* (material on which the item is written), *consistenza* (amount of papers), *formato* (size), *stato di conservazione* (state of preservation), *lingua* (language), *provenienza e segnatura originaria* (city, archive and collection holding the original document).

4) *Relazioni* – The two fields of this section, *documento padre* and *documenti allegati*, shows whether the evidence has some related documents.

While entering data, we had to take on a few conventions:

- All the information written in square brackets is likely conjecture, but they don't appear in the document in that form.

- As the number of minor figures is so large, the spelling of their names is not standard. The same rule applies to foreign words. Moreover, sovereigns are generally indicated with their title and not with their name: e.g. Duca di Mantova, Re di Francia, Imperatore.

- In the case of *epistular* exchanges, sender and receiver are written both in the *titolo* field and either in *comici* or in *persone notevoli*.

- The field labelled *Comici* includes only *Commedia dell'Arte* comedians. In this field we insert name and surname of these actors, while their stage name (if known) goes in round brackets. As far as women are concerned, we also write their married name: e.g. *Tristano Martinelli (Arlecchino), Virginia Ramponi/ Andreini (Florinda)*, etc.

- All the other interpreters (musicians, singers, occasionally actors, etc.) are entered in *persone notevoli* field.

- Files with an S in their call number don't have any keywords or *categorie*, which are entered in all the connected records instead.

Pier Maria Cecchini a ignoto della Corte di Mantova: "Questo è l'ano delle mie disgracie..."			
Luogo	Torino	Data	13/01/1606 -
Struttura	1.1 Firmata da comici	Segn. Defin.	C 914
Definizione	Lettera	Supporto	Cartaceo
Consist.	2 carte	Formato	Fino a 21 x 29,7 cm
Stato Cons.	Buono	Lingua	Italiano

Città Prov.	Mantova, Archivio di Stato – Autografi

Segn. Orig.	b. 10, cc. 86-87

Abstract	Frittellino si rammarica di come il Duca sia certo della sua responsabilità nell'impedire alla compagnia di ritornare a Mantova. Una lettera anonima accusa il comico di essersi innamorato di Flavia e di aver per questo licenziato un servitore. Nel respingere le accuse Cecchini chiede protezione per far conoscere la propria innocenza.

Note	Cf. C915

Parole Chiave	Attori	Persone Notevoli	Luoghi	Opere Citate
lettera, servitore	Pier Maria Cecchini (Frittellino), Margherita Luciani (Flavia), Compagnia del Duca di Mantova	Duca di Mantova, Alessandro da Rho, signor Brusco	Torino, Mantova	

Categorie	Documento padre
1.1 Comici	
3.2.2 Protezione e richiesta di favori	Documenti collegati
3.1.4 Avvento dell'attrice	

The record: the card shows the entered data in a specific order.

1. *titolo* and *descrizione* (title and archival description of the document): place, date, structure, call number, definition, material, amount, size, state of preservation, language, original source.

2. abstract and possible notes

3. *parole chiave* (keywords)

4. *categorie*

The Search tools: Herla offers two search options.

Ricerca Generale – the user can fill in one or more of the boxes in the screen. Multiple-term searches may give a restricted list of documents, as the records will match all the information entered.

Searching, for instance, in how many records we can find the actor Tristano Martinelli, we get a list of 182 documents (Fig. 5).

Ricerca per categorie – this option allows choosing one item or more from the *categorie* complete list. As before, multiple-term searches will give more focused results.

Although the searches available on our Website give only a part of the information included in Herla (the original source and other minor data are not on line), students all over the world can already find information about documents scattered all over Europe in one comprehensive electronic database, which is updated three times a year (Fig. 6). In a later stage of our "work in progress", the complete version of Herla will be available in Mantua at the Foundation offices[3].

---

[3] Umberto Artioli tragically passed away in July 2004 and the Foundation was renamed after him to pay homage to the relevance of his studies. Since 2005 the original source of the document has been made visible in the on-line version of the Herla database. At present the following group of researchers and archivists has been given the task of selecting and filing documents: Cristina Grazioli (University of Padua), Simona Brunetti (University of Verona), Licia Mari (Catholic University of Brescia and vice-director of the *Archivio storico Diocesano* in Mantua), Barbara Volponi, Roberta Benedusi, and Vittoria Asioli. In the past few years the Foundation cooperated with the following scholars: Raffaele Tamalio (the Spanish area); Otto Schindler (Wien and the Austrian area); Angela Ghinato, (the Estensi court); Marzia Maino, (Vicenza and the *Accademia Olimpica*); Federica Veratelli and Marco Prandoni (The Netherlands). For a close view on new stages in the project, recent publications and conferences organised by the Foundation refer to our Website: www.capitalespettacolo.it. On-line Herla database last update: 14 April 2011 with 10,022 records.

Fig. 1 – Homepage

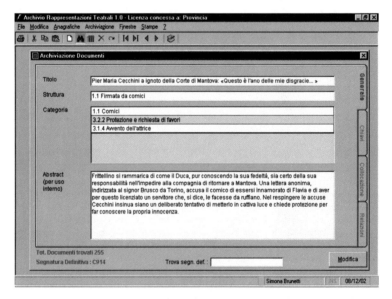

Fig. 2 – Data Entry

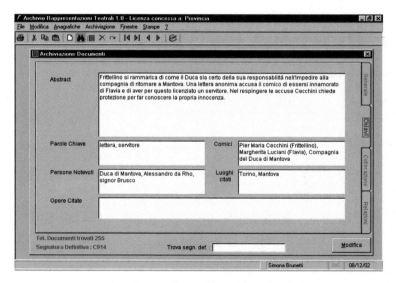

Fig. 3 – Data Entry: Keywords

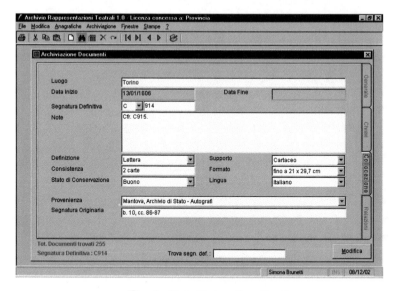

Fig. 4 – Data Entry: Localisation

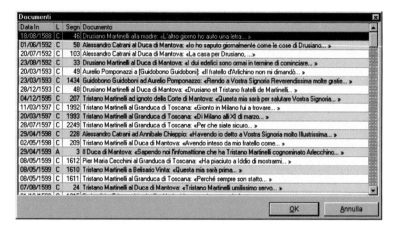

Fig. 5 – Search Results

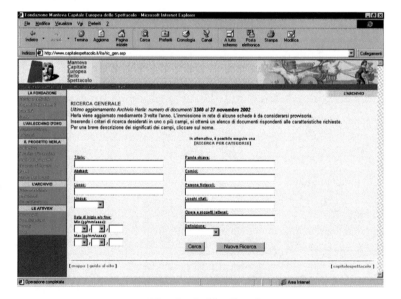

Fig. 6 – Online Database

The Archives
of the Teatro Comunale of Florence

Now Called
the Teatro del Maggio Musicale
Fiorentino – Fondazione: 1933-2002

Moreno BUCCI

Archivio storico del Teatro del Maggio Musicale Fiorentino
(Florence - Italy)

At the start of this paper, I want to highlight two negative, but no less important, aspects of the archives of the Teatro Comunale of Florence. Firstly, there is no space to consult them; and, secondly, there are no funds for their conservation and computerisation. On the other hand, we have plenty of material, as well as ideas, for projects about making this important resource for the musical and theatrical history of 20th century Italy more available.

We do our best to make the archive available to the many students and scholars who come to consult it. Proof of this is the number of Italian university graduate theses on many of the most important European set designers who have worked in the Teatro Comunale di Firenze. We also lend material to many exhibitions. And, not least of all, in the last few years we have organised many exhibitions with the Galleria degli Uffizi, which have been installed in the Gabinetto Disegni e Stampe of that museum. These last exhibitions in particular have been invaluable for making this collection better known.

The Archives of the Teatro Comunale are largely concerned with the story of the theatre's festival, the Maggio Musicale Fiorentino, the most important and oldest musical festival in Italy, and, in Europe, second only to Salzburg. Founded in 1933, the Maggio will celebrate its 70th anniversary in May 2003. The festival's long history of uninterrupted musical activity is a telling testimony of artistic vitality so essential to our country's culture.

No one who loves the theatre will doubt that many different types of energy and effort are needed to make a production. The Archives of the Teatro Comunale di Firenze cover all these different intellectual and physical forces, and contain, besides the material on the Maggio Musicale, documents about the normal opera repertory of the autumn, winter, and summer operatic seasons as well as dance and concerts.

There are five main sections of the archive and they are named after the offices that generated them:

1. the Musical Archive;
2. the Press Archive;
3. the Stage Production Archive
4. the Photographic Archive
5. the Historic Archive (of which I am the curator).

Before addressing this last one in detail, I would like to say a few words about the other archives which have survived thanks to the conscientiousness of the persons who have worked in them as well as the tradition of keeping records that has existed at the Teatro Comunale di Firenze ever since the creation of the Stabile Orchestrale Fiorentina in 1929 by Vittorio Gui.

The Musical Archive provides concert, opera, and ballet scores for conductors, orchestras, singers, chorus, directors, and choreographers. It audiotapes the performances, if permitted by contract with copyright holders, and, since 1980, has videotaped operas and ballets. The inventoried material consists in 5,100 scores for all users (the conductors, musicians, singers, stage directors and choreographers), 3,500 audiotapes dating from 1949, and 600 videotapes dating from 1982. It is run by the director of the Musical Archive, who is a full-time employee of the theatre.

The Press Archive, run by the Director of the Press office, a profession on contract, conserves a full collection of programmes, posters, and the so-called *Numeri Unici*, or special programmes printed for the Maggio Musicale Fiorentino, photographs of artists and of performances, and almost all the press articles about the theatre since 1928. The material is kept with care, but it does not have a computer catalogue. The office has, however, recently published two volumes and a CD with a list of all the theatre's events from 1928 to 1997.

The programmes are kept according to season or Maggio Musicale and number about 43,600 copies. There are 56 *Numeri Unici* and 6,000 posters. The circa 311 press books are kept in large volumes arranged by year and Maggio Musicale. The circa 30,000 black and white and colour printed photographs of artists and performances date only from 1970-1971 because the earlier material was destroyed in the 1966 Flood. There are also about 6,000 colour transparencies.

The Stage Production Archive conserves in individual folders all the technical material and drawings needed for putting on a performance of an opera or a ballet (plans of the staging, lists of the characters and notes on their costumes, props and other stage objects, and photographs of the scenery, set and costume designs). Each of the 700 folders measures 30 x 40 cm. They are arranged in alphabetical order by title of the opera or ballet. A lot of material has been lost, which is a shame since the files are of the utmost importance for the history of 20th century Italian stage performance. The stage director who has a professional contract with the theatre runs the archive.

The Photographic Archive, preserved in progressively numbered boxes measuring 18 x 24 cm, conserves images of performances from 1933 onwards. Over time the material has been ransacked for various uses and therefore the contents of the boxes are spotty. For the years 1940-1960 there are also innumerable glass negatives, which have not been catalogued. This archive is also the responsibility of the director of stage production.

The Historic Archive, of which I am the curator, holds, from an economic point of view, the theatre's most important patrimony. Five years ago it was assessed for the Fondazione del Teatro for a total of more than 21 billion Italian lire (11 million Euros). This archive contains the theatre's set and costume designs and models from 1933 and the theatre's correspondence from 1928. There are 3,325 set designs, 8,270 costume designs, 25 models, and 515 boxes of correspondence.

The drawings in the collection are by some of the best Italian and European painters, sculptors, architects, and set and costume designers of the 20th century. They are all either in tempera or oil on paper. And they have been computer catalogued and inventoried. They are conserved in chronological order starting with the first Maggio Musicale Fiorentino in 1933 and kept in a large air conditioned room with its own alarm system.

Some of the painters are Giorgio de Chirico, Felice Casorati, Mario Sironi, Gino Carlo Sensani, Gino Severini, Primo Conti, Gianni Vagnetti, Mino Maccari, Toti Scialoja, Renato Guttoso, Alberto Savinio, Corrado Cagli, Gregorio Sciltian, Pietro Annigoni, Mario Schifano, Franco Angeli, Vladimir Kara, Piero Vignozzi, and Giulio Paolini. Among the sculptors one finds Fausto Melotti, Pio Manzù, Dani Karavan, and Piero Cascella, and, among the architects, Pietro Aschieri, Erasmo Valente, Giovanni Michelucci, and Oskar Strand. Professional set and costume designers are represented by: Aldo Calvo, Pier Luigi Pizzi, Anna Anni, Maria De Matteis, Piero Tosi, Pierluigi Samaritani,

Joseph Svoboda, Emil Preetorius, Franco Zeffirelli, Dante Ferretti, Ferdinando Scarfiotti, Margherita Palli, Gabriella Pescucci, Vera Marzot, and Stefano Lazaridis.

Cataloguing began in 1980, and, as far as I am aware, the Teatro Comunale di Firenze is the only Italian theatrical foundation that, for about six years now, has a fixed curator – with a degree in art history – of its artistic collection even if only on a contractual basis. This position was created at a time when no one ever imagined that theatres conserved "museums" of this type. Over the years I have developed a type of catalogue entry that has been approved by the Soprintendenza per i Beni Artistici e Storici di Firenze (the state office for the artistic and historical heritage of Florence) with which I have closely worked. In addition, the Opificio delle Pietre Dure di Firenze (a separate state office specialising in restoration) worked with the theatre on a programme of conservation of the works and of climate control of the room in which they are kept.

It is not always easy to evaluate set and costume designs artistically. Sometimes the pictorial or graphic quality of an individual drawing is of high enough quality to consider it an aesthetic object of its own whereas in other cases its importance relates only to its function for the stage.

The data entries that have been developed for our archive are simple and concise. For the set designs we have included the inventory number that is on the back of the drawing, the number of the drawer in which it is located, the date, the context (either the Maggio Musicale Fiorentino or the regular opera season), the artist, the title of the opera or ballet, the composer, the act, the technique, the dimensions, its value, indications of a signature and other autograph notations, and the state of conservation. For the costume designs the entry consists of the same information, but instead of the act, the name of the character is indicated. The artist, the composer, and the title of the production are also identified by a number assigned by the theatre's computer programmer and which is the same for the computer programmes used by the Musical Archive and the central administration.

We have consulted with other Italian theatres about this type of inventory, and on a number of occasions I have tried to develop a uniform system so that information could be easily interchanged between theatres and scholars. These attempts, however, have been unsuccessful. I have noted, with a certain humour and/or anger, that when works like these are exhibited (and this is happening more and more frequently) there is a great variance and imprecision in cataloguing. I personally cannot stand it when, instead of citing the act of the opera, the location of the scene is taken from the libretto. Therefore, instead of "Act I" one finds "Royal den" or "Mysterious place near a forest at dusk" or "Moonlit cloister". This is of no use. I am convinced that entries need to be factual, precise, and straightforward. Iconographic and artistic considerations should come second.

The Historic Archive possesses a single computer dating from 1982. All our work has been done on that and though the archive can be consulted through any number of categories in the programme (opera, composer, season etc.), this can only happen at the archive itself and on its ancient computer. Unfortunately, none of the theatre's computers are on a network system nor is it possible to update information automatically without reworking the whole entry. However, scholars and students can visit the archive and there are also group visits. Soon we hope to inaugurate a museum space that will also be open during performances.

The Historic Archive also takes care of correspondence between the theatre, artists, government officials, musicologists, and other professionals from the years 1928-1952. These circa 515 folders are of great importance for 20th century music history. The Maggio Musicale Fiorentino promoted and commissioned many contemporary musicians like Alfredo Casella, Luigi Dallapiccola, Goffredo Petrassi, Gian Francesco Malipiero, Mario Castelnuovo Tedesco, Luciano Berio, Sylvano Bussotti, and Salvatore Sciarrino. The correspondence contains invaluable information about the Maggio Musicale Fiorentino and its relationship to the Fascist Regime and the Minculpop[1] in the 1930s and 1940s as well as about the post-war reconstruction.

The Teatro del Maggio Musicale Fiorentino-Fondazione and Sovrintendenza Archivistica della Toscana supported my project for revaluating and cataloguing these papers. The theatre also received 50 million lire (circa 25,000 Euros) for the computer inventory of each folder from the Ministero per i Beni e le Attività Culturali (Direzione Generale per i Beni Archivistici). The three year project employed three experts from different backgrounds (theatre, music, and art), who, under my direction, have been inventorying the folders according to the *Arianna* program of the Scuola Normale Superiore di Pisa. Periodical meetings with the Ministero and the Sovrintendenza Archivistica have yielded good results even if getting started was not easy because it took some time to develop a mutually acceptable catalogue entry. The work will be published in 2005 in the series of the Archivi del Ministero and will be easily consultable at the theatre and in the near future on the Web.

On the basis of all this work, I would like the Teatro del Maggio Musicale Fiorentino and its Historic Archive to become the living memory of Italian 20th century music and its production. We would

---

[1]   Italian Ministry of Culture (Editor's note).

become the one place in Italy where owners of this type of material can leave it for future generations instead of dispersing it in auctions or misguided donations that often put the material outside of the reach of scholars. I have often had to fight against the feeling of those in possession of such documents who jealously guard them as their own and who do not want to make them available. These people act just like those curators of the Italian fine arts administrations who do not let the public or scholars see works of art in storage because they think that someday they will personally find there some great unknown masterpiece. I look forward to your suggestions, your visits, and your support[2].

---

[2] Addendum (June 2011): I would like to note in 2008 the inventory of the theatre's correspondence from 1928 to 1952 was published (Moreno Bucci, *Le carte di un Teatro*, Florence, Leo S. Olschki). The book was underwritten by the Fondazione Carlo Marchi of Florence, which is also financing the computerisation of the drawings belonging to the Archivio Storico. The first volume of that inventory was also pubished in book-form (Moreno Bucci, *I disegni del Teatro del Maggio Musicale – I [1933-1943]*, Florence, Leo S. Olschki, 2010). The second volume covering the years 1943-1953 is now being prepared.

DEUXIÈME PARTIE

CONSERVATION ET ORGANISATION DE L'ESPACE

SECOND PART

PRESERVATION AND SPACE ORGANISATION

Reorganisation of Stack Space in the Performing Arts Collection at the Harry Ransom Humanities Research Center

Helen ADAIR

Harry Ransom Humanities Research Center,
University of Texas (Austin – United States)

In the Harry Ransom Humanities Research Center at the University of Texas at Austin, the organisation of space for the storage of manuscript and book collections pertaining to the performing arts has been a longstanding problem. From September 2000 to August 2002, the Performing Arts Collection underwent a major stack reorganisation project which completely reconfigured its storage space and alleviated a host of collection management problems affecting public service, cataloguing, conservation, and building-wide space issues. This paper will explain the goals of the project, outline the steps involved, and comment upon the results.

The Performing Arts Collection is a research collection documenting the history of theatre, dance, costume and scenic design, opera, and popular entertainment in Britain and America from the 18th through mid-20th centuries. In addition to playscripts, promptbooks, correspondence, playbills, programs, and clippings, the collection is rich in visual material such as production photographs, set and costume renderings, posters, prints and engravings, and set models. Performing Arts is divided into 142 discrete collections stored in two rooms on the seventh floor of the Ransom Center, and its overall size is estimated to be about 3,300 linear feet. The archival collections are supplemented by the Theatre Arts Library, which consists of 30,000 books related to the performing arts. Although Performing Arts no longer operates its own reading room, it occupies separate stack space and has traditionally been administered independently of other units within the Ransom Center.

Since the University of Texas' first major theatre acquisition in 1956, the size of the Performing Arts Collection and the Theatre Arts Library has increased regularly, but stack space did not expand significantly after 1986. That year, the stacks in the main stack room, 7A, were partially reconfigured, and space in a smaller room, 7C, was provided for flat files and file cabinets which could not fit in the main room. As new acquisitions came in, the collection outgrew the 1986 reconfiguration, and by the mid-1990s there was no room for new collections, no room to install more shelving, and no room to shift the existing collections in hope of arriving at a more efficient layout.

The utter lack of workspace in the stacks, and the crowded condition in which collections were stored, had negative consequences for reference work and for the long-term conservation of the materials. Some collections with oversize material were split into numerous stack locations, causing considerable inefficiencies in paging and reshelving materials, and contributing to the general difficulty in training new staff for public service duties in the collection. Everyday work was hampered by the collections not being clearly labelled, and by boxes being stacked too high for easy access. Unbraced and overloaded ranges of shelving threatened to become a safety issue. Because file cabinets were a mainstay for collection storage, materials were not readily transportable for paging, and the opening and closing of file drawers frequently caused damage due to overfilling or oversize materials. Unhoused materials (mostly models and realia) were difficult to page and poorly conserved.

Cataloguing and general collection management were also affected by the lack of space. Some archival containers were not space efficient, such as pamphlet boxes, which occupied twice as much shelf space as standard document cases. Substandard, narrow shelving was inadequate for standard document cases and incompatible with shelving elsewhere in the Ransom Center. Oversize storage in flat file drawers was almost completely full, with the largest drawers filled to 93% of capacity. Archival cataloguing of Performing Arts collections, which began in early 1999, was occasionally made more challenging by the dispersed state of many collections. Finally, within the entire Ransom Center, little space was available for new collections, yet 7A and 7C as currently configured could clearly only be occupied by the Performing Arts Collection.

In spring 1999 the stack maintenance supervisor and the theatre curator presented separate proposals to alleviate some of the immediate space problems, but because the Ransom Center lacked a large, empty space into which some collections could be shifted temporarily, only minor recommendations could feasibly be acted upon. Both plans pointed to the need for a major reassessment of the current floor plan.

In Fall 1999 a task force was appointed to address the organisation of space in the Performing Arts Collection. Its charge was to present a plan for the reorganisation of stack space, including oversize storage, flat files, and file cabinets, a plan which would maximize space for current collection materials and future acquisitions, as well as eliminate non-standard shelving, storage, and housings. The collection was surveyed to determine how much space it would occupy when placed onto standard shelving. The task force's options were limited by three incontrovertible facts: there was no space within Performing Arts to shift materials, no room elsewhere in the Ransom Center which could be used as a staging area, and the collection could not be closed to the public at any time during the reconfiguration. After examining a broad range of options, the task force recommended a comprehensive, long-term solution to the space problems rather than short-term or piecemeal approaches. The task force endorsed a phased approach to the reconfiguration which could be accomplished within two years.

The project was budgeted at $206,000 which covered the cost of equipment (shelving, flat files, and lateral file cabinets), conservation supplies, the salary of two half-time office assistants, and the services of professional movers and a carpenter. (Project expenses are summarised in the table "Expenses for Performing Arts Stack Project, 2000-2002") The goals of the project, which began in September 2000, were to maximize efficiency by upgrading or reconfiguring existing shelving and cabinets; eliminate all temporary, unbraced wooden shelving; standardise collection housings wherever possible, such as by rehousing materials from file cabinets into document cases; when possible, consolidate dispersed portions of individual collections for cataloguing and paging efficiency; and label all parts of the collection according to current Ransom Center standards. These goals were accomplished in three phases, preceded by a period of preparation.

Pre-project

In the summer of 2000, shelving equipment, conservation supplies, and labour were secured with the help of the University of Texas administration which contributed $168,000 for shelving and installation costs. Collection staff weeded out-of-scope and seldom used materials which were then transferred to other units within the Ransom Center, moved offsite, or deaccessioned. The Ransom Center's Conservation Department unframed about 80 works of art, which had been stored in a set of unwieldy, and space-inefficient slot files, which were then removed. The Conservation Department also constructed several oversize poster portfolios for theatre posters and other materials such as design renderings which did not fit into the largest flat file drawers. Though the portfolios were not a part of the project *per se*, they proved to be an excellent solution to another long-term storage problem.

During this period and throughout the project, collection staff made a series of curatorial decisions regarding further unframing, deaccessions, transfers to other Ransom Center departments, the disposition of collection material, and the integrity of collections. In this regard, the presence of a visiting theatre curator in the springs of 2000, 2001, and 2002 was invaluable.

Phase 1: Reconfiguration of Staff Space (Months 1-3)

Because the Ransom Center's Art Collection shared space with the Performing Arts Collection on the seventh floor, the project had a major impact on office space for the Art Collection. The Art Collection's files, work areas, and finding aids were moved into former gallery space and other offices nearby. The Performing Arts Collection's business files and provenance records, which had been stored some distance away from the main work area, were moved to a much more convenient area in 7A. Performing Arts' workspaces were consolidated and reduced as much as possible by transferring archival supplies to supply storage on other floors.

Phase 2: Reconfiguration of the Theatre Arts Library (Months 3-6)

Ranges of book shelving were installed in the space that had been occupied by the Art Collection. Next, the Theatre Arts Library was shifted onto the new shelving and compacted so that the books fit into a smaller space. Space was also saved by narrowing the stack aisles during this process. Steps were taken to insure that no further growth would take place in the Theatre Arts book collections, and space-consuming runs of two daily periodicals were deaccessioned. Phase 2 resulted in enough "new" space to install 70 sections of standard shelving (1,225 linear feet) and 11 sections of oversize shelving (165 linear feet) on which to place archival collections when the re-housing phase began.

Phase 3: Reconfiguration of Archival Collection Space (Months 7-24)

The general reconfiguration was accomplished via the ongoing process of rehousing collections from file cabinets into archival boxes, while simultaneously replacing most of the file cabinets with more space-efficient ranges of free-standing shelving in the space vacated. Because of the lack of space, this phase was completed in many stages, by repeatedly moving materials and building new shelves. At the same time, we replaced the temporary wooden shelving with wall-mounted shelving that made use of most of the available wall space. The new shelving had various widths suited to archival materials ranging from document cases to large scrapbooks.

Oversize storage often required specific solutions. We purchased six lateral file cabinets for our playbills collections and transferred some playbills from flat files into these cabinets and into document cases. By doing so, the fullness of the medium- and small-sized flat file drawers was reduced to approximately 70% and 50% of capacity, respectively. For certain collections, the existing storage could not be improved upon with project staff, and the materials will be left in file cabinets until a cataloguer can properly address the housing problems. For this reason, we kept ten oversize file cabinets for current materials and future expansion, the tops of which can double as storage space for set models and other oversize objects.

When the project was completed in August 2002, shelf space had increased from 1,665 linear feet to 5,127 linear feet, or 308%. The benefits of the reconfiguration extended beyond collection management. Most of the collections had been dispersed and uncatalogued, but we were able to unite dispersed materials and arrange or at least provide box lists for most collections. Because collections are now clearly labelled, staff from other departments can more easily locate materials without assistance, freeing Performing Arts staff for public service and collection management activities. The process of reviewing each collection contributed immeasurably to the revision of the Ransom Center's Website in spring 2002, and invited a level of discussion and exchange within Performing Arts and with other Ransom Center units that was unmatched in recent memory.

Although the project ran smoothly from start to finish, it was complicated by a long-planned renovation of the Ransom Center and by the loss of collection personnel. The building renovation, which began in August 2001, limited access to elevators occasionally and to the loading dock and basement regularly, affecting access to shelving and forcing us to find other places to move surplus shelving and file cabinets out of the stacks. Work on fire protection systems compelled a change in the order of the work plan, and some of our new shelving was requisitioned as temporary storage for books that were displaced from one of the renovation sites in the Ransom Center. Halfway through the project, Performing Arts' full-time reference position was eliminated when that staff member left. Remaining collection staff were hard-pressed to take on reference duties, continue cataloguing, consolidate workspaces, and complete other projects in a timely fashion.

From the curatorial standpoint, the task force underestimated the complexity of the collection material that had been dispersed into artificial collections over many years, under the supervision of several curators. Past decision-making processes were not well documented as regards the disposition of this material which lacked unity of provenance, and the learning curve was steep even for experienced staff. We were fortunate to have a visiting curator before and during the project as we struggled to define the purpose and composition of certain collections. Now, difficult questions remain as to our identity, who our primary audience should be, and which areas we will build upon for future growth. But with most of the immediate storage problems solved and with access to the Performing Arts Collection vastly increased both physically and intellectually, the Ransom Center is much better prepared for the expected increase in use of the collection and to plan for its future.

Expenses for Performing Arts Stack Project, 2000-2002

Personnel	$ 32,000
University of Texas transportation services (movers)	$ 1,000
Shelving equipment	$ 150,000
Installation of shelving equipment	$ 18,000
Conservation supplies	$ 5,000
Total	**$ 206,000**

Using New Technologies to Overcome the Problem of Museum Space

Ksenija RADULOVIĆ

Museum of Theatre Art of Serbia (Beograd – Serbia)

The problem of space, and what comes out of it, is not a problem that only theatre museums have to face. Also, this problem may not manifest in the same form under different circumstances. Since the activities of theatre museums are rather specific, above all because of the ephemeral, momentary nature of the theatrical act, I believe this issue is worth discussing.

When I started working in the Museum of Theatre Art of Serbia a year ago, one of my university professors, who had been living abroad for years and who had gained broad experience as the head of a big theatre institute that includes a theatre museum, told me: "Unfortunately, many theatre museums in Europe turned into small, quiet, out-of-the-way and dusty places and in time became repositories of heirlooms and similar things. About such places we feel sentimental." This did not sound encouraging to me. Not that I dislike sentimentality and nostalgic contemplation of bygone days, but I believe that this is simply not enough.

Namely, in our museum, in the room of some 200 square metres, the entire history of the Serbian theatre is to be stored, exhibition halls and offices included. Trying to obtain more space, we have to think simultaneously about newly obtained materials and we have to plan well in advance.

The new museology in Europe and the world has already rejected the stereotypical idea of a museum as a kind of storage place, a stockroom for objects of art and heirlooms, and has helped to turn some museums into lively, open places that foster the atmosphere of polemics, taking an active part, together with other institutions, in creating the cultural policy and launching various cultural trends in the community instead of being "passive" exhibition and "consumer" places.

However, I think that even this should not satisfy us: theatre art belongs to one moment, and then it simply disappears – this makes it different from a painting, a book or a film. So, what is to be done with the "remains" of a theatrical performance stored in the museum when we know that they represent the sole material for researchers and future reconstructions, and that they are a document about a specific time?

In this area, we can understand the important role of new technologies. In the Museum of Theatre Art of Serbia we are developing a programme package for museum collections and the national theatrical repertoire. This future documentation centre would represent the first comprehensive database in the field of performing arts in Serbia. As far as I know, the plan to create a joint programme package for theatre museums of various countries has not been carried out yet. Also, as a national museum, we have to coordinate our activities with local museums in Serbia, which practically means that our future programme package will be a part of a wider museum network developed at the national level. The authorities in this field have promised that they will take into account the specificities of certain museums, as well as our specific needs – in our case, for example, it is the repertoire database, which does not represent a classical museum collection.

Once we have created the programme package, a long and toilsome job of feeding in the data will follow, for which we expect to engage a few collaborators who would help us. Some of the materials in our possession can be scanned and stored on CDs, while the originals can be stored in a repository and thus protected from wear and tear, which will at the same time create more space in the museum. This brings us back to the notion that museums should not be just storerooms covered with patina – places that make us feel sentimental and nostalgic.

Furthermore, the database would be continually upgraded with incoming materials, and it is needless to say how useful this would be for the museum activities, as well as for our collaborators, researchers, the media and the public at large.

One important issue that still remains open for discussion is if the public should have access to the whole database via the worldwide Web, in which form and under which circumstances. This is something that should be regulated by law. I must admit that I am rather ignorant about legal regulations, and particularly because I come from a country where the black market was prevalent in various fields in the last decade. Another issue is the exchange of the database – or parts of it – among different museums. Of course, any experience in developing programme packages and making them available online can be of great help.

As far as our Website is concerned, we have a relevant and informative site, which is regularly updated and which offers general information concerning the activities of the museum (including exhibitions, presentations, our journal, etc.). It is also possible that museum exhibitions will soon include their Web presentations (now they are classical), which will give opportunity to those who cannot visit the museum to see them. In the same way, some interesting collections or their individual sections can become accessible to the public.

There is one more thing I would like to touch on. As our programme is mostly based on preserving and presenting the national theatrical heritage, we have been thinking about our fellow countrymen – Web users – who have recently moved abroad. Namely, they are the typical Internet population because they are young and educated people who left Serbia in the last decade during the big economic depression and the war. They use the Internet to keep in touch with their mother country and mother tongue. As there are many emigrants of this type, it is not impossible that some parallel Serbian Web culture could be developed in the future. Although in a different technological milieu, other nations also developed their parallel cultures in the past – let me remind you of the valuable Russian emigrant literature created after the October Revolution. We also plan to put on the Web the museum's journal, entitled *Teatron*, which now follows a new, modern trend. Readers will have access to our articles in Serbian on the Websites of some departments of Slavic studies at universities worldwide (some have already expressed their interest), and some articles will also be translated into English when we think that they could be interesting to a wider audience.

In conclusion, I believe that the Internet will help us to extend the scope of the museum's activities, which will in turn attract a larger audience. New technologies can be used to upgrade the work of theatre museums, to make it more efficient, more accurate and much faster. I believe that in this way the public will stop looking down on this kind of institutions, regarding them as "small, quiet and dusty places"[1].

---

[1] In the meantime, The Museum of Theatre Art of Serbia has realised a digital database consisting of all relevant facts based on collections and theatre history in Serbia.

TROISIÈME PARTIE

LES RÉSEAUX ET LES RÉPERTOIRES EN LIGNE

THIRD PART

NETWORKS AND ONLINE DIRECTORIES

The SIBMAS International Directory of Performing Arts Collections and Institutions Online

The Transition from Printed Volume to Online Service, How It Was Done, Why Was It Done, How Is It Being Received?

Paul ULRICH

(Berlin – Germany)

At the beginning of the 20th century theatre was recognised as a field of study in its own and not merely a branch of other fields, most particularly literature. The problem of locating primary sources soon became painfully clear: what had been preserved was scattered in numerous museums, archives and libraries throughout the world. Just as no one knew how many theatres and performances there were, likewise no one knew where the multitude of records and traces of the theatre could be found. The multi-faceted institution theatre, encompassing theatre, music, art, architecture, technology, public administration, to mention only a few of the aspects, meant that the necessary sources were scattered, often hidden within collections which would initially seem to have nothing to do with the theatre itself. The question for the theatre researcher was thus: where are the materials for research? The extensiveness of this problem was elucidated in 1960 by Julien Cain, General Administrator of the National Library:

> The staggering amount of material in the field of the performing arts which has accumulated throughout time, whether it be handwritten, printed, designed, engraved, photographed, or microfilmed, such a variety of documentation, where even the most divers objects, set designs, and costumes

themselves, have their part, all this material deserved to be more widely known so that more use could be made of it.[1]

History of the Directory

The late André Veinstein (1916-2001), founder and former President of sibmas, George Freedley and Rosamond Gilder convinced the members of the International Section for Performing Arts Libraries and Museums of the International Federation of Library Associations[2] that producing an international directory with information about these institutions should be a continuing project for the association. The first edition finally appeared after seven years of preparation[3].

In her introduction to this first directory, Rosamond Gilder described the work which others had previously done to make information about performing arts collections available:

[...] One of the fields that seemed to her[4] of primary importance was the theatre collection - As early as 1933 Theatre Arts ran a series of articles on the great theatrical collections of Europe and America. In 1936 it published the first handbook on the subject: Theatre Collections in Libraries and Museums, by Rosamond Gilder and George Freedley. The studies made to secure the material for this modest volume both by correspondence and by the actual visits of George Freedley, Curator of the Theatre Collection of the New York Public Library, to the major collections of the continent and England revealed an extraordinary wealth of material that few had realized was so extensive or so important both in quality and quantity. So keen was the interest in the subject that the handbook published in 1936 was soon out of print.

A new edition, revised and brought up to date had long been needed and work on the American section was undertaken in 1952 by Paul Myers as Chairman of the Library Project of the American Educational Theatre Association. Shortly thereafter, Dr. André Veinstein of the Bibliothèque de l'Arsenal (Paris), became keenly interested in the whole subject of bibliography and collections in the field of the performing arts

---

[1] Julien Cain, "Préface", in André Veinstein, Marie Françoise Christout and Denis Bablet (eds.), Bibliothèques et musées des arts du spectacle dans le monde = Performing Arts Collections, an International Handbook, Paris, Centre national de la recherche scientifique, 1960, p. 9.

[2] This section within the International Federation of Library Associations was the beginning of SIBMAS.

[3] André Veinstein, Marie Françoise Christout and Denis Bablet (eds.), Bibliothèques et musées des arts du spectacle dans le monde, op. cit.

[4] Edith J.R. Isaacs, editor of Theatre Arts Monthly.

and as President of the Committee of the International Federation of Library Associations launched early in 1955 an exhaustive, world-wide inquiry on theatre libraries and theatre collections. His questionnaire, cast in a somewhat different mould from that of the Gilder-Freedley handbook, which, with the approval and cooperation of its authors he used as a springboard, was addressed not only to the collections listed in that volume but to other libraries and museums both public and private.[5]

From the very beginning it was clear for Mr. Veinstein how the directory was to be used:

> The use of the present work will permit librarians to offer their readers an enlarged scope of information, to increase their network of foreign correspondents, and to know better the activities of certain of their colleagues on the national level in order to avoid duplication of effort. Moreover, the diversity and the particular nature of the documents brought together in the different fields of the performing arts and the use made of the various institutions by certain categories of specialists will facilitate the spreading of solutions which have been made with respect to classification, cataloging, and ordering of places; will allow the organization of meetings designed to try to resolve problems of a professional order; and, finally, will go forward with collective projects; e.g., the editing of catalogs, bibliographies, etc.
> Still, using the present book as a point of departure, useful observations will be drawn from the orientation taken by certain collections (the rejection of the principle which accords precedence to books over documents, of the radical separation of museums and libraries, and of the documentary value of such recent supports as films and magnetic tapes); from the increase in holdings and reference systems in response to the expansion of sciences, besides history, which are interested in the performing arts; e.g. aesthetics, psychology, sociology, pedagogy, phonetics, and electro-acoustics; and from the growing needs of artists and technicians with respect to authentic documents, that is to say, those which are not, interpreted and are not foreign to the production of their art.
> Scholars and students will be able to find in this book subjects bearing, for example, on the geographic distribution of documentary resources, the conditions under which they were set up, the conditions and general make-up of holdings, in different countries, devoted to certain subjects or personalities, and the particular nature of certain institutions; e.g., those set up by the theatres themselves; those devoted to the documenting of professionals (artists,

---

5   Rosamond Gilder, "Theatre Collections: Present and Future", *in* André Veinstein, Marie Françoise Christout and Denis Bablet (eds.), *Bibliothèques et musées des arts du spectacle dans le monde, op. cit.*, p. 15-16.

technicians, or administrators); or those recently created by radio and television stations."[6]

André Veinstein and those assisting him wanted not only to provide basic information about the respective institutions (name, address, telephone numbers and opening hours), they also strove to provide a glimpse into the actual holdings of the institutions. In order to gather all this information, extensive – 7 page – questionnaires (both in French and in English) were mailed out to all those institutions which were known to have holdings relating to the performing arts. The institutions were encouraged to write descriptions about the history, holdings and other interesting facts about their institution.[7] As is always the case with questionnaires, the recipients did not always return them to the editors, hence an extensive apparatus was needed to follow up and remind those who had not returned the questionnaire that information from them was missing.[8]

In keeping with the bilingual (French/English) policies of SIBMAS, all of the replies not only needed to be edited to correspond to editorial guidelines they also had to be translated into either English or French. This procedure was maintained for the first 4 editions,[9] the only major changes being in modifications in the wording of the questions asked.

---

[6] André Veinstein, "The Book and Its Use", *in* André André Veinstein, Marie Françoise Christout and Denis Bablet (eds.), *Bibliothèques et musées des arts du spectacle dans le monde*, *op. cit.*, p. 24.

[7] A major problem here is that institutions do not like to respond to such questionnaires, since it takes a long time to formulate answers. For institutions where English or French is not a native language, there is either a hesitancy to avoid answering such forms, put it off indefinitely, or to have someone translate a text into either French or English – the quality of the translations often being very poor.

[8] Experience with other mailings of questionnaires has shown that this procedure requires extensive follow-ups to get the questionnaires returned.

[9] André Veinstein, Marie Françoise Christout and Denis Bablet (eds.), *Bibliothèques et musées des arts du spectacle dans le monde*, *op. cit.*, 761 p.
André Veinstein and Cécile Giteau (eds.), *Bibliothèques et musées des arts du spectacle dans le monde = Performing Arts Libraries and Museums of the World*. 2nd ed., Paris, Centre national de la recherche scientifique, 1967, 803 p.
André Veinstein and Alfred S. Golding (eds.), *Bibliothèques et musées des arts du spectacle dans le monde = Performing Arts Libraries and Museums of the World*. 3rd ed., Paris, Centre national de la recherche scientifique, 1984, 1181 p.
André Veinstein and Alfred S. Golding (eds.), *Bibliothèques et musées des arts du spectacle dans le monde = Performing Arts Libraries and Museums of the World*, 4th ed., Paris, Centre national de la recherche scientifique, 1992, 740 p.

The Directory, which was published with a blue cover, was affectionately known within SIBMAS as the "Blue Book"[10]. At the biannual SIBMAS congresses the Blue Book Commission would discuss the problems of the preceding volumes and make decisions on the next edition.

At the 1988 SIBMAS Congress in Mannheim there was a general consensus within the Blue Book Commission, that it was increasingly difficult to continue the work in the present form. A major concern was the extensive time required to make the translations for a bilingual publication; this time factor decreased the currentness of the content. Furthermore, the translators – even in the first edition – noted the problems in making adequate translations[11]. It was suggested that for many sections the use of symbols would streamline the presentation and also make repetition in French and German superfluous[12].

For the 3rd and 4th editions, André Veinstein passed on much of the editorial work to Alfred S. Golding, who retained the general content and structure of the publication. After the appearance of the 4th edition, Alfred Golding turned over the editorship to a new editorial team[13], which began implementing the suggestions which had been discussed at Blue Book Commission meetings since 1988 in Mannheim.

At the 1992 Blue Book Commission meeting in Stockholm, the structure of a very simplified, one-page questionnaire[14] was accepted, with minor changes, by the members and the necessary preparation was

---

[10] Not to be confused with the *FIRT/IFTR-SIBMAS Bulletin*, which also had a blue cover. The Bulletin was published several times a year and contained current information about conferences, publications, exhibitions and other matters pertaining to the performing arts. It ceased publication in paper form in 2001.

[11] This problem was prominently mentioned in George Miller's "Translator's Note" in the first edition: "The particular difficulty for the translator in the present book has been that it is a work which describes specific things, unknown, for the most part, to the translator. For this reason, where alternative translations have presented themselves, particularly in the many lists and catalogues of holdings, educated guesses have been more the rule than the exception. Inevitably, some of these have been unfortunately incorrect. The translator can only hope that no one will have journeyed half way around the world because of one of these presumed mistranslations."

[12] This suggestion was partially realised in the 4th edition with the use of abbreviations.

[13] This editorial team was composed of Richard M. Buck (New York Public Library of the Performing Arts), who as general editor was also given the task of finding a publisher who would help finance the project, Paul S. Ulrich (Amerika-Gedenkbibliothek, Berlin), Ruth Freydank (Märkisches Museum, Berlin) and Roger Rennenberg (Stadsbibliotek Antwerp), who were to do the actual preparation of the next edition.

[14] Prepared by Ruth Freydank and Paul S. Ulrich.

done to transfer the information from the 4th edition to this new form. The instrument for gathering information was no longer called a questionnaire, but rather a proof sheet. Institutions would be asked to review the information already known about their institution and make the necessary corrections. The information on the proof sheets was what would be printed if the institution did not make corrections[15].

There were numerous reasons for streamlining the information-gathering instrument:

- Erroneous information would be more likely to be corrected, if the institution was aware that the proof sheet was the basis for a publication[16].

- It made it as easy as possible for the institutions to provide the information. If all the head of the institution had to do was make corrections of what was wrong with the information available to the editorial board, the chances were very great that he would be able to do this very quickly. Furthermore he would not have to spend time formulating texts.

- It made it as easy as possible to make additions and corrections to the database[17]. This reduced the editorial preparation of the 5th edition to less than 4 months (compared to the several years needed for the 4th edition)!

Richard M. Buck succeeded in finding a new publisher, who would be willing to finance the directory, and in 1994 at the SIBMAS Conference in Antwerp, the decision was made to sign a contract with Jim Emmett of Emmett Publishing in England. Emmett Publishing agreed to finance the mailings to the institutions, cover the costs of publishing and distribution[18].

---

[15] In a cover letter the institutions were informed that not returning the proof sheets would be interpreted as approval of the information. In the printed directory those institutions which had not returned the proof sheets were thusly indicated.

[16] No one likes to have erroneous information printed about themselves, and they will do what they can to correct errors. This increases the possibilities of returns being made.

[17] This was possible because only the fields containing positive information needed to be entered in the database. Furthermore extensive simplification in the number of characters entered in each of the fields reduced both data entry time and typographical errors.

[18] Because of the high production costs – primarily arising from mailing 5,000 proof sheets –, the original intention to keep the price of the directory under $50 was not possible.

For a directory of German-language institutions[19], a different approach to gathering information had been used, which seemed transferable to collecting and verifying the information about the institutions which would be included in the directory. Instead of sending out a questionnaire, the institutions were sent an extremely simplified one-page proof sheet with information about the respective institution. The institution only had to make the necessary corrections and return it to the editors. The institutions were informed that the information the way it was on the proof sheet would be printed, "as is", unless the institution made corrections. Failure to return a proof sheet would be interpreted by the editors to be approval of the content. Instead of the usual 30% return rate for most questionnaires, the German directory achieved over 60% returns[20].

Prior to sending out the proof sheets, the information about the institutions in the 4th edition was standardised and put into a structured ASCII flat file[21] for later import into a database. Other regional performing arts directories, which had been prepared by national/regional members of SIBMAS, were used to verify and augment this information[22].

---

[19] Peter Schmitt and Paul S. Ulrich (eds.), *Archive, Bibliotheken, Museen, Sammlungen und Gedenkstätten mit Beständen zum Bereich „Darstellende Künste" in der Bundesrepublik Deutschland* = *Archives, Libraries, Museums, Collections and Memorials with "Performing Arts" Holdings in the Federal Republic of Germany* (SIBMAS-Brief. Sonderheft 1.), Erlangen, Bundesverband der Bibliotheken und Museen für Darstellende Künste, 1992.

[20] Of the 350 institutions sent the questionnaire, 310 responded.

[21] A flat file is a text file, with the information so structured that it can be automatically transferred to the respective categories in a database. The advantage of working with information in this form is, that it is independent of the database used, it can be processed in any word processor, it does not need a data-entry interface, it is easily transported and can be imported into almost any database.

[22] Joke Elbers (ed.), *Theater collecties in Nederland en Vlaanderen*, Amsterdam, Nederlands Theater Instituut, 1991.
Lennart Forslund (ed.), *Teatersamlingr i Norden. Katalog over teatermuseer, -bibliotek og -arkiv i Danmark, Finland, Island, Norge og Sverige*. 3., revised edition, Umea, Nordisk Center for Teaterdokumentation, 1991.
Heather McCallum and Ruth Pincoe (eds.), *Directory of Canadian Theatre Archives*, London, Vine Press, "Dalhousie University, School of Library and Information Studies. Occasional Paper Series", 1992.
Roger Rennenberg (ed.), *Bibliotheken, Archieven, Musea en Documentatiecentra over de Podiumkunsten in Vlaanderen en Brussel* = *Libraries, Archives, Museums and Documentation Centres of the Performing Arts in Flanders and Brussels*, Antwerp, National SIBMAS Centrum Vlaanderen, 1992.
Theatre Communications Group (ed.), *Theatre Directory*, Vol. 20, New York, Theatre Communications Group, 1992-93.
Nicole Leclercq (ed.), *Les Bibliothèques et musées des arts du spectacle en communauté française de Belgique* = *Libraries and Museums of the Performing Arts*

Furthermore, numerous international directories[23] were consulted and relevant material was added to the information already present. In contrast to previous editions, which primarily focused on the major international institutions with material on the performing arts, the editors of the 5th edition[24] tried to identify less-known institutions with smaller collections[25], since it was particularly these lesser-known collections which were of particular interest to scholars. The result was a database of over 5,000 institutions.

The database was sent to Emmett Publishers, where the preparation, printing and mailing of the proof sheets was managed. The institutions were asked to return the proof sheets to Paul S. Ulrich in Berlin, who made the necessary changes to the information in the database, and after all the proof sheets had been received and the corrections made in the entries (some of the members of the Blue Book Commission put pressure on institutions which hadn't sent in their proof sheets, and this made many of the entries better than they would have been), the final database was sent to Emmett Publishers, which then printed the directory, which had a new name (*SIBMAS International Directory of Performing Arts Collections*) and was printed with a gray cover.

Institutions which were members of SIBMAS were indicated as such in the directory[26]. Cross-linking[27] was already present in a passive form in the 5th edition with inclusion of their URLs and email addresses. Since then many institutions now have Websites that have had to be included. Even more important, additional databases with information about collections have become available on the Web[28].

---

in Belgium's French-speaking Community, 4th ed., Brussel, Centre SIBMAS Communauté française de Belgique, 1994.

[23] In particular the *World Guide to Libraries, Museums of the World and the World Guide to Special Libraries*.

[24] *SIBMAS International Directory of Performing Arts Collections*, General Editor: Richard Buck, Editors: Paul S Ulrich, Ruth Freydank and Roger Rennenberg. Haslemere, Emmett Publishers, 1996, 651 p.

[25] This change was also reflected in the title which replaced the words "Libraries" and "Museums" with "Collections".

[26] This has also been retained in the Web-based directory, where all SIBMAS institutions are indicated by a blue "S".

[27] Active links from the Directory to Websites of the institutions and email addresses.

[28] At the SIBMAS Congress in Rome, it was decided that links to these databases should be included in the entries. The addition of this material has begun to be implemented, beginning with those databases presented at the SIBMAS Congress in 2002 in Rome.

The Migration to a Web-based Directory

Indications of potential long-range problems became increasingly apparent during the preparation of the 5th edition. The number of institutions which needed to be sent proof sheets was so large (over 5,000) that postage costs were high. Even though the layout and content had been streamlined, the space needed for the increased number of institutions and the indexes was such that the price for the printed edition could not be kept under USD 100. The price of the printed version (USD 150) was too high for many institutions to afford. This resulted in a low number of purchases. Parallel to this, the international publishing scene was experiencing major changes by increasingly using electronic methods of distribution (CD-ROM and Internet) particularly for reference works.

Already in 1996 there were numerous requests for an electronic version of the directory, primarily from academic institutions in the USA and the United Kingdom. Within SIBMAS there was still a feeling that the printed version should be maintained for institutions which were not capable of accessing electronic versions. Supporting this argumentation became increasingly difficult when one examined the sales of the printed version: the institutions which did not have the resources for accessing an electronic version of the directory were not purchasing the printed version, and those institutions which were purchasing the printed edition were also those institutions desiring an electronic version.

Following the publication of the 5th edition in 1996, there were numerous discussions about the future of the directory. Transferring the directory to CD-ROM was rejected, since many of the problems of the printed directory would merely be transferred to the new medium. In addition new problems would need to be addressed, among them creating at least two versions (Macintosh and Windows) and developing an appropriate user interface which could be used internationally.

The increasing acceptance and accessibility of the Internet seemed to offer an alternative which might solve many of the problems: no printing costs, ease in making corrections and keeping the information current. Emmett Publishing already had made several of its databases accessible by subscription on the Internet, so such a move would have been possible. They already had a structure which could be transferred to an online version of the directory. The question still remained, whether or not institutions would be willing to pay for online access to the directory, or whether the non-use would continue because of an unwillingness to pay for online databases. An early decision was made that should the directory be offered as a subscription database, a demo version would be made available free-of-charge for potential users to evaluate the usefulness of the offering. In order to increase the attractiveness of being a SIBMAS member, it was decided that only institutions which were members of SIBMAS would have access to this demo database[29].

With the cessation of Emmett Publishing in the summer of 2000, SIBMAS was forced to reevaluate the continuation of the directory. At the SIBMAS Conference in Paris in September 2000, the decision was made to migrate the directory to the Web and to make it available free-of-charge on the SIBMAS Website[30]. The administrative costs of maintaining a fee-based directory were such that it was unrealistic to expect that it would be able to generate income for SIBMAS[31]. Furthermore usage would probably not be very high, since most institutions felt that what was on the Internet should be free-of-charge anyway.

Maria Teresa Iovinelli, the Webmaster of the SIBMAS Website, indicated that there was sufficient space available on the server to house the Web-based directory[32]. Paul S. Ulrich was given the task of migrating the information in the database (which had increased to almost 7,000 institutions) to the Web.

At the Executive Committee meeting in Rome in October 2001, the Web directory was presented for approval and it was proposed that it be mounted on the Website prior to the end of the year. The members of the committee had numerous suggestions for improving both the presentation and the content. It was then decided to postpone the start of the Web-based directory until March 2002[33]. After the official start of the directory on the Web, the URL was sent to numerous mailing lists and online news services, so that it would be known. Since its

---

[29] Since it could be assumed that institutions with large holdings were SIBMAS members, this would give the demo database a high feeling of quality and usefulness and thereby be a good way of promoting the value of the complete database.

[30] http://www.theatrelibrary.org/sibmas/sibmas.html.

[31] Among these problems are managing payments (collecting the money), controlling access to the directory (entering and maintaining passwords) and maintaining statistics for the users.

[32] It was estimated that the directory would require between 30 and 50 megabytes of disk space.

[33] The Web-based directory was actually available on the Web in December 2001. Initially only members of the Executive Committee had the URL. This permitted them to check the content and send corrections to Paul S. Ulrich, who then made the respective changes. When several institutions linked to this URL on their Websites, it was picked up by the robots of several search engines, which meant that prior to the "official" presence of the directory on the Web, the directory was already being used by people who had found it via search engines. This put pressure on SIBMAS to make the presence known officially.

appearance on the Web, there has been a noticeable increase of the usage of the SIBMAS Web offerings.

The Structure of the Directory

Users of the directory have different needs at different times. The printed directory already provided the basis for the types of access needed for the Web-based directory: geographic (what institutions are in a city?), name of institution (where is information about a specific institution?) and names of special collections (which institutions have material on a special topic?). Transferring these points of access to the Web meant that the information in each Web page be broken down into the smallest possible units[34]: geographic by city, institution and collection names alphabetical in many short lists rather than one long list.

The Web version of the directory has over 3,000 Web pages. With this many pages (= files), the organisation on the server plays an important role, both in generating the files from the database, making updates on the server, as well as for the navigation and later use.

The main information about an institution is contained in the geographic (city) files. These are grouped by geographic region[35], each region having its own directory on the server. Each regional directory has an index file ("index.html"[36]) for all the countries in the region and each country has its own index file for the cities. All file names have no more than 8 characters plus the "html" extension. The file names for the cities all have the same structure: ISO country code, first letter of city name, 3 digit number padded with "0" to indicate how many other cities from the country have the same beginning letter. These file name conventions make it very easy to isolate and copy files with wild cards for

---

[34] There are numerous reasons for having so many files: it corresponds to the needs of the users: if he is interested in the institutions in a town, providing him with additional information about other towns distracts him from what he is looking for. The more towns in a file, the larger it will be; this means that the user will be forced to find what he is really interested in on the page. A large file also takes longer to download. Furthermore, by not having long lists on one page it makes it more difficult for institutions looking for lists of addresses for commercial mailings to simply download the addresses and make them commercially available.

[35] Africa, Asia, Australasia, Caribbean, Central America, Europe, Middle East, North America and South America.

[36] This corresponds to the default file name of the server. Using this name means that it is not necessary to provide the file name in the URL, since it will automatically be used by the server. For example, the URL of the home page of the directory http://www.theatrelibrary.org/sibmas/idpac/index.html.
The URL http://www.theatrelibrary.org/sibmas/idpac/ automatically loads the actual file and is shorter to use.

the administrators of the system[37]. It also makes it very easy to create file names by the program which exports the information from the database to html-files. This convention also guarantees that a name will not be given twice to a file when, for example the name of a city is the same in two countries (for example, San Francisco in California and in Spain).

There are two additional indexes on the server which make it possible for a user to go directly to the main entry: Institutions and Collections. In addition to the "index.html" file, which lists all the files in the respective directory, the names of the individual files have the following structure: the first two characters of the name of the institution or the collection. These files are also easily generated by the program.

Findability and Usability

The first important decision was that the directory would have to attract as many possible visitors as possible and offer as many points of access as possible. This meant that the content could not be presented as a database[38] on the server, which would only offer one point of entry, but rather all the information would be on individual pages, i.e. the presentation on the Web would be with static rather than dynamic pages. Furthermore, frames would not be used, since the content of frames provides indexing problems for search engines, and it is very difficult to link to a specific page within a frames environment.

Much of what is necessary to make it easy find a page is not really new or special, rather it is a matter of logic. In order to create a usable Website it is necessary to understand how search engines gather their information about a Website and how they process it for presentation in their lists of "hits". Likewise it is important to be aware of how people using the Internet react to the presentation of Web offerings. This knowledge must then be transferred to the actual presentation so that it supports rather than discourages use.

There are generally two ways that people find a Website:

---

[37] A negative aspect of this convention is that the name of the file does not reflect the content. If the name of the file contained the name of the city, it would increase the ratings on search machines. Creating an algorithm to make use of this negative aspect would not be easy. This disadvantage is not so serious, however, that the administrative advantages of the file name conventions are overridden.

[38] Databases belong to the "invisible Web" and their content is not indexed by search engines. Hence someone looking for information on a search engine is not directed to the individual entries. This is comparable to library OPACs on the Internet, their content cannot be found with a search engine.

1. They find a reference to it a thematic directory (such as Yahoo, the Open Directory), in a clearinghouse or in a link collection. In such instances they are directed to the home page of the offering. These link collections are manually maintained and links are added when those managing the directories are made aware of the presence of a new site. As a rule a link is only made to one location – the home page –, and the Web offering may or may not reflect where the creator of the offering feels it should be placed[39].

2. They use a search engine (such as Google, AltaVista, AllTheWeb, etc.) to find it; more specifically they find a page with words corresponding to terms they are looking forward to, whether or not the terms are on the home page or somewhere within the offering.

These search engines are fed with information picked up by robots. Each individual page is analysed and the words on the page are entered into the search engine database, i.e. each word on the page (or combinations of the words) serves as points of entry for someone looking for information. Complicated mathematical algorithms ultimately determine how easily or poorly one's page is rated, and this determines whether or not one lands among the first 10 to 20 offerings.

After a page has been found, it must also be used. The easier a page can be used, the greater the chances are that it will be used again in the future. A page which is difficult to use discourages users from returning to the site in the future, since negative experiences are counterproductive.

Within the past few years the concept of usability is of central concern to designers of high-usage Websites. They realise that the greater emphasis they place on making a Website usable, the greater the usage will be. The recommendations of such usability studies have been incorporated in the SIBMAS directory.

There are many factors which must be taken into consideration when planning the presentation. Too frequently designers are so interested in making a Web presentation look nice that they forget the behaviour of themselves and others when actually using the Web. Before a Website is used, it must first be found. It is not enough to inform search engines that a site is present; it must also land in the top 20 results of a search

---

[39] This is comparable to the traditional way of finding information in a library via the catalogues: the primary source of information is what is found on the title page of the book. One must "guess" what information is hidden within the book, since it is not indexed in catalogues.

engine for it to be found. This means that choice of page title, choice of wording, coding the text all play a role in the findability.

- *Minimum hierarchical depth.* From the home page to a page with the sought information, a user should ideally only have to click a maximum of three times[40].

- *Navigational elements at all points.* Every page should provide information to the surrounding environment and have links to the various points of entry[41].

- *Each page has its own distinctive title*, with the page specific information at the beginning of the title.

The title plays a role not only in being found, but also when navigating within a Website. The most import differentiating part of the title of the page should be placed first, not at the end of the title. The title has several functions:

a) it is always indexed by all search engines;

b) the words in the title have added weight in mathematical algorithms for search engine placement;

c) the title is what is automatically given for the entry in the favourite (Internet Explorer) or bookmark (Netscape Navigator[42]) listings;

d) the title is what appears in browser "history" listings;

e) the title is printed on all print-outs[43].

For this reason, the title of each main entry page begins with the name of the city, followed by the country and ending with "SIBMAS International Directory of Performing Arts Collections and Institutions".

- *Page renewal coding* to guarantee that the current version of a page is viewed by the user. Most designers forget that if a user has already viewed a page recently, his browser will load the version from the cache and not the version on the respective server. By putting a command in the html text[44], it is possible to override

---

[40] For practical reasons this principle was rejected for the geographic access, which requires four clicks to access the information: home page, geographic region, country, city.

[41] Since each page of the directory is a point of entry when it is found by a search engine, it is important that navigation elements for the entire directory be present on each page.

[42] Now Firefox.

[43] Assuming that this is not intentionally suppressed by the user.

[44] "<meta http-equiv="expires" content="43200">", whereby the value "43200" corresponds to the number of seconds in a day, hence the cached copy of a file on the

the use of the local cache and be more certain that the viewed information reflects the current status of a page.

- *Index at top and bottom of each page.* Not only does this facilitate navigation on the page, it also has a few other important advantages: the user sees at the beginning of the page, what is on it and can quickly jump to the entry which he is interested in; equally important, it means that for all the institutions on the page the name appears three times; this in turn means that there is automatically a greater weight of the page for search engines.

- *Names of institutions coded as heading.* Since search engines give greater weight to terms listed on a page as "headings" [45], the name of the institution in the main entry is coded as a heading and is not merely in bold text[46].

- *URL on every page.* The full URL is included on every page. This is equivalent to professional journals including the name and issue of the journal on every page and guarantees that on every printout or download of the page, that its source will be retained. Furthermore, having the URL on each page is good public relations and it guarantees that the source is always provided with the page content – particularly when it is downloaded[47].

- *Content on the left side of the page, navigation elements on the right.* Just as most people read from left to right, so do the content evaluation programs of search engines. Text on the left-hand side of a page has greater weight than text on the right-hand side. The navigation elements are important, but should not be given additional weight for search engines.

Putting the main text on the left side of each page also makes the page easier to use. This is particularly true for handicapped viewers who use auxiliary programs to magnify the text: it is easier to jump to the left or right side of a page than to locate text which is in the centre of the page[48].

---

user's pc (and also that cached on the servers) should automatically be replaced with the current file from the sibmas server if it is older than one day.

[45] The html coding is "<h1>.... </h1>" to "<h6>...</h6>" as opposed to "..." for bold face.

[46] To the naked eye there is no difference between the appearance of text marked as a heading or in bold face, the difference is the weight given to them by search engines.

[47] When a file is downloaded to a disk, the URL is lost if it is not included in the file itself.

[48] Since increasingly countries are passing legislation which require that everything should be done to make information equally available to handicapped persons, it is

Equally important is what information about the page appears on the upper left portion of the screen, since this is the first information about the page and very often determines whether the whole page is viewed or not.

- *Quick loading.* The file must load quickly, otherwise the viewer will click and go on to another page[49] – no one has time to wait for a page to be loaded. As a general rule the designer of a page must do everything in his power to reduce the loading time of a file to a minimum. This means that the file should be less than 50 KB in size and have as few graphics as is necessary[50].

Use of the Directory

After spending so much time designing the Website so that it would be visible on the Web and also be usable, the big questions remain: is it being found, is it being used?

An examination of the log files[51] on the SIBMAS server clearly shows that since the presence of the directory the usage of the SIBMAS Website has increased considerably. Not only have the number of visits to the server by search engine robots increased considerably[52], the number of visits to the directory by users has increased dramatically. Log files also give a good indication of how the directory is being accessed. Although

---

only logical that Web designers should begin making usability for handicapped persons a prime requirement in their design.

[49] A rule of thumb is that one has 20 seconds after a page has begun to be loaded to catch the attention of the viewer. If within these 20 seconds his interest is not caught, he will return to the page he came from and the page will not be viewed.

[50] It makes good sense to keep the loading time short, since time is money: viewers expend a lot of valuable time waiting for information to become visible on a browser. Furthermore, in many countries the user's telephone fares are calculated by the length of time they have telephone connection to their Internet provider. Long file loading times mean higher costs for the viewer.

[51] Statistical information collected by the server. These records include information about where the visitor to the page came from, how long the page was viewed, where the user went from the page, errors encountered using the page etc. By regularly evaluating this information, corrections can be made to the Website in order to optimise usage.

[52] The increased visits by search engines means that the information from the directory can potentially be found among the results of queries on the search engines. Likewise it means that search engines are regularly checking to update their information about the site.

many visits are over the regional pages, the largest number of visits and usage is over the indexes of the special collections[53].

Likewise, regular checks for Websites linking to the directory have pleasantly revealed an increasing awareness of Webmasters who are including links to the directory. This is doubly important:

1. the more pages on the Internet linking to the offerings, the greater the chances of somebody finding it;

2. particularly in the last year, and in particular popularised by Google, the placement of a Web page in a list of hits by a search engine is to a large extent governed by how many pages link to it: the more links, the closer to being number one on a search engine hit list.

A further indication of the use of the Web-based directory is evident in the number of emails which the editor receives from visitors to the Website. Almost daily emails requesting information about the holdings of various institutions are received.

Even more interesting are the emails which report corrections for the directory. Whereas in the past all modifications were either identified by the editor or members of SIBMAS, now potentially all the users of the directory are potential sources for corrections or additions to the information. Many institutions have noticed that their listing is not correct and have directly contacted the editor and requested that corresponding changes be made to their entry.

Future Plans for the Directory

It would be wrong to assume that the directory should remain in its present form. By reviewing usage of the presentation, changes are continually being made to the layout: some of the changes are major and easily recognisable; others are minor and not noticeable. Changes in the Web presence of information from others means that this needs to be regularly reviewed and either incorporated in the directory or made available via SIBMAS in other forms.

New browsers and new expectations of users mean that the layout and page coding must be carefully examined on a regular basis to see that it conforms to the current standards and still not only be viewable by the most popular browsers.

---

[53] This has led to an in-depth evaluation and standardisation of the entries in the index. In particular the names of persons with special collections are being standardised and expanded to include full names (with variants), dates of birth and death, and professions.

Currently SIBMAS is not capable of financing extensive mailings to update the information on the various institutions. Since the number of institutions with email is rapidly increasing, it would seem logical that at regular intervals these institutions be sent emails in which they could be requested to update the information about themselves.

Currently the editor makes the changes to the database on his computer and then generates the pages for the Web, which then must be manually updated to the server. In the near future it will be necessary to move this database to the server directly and install programs which will automatically update the pages on the server. Such a move would also make it easier to email requests for corrections to the institutions in the directory. Likewise it would make it possible for numerous persons to do the actual editing of the database.

Conclusion

From its inception as a book in 1960 to the present electronic Web version, the SIBMAS directory has been an important instrument for locating which institutions had material on the performing arts and where specific material could be found. The many changes which have been made reflect not only the rise in the number of institutions collecting this material, it also reflects the changes in how information is made available in an increasingly changing world. The use of the SIBMAS International Directory of Performing Arts Collections and Institutions both in the past and at the present is an indication of the need of such resources. In the future the need for such a tool will not decrease, but will be even more necessary. The content and the presentation will not necessarily remain the same. It should, however, reflect the needs of both the institutions for making their holdings known and for those looking for these holdings[54].

---

[54] Addendum (2011): Since this paper was presented at the SIBMAS Congress in Rome, there have been several changes. The address of the SIBMAS Website was changed and is now http://www.sibmas.org. That of the directory is http://www.sibmas.org/idpac. Upon my retirement at the end of 2008 I gave up being the editor of the directory. I very much hope that there will be enough willingness on the part of SIBMAS members to continue the work of making the directory even more useful in the years to come. The value of the directory both to researchers and SIBMAS can be seen in the usage it has had. It is now up to others to continue making the directory better and more useful. The need is most definitely there.

Le *Répertoire des arts du spectacle* (RASP)

Christelle CAZAUX

Bibliothèque nationale de France (Paris – France)

Le *Répertoire des arts du spectacle* est un instrument de recherche destiné à guider les chercheurs, les professionnels du spectacle et le grand public à travers les sources patrimoniales ou documentaires qui constituent la mémoire du spectacle en France. Accessible depuis 2001 sur le site Internet du ministère de la Culture et de la Communication, sous la forme d'une base de données, le *Répertoire des arts du spectacle* recense, localise et décrit les fonds relatifs aux arts du spectacle en France, quelle que soit leur nature ou l'établissement qui les conserve.

Histoire du projet (1997-1999)

Pourquoi un Répertoire des arts du spectacle *?*

Né en 1997, à l'initiative du Département des arts du spectacle de la Bibliothèque nationale de France, le projet de *Répertoire des arts du spectacle* s'est imposé devant l'absence de moyen pratique et efficace pour identifier et localiser les sources de l'histoire du spectacle en France. En effet, à l'exception de l'annuaire publié par la SIBMAS, qui du fait de sa couverture géographique ne décrit pas en détail les collections des établissements qu'il répertorie, il n'existait jusque-là aucun guide des sources conservées en France.

L'objectif du projet de *Répertoire des arts du spectacle* était donc avant tout de fournir un guide des collections concernant le théâtre, le théâtre lyrique, la danse, le cirque, le mime, les marionnettes, mais aussi le music-hall, le cabaret, le café-théâtre, la variété, conservées dans les bibliothèques, les musées, les archives, les théâtres, les compagnies, ou encore les conservatoires, les écoles de spectacle, les associations professionnelles et autres établissements de recherche et de promotion du spectacle.

Des recensements avaient déjà été entrepris dans ce domaine, mais leur champ d'investigation ne couvrait qu'une partie des établissements susceptibles de conserver des documents sur l'histoire du spectacle ou s'étaient limités à certains domaines seulement : ainsi l'enquête *Mémoire des lieux de théâtre*, menée conjointement par le Centre national du théâtre et la Direction des archives de France en 1998, dont le but était d'étudier les pratiques des théâtres subventionnés en matière de classement et de conservation des archives.

Aussi était-il nécessaire d'étendre le champ d'investigation du *Répertoire* au plus grand nombre d'établissements et de domaines possibles, en instituant un partenariat entre les différentes directions du ministère de la Culture et de la Communication. Un comité de pilotage composé de représentants de la Direction des musées de France, de la Direction des archives de France, de la Direction de la musique, de la danse, du théâtre et des spectacles, du Comité d'histoire du ministère de la Culture et de la Mission de la recherche et de la technologie ainsi que de la Bibliothèque nationale de France fut constitué et placé sous l'égide de la Direction du livre et de la lecture du ministère de la Culture et de la Communication. La réalisation matérielle du projet fut confiée à la Bibliothèque nationale de France.

L'enquête

La première étape du projet fut une vaste enquête, auprès des services d'archives, des bibliothèques, des musées et des théâtres, commencée en octobre 1998. Un questionnaire détaillé fut envoyé à plus de 2 600 établissements : 563 services d'archives, 453 bibliothèques, 946 musées et 630 théâtres.

Une campagne active de relances, soit par courrier, soit par téléphone, qui s'est poursuivie jusqu'en 2002, a permis de recueillir près de 800 réponses positives à l'enquête. Ce nombre, qui paraît considérable, montre à la fois l'éparpillement des collections sur le spectacle dans des établissements à vocation pluridisciplinaire (bibliothèques municipales, musées des beaux-arts, dépôts d'archives), et, au contraire, le faible nombre d'établissements spécialisés dans le domaine qui nous intéresse.

Il ne faut cependant pas se laisser trop fortement impressionner par un tel résultat, qui recouvre des réalités très diverses. En effet, le volume des collections signalées varie considérablement d'un établissement à l'autre. À côté de pièces isolées, parfois arrivées par hasard, ou de collections précieuses mais modestes, souvent liées à l'histoire locale, que l'enquête a permis de (re)découvrir, on trouve quelques grandes institutions conservant des centaines d'œuvres ou de fonds dont il est difficile de faire le tour. Mais nous reviendrons plus précisément sur la nature et la répartition des collections que le *Répertoire* a permis de recenser dans la suite de l'exposé.

La base de données

La première base sous Mistral (2000-2002)

Dès l'origine du projet, l'idée du comité de pilotage était de verser les informations recueillies lors de l'enquête dans une base de données. Le but était de permettre, à partir d'un sujet de recherche donné – une personnalité du spectacle, un théâtre ou l'histoire théâtrale d'une ville, mais aussi un thème comme le décor ou l'architecture –, de retrouver tous les témoignages documentaires ou artistiques parvenus jusqu'à nous, de les décrire brièvement et d'indiquer les modalités pratiques de leur accès. Afin de rendre les informations recueillies très largement accessibles, le *Répertoire* devait être accessible sur Internet.

Les réflexions sur la structure de la base ont commencé au printemps 1999 et ont été menées en collaboration avec le service informatique du ministère de la Culture et de la Communication. Le logiciel Mistral, déjà utilisé pour d'autres bases de données documentaires réalisées par le ministère de la Culture, a été adopté. La structure des notices du *Répertoire*, qui comprend une trentaine de champs, permet de signaler un ensemble de documents comme une pièce isolée, avec des informations pratiques sur l'établissement qui les conserve.

La saisie des informations recueillies grâce à l'enquête a commencé en juillet 2000. Elle s'achèvera à la fin de l'année 2002. En effet, si presque tous les questionnaires reçus depuis 1999 ont été saisis, le signalement des collections de certains grands établissements aux collections pléthoriques nécessite encore des recherches et un effort de synthèse particuliers. C'est le cas des différents départements de la Bibliothèque nationale de France et du Musée national d'art moderne, entre autres.

La base a été rendue publique en mai 2001[1] sur le site du ministère de la Culture.

Cette mise en ligne précoce, alors que la saisie n'en était qu'à la moitié des questionnaires reçus, a permis au *Répertoire des arts du spectacle* de commencer à se faire connaître du public. Nos partenaires du ministère de la Culture sont très soucieux de la promotion de la base et œuvrent dans ce sens. Les statistiques de consultation ont crû régulièrement entre mai 2001 et octobre 2001, puis se sont stabilisées autour de 900 à 1 000 interrogations par mois.

---

[1]   Addendum (2012) : Le site est consultable à l'adresse http://rasp.culture.fr.

2002 : la conversion en XML

Au printemps 2001, une réflexion sur l'avenir de la base et sur les limites, en matière d'interrogation et d'interface Web, du logiciel jusque-là utilisé, a conduit à envisager une conversion vers un outil plus moderne et plus souple. Le choix s'est porté sur SDX (Système Documentaire XML), une application développée par Martin Sévigny, de la Société AJLSM (Bordeaux), une « plate-forme » qui permet de gérer des données documentaires en format XML.

SDX présente un certain nombre d'avantages : il n'utilise que des logiciels libres de droits, fondés sur des normes et des formats standards. Spécialement conçu pour des applications documentaires diffusées sur Internet, SDX a la particularité d'associer un moteur de recherche en texte intégral à une interrogation traditionnelle utilisant la structure de la base en différents champs. Par exemple, et c'est le principal atout de ce nouveau logiciel par rapport à Mistral, il est désormais possible de rechercher un mot dans un champ ou dans l'ensemble des champs de la notice. Avec Mistral, au contraire, la recherche passait obligatoirement par la consultation du lexique d'un champ, car il fallait connaître l'expression exacte telle qu'elle avait été saisie dans la base pour que la recherche donne un résultat.

En somme, la conversion vers SDX permet de bénéficier de tous les avantages de la norme XML : une interface plus conviviale, une souplesse et des possibilités d'interrogation accrues, pour l'usager comme pour le gestionnaire de la base. L'usager a désormais le choix entre plusieurs modes d'interrogation : recherche simple à partir d'un ou plusieurs mots tapés dans une fenêtre unique d'interrogation, recherche guidée par domaine du spectacle ou par région, recherche avancée permettant de croiser les critères et d'utiliser les opérateurs booléens. Enfin, SDX permettra, d'associer facilement des images numérisées à certaines notices du Répertoire.

Le patrimoine des arts du spectacle en France : bilan de l'enquête

Bien que la base ne soit pas encore tout à fait achevée, son volume actuel et le faible nombre d'établissements qui ne sont pas encore saisis nous autorisent désormais à analyser son contenu et à tirer quelques conclusions sur la nature et la localisation des fonds sur les arts du spectacle en France.

Au mois de juillet 2002, la base comprenait 1 203 notices décrivant les collections de 711 établissements, dans 342 localités. Toutes les régions sont représentées, y compris un département d'outre-mer (la Guadeloupe) et la principauté de Monaco.

Répartition par type d'établissement

La localisation des collections sur les arts du spectacle révèle une nette prédominance des musées sur les autres types d'établissements. Par le nombre d'établissements concernés (39 % des établissements recensés) comme par le nombre de fonds conservés (37 % des notices de la base), les musées arrivent en tête. Viennent ensuite les dépôts d'archives, qui conservent 33 % des fonds signalés dans le Répertoire, alors que par le nombre d'établissements ils ne sont qu'au troisième rang (20 %) derrière les bibliothèques (22 %)[2]. Le calcul du nombre moyen de notices, donc de fonds, par établissement laisse clairement apparaître que si les musées sont très nombreux, ils conservent généralement moins de fonds ou d'ensembles de documents que les archives[3].

La part des établissements dont la vocation principale n'est pas la conservation du patrimoine reste importante : les théâtres, compagnies, festivals et autres établissements représentent presque un cinquième des établissements recensés, mais seulement 11 % des fonds[4].

Répartition géographique

La répartition entre la région parisienne et les autres régions est plus favorable à ces dernières qu'on ne pourrait le croire : en effet Paris et l'Île-de-France ne représentent qu'un quart des établissements et des collections recensées[5]. Il est vrai que la proportion de fonds conservés dans des établissements parisiens et d'Île-de-France risque de croître un peu lorsque les derniers grands musées et la Bibliothèque nationale de France, dont les collections nécessiteront des dizaines de notices, seront saisis. Le sud-est de la France (Provence-Alpes-Côte d'Azur et Rhône-Alpes), le Nord-Pas-de-Calais et les Pays de la Loire, mais aussi le Centre, l'Alsace, l'Aquitaine et la Basse-Normandie sont les régions les mieux représentées dans le *Répertoire*. Les plus pauvres en fonds sur les arts du spectacle sont la Corse, le Limousin, l'Auvergne[6].

Outre la présence relativement forte des établissements de province, l'enquête a révélé une extrême dispersion des documents patrimoniaux sur les arts du spectacle en France. L'analyse de la répartition des collections par ville met bien en évidence ce phénomène. Hormis Paris (15 % de la base), les 20 villes qui, après elle, conservent le plus de

---

[2] Voir, dans ce chapitre, Annexes 1 et 2.

[3] Voir, dans ce chapitre, Annexe 3.

[4] Voir, dans ce chapitre, Annexes 1 et 2.

[5] Voir, dans ce chapitre, Annexe 4.

[6] Voir, dans ce chapitre, Annexe 5.

fonds sur les arts du spectacle ne représentent que 19 % des établissements recensés. Ces villes sont : Paris, Bordeaux, Lyon, Strasbourg, Marseille, Avignon, Nice, Rennes, Besançon, Toulouse, Montpellier, Lille, Caen, Amiens, Dijon, Nîmes, Nantes, Limoges, Bourges, Angers, Versailles. On retrouve dans cette liste la plupart des grandes métropoles régionales, qui réunissent généralement un, voire deux services d'archives (départementales et municipales), une bibliothèque municipale classée, un grand musée et un ou plusieurs théâtres. Si ces 20 villes détiennent donc près de 29 % des fonds recensés (44 % avec Paris), le reste de la France représente encore 56 % des notices de la base de données, soit plus de la moitié de la base, et, signe encore plus évident de la dispersion de ces collections, 67 % des établissements[7].

Répartition par type de document

L'étude de la répartition des documents dans le *Répertoire des arts du spectacle* se heurte à quelques difficultés. En effet, il s'agit d'analyser le contenu du champ « nature des documents » qui ne renvoie ni à un nombre de notices, ni à un nombre de documents, mais simplement au nombre de fois où un type de document est signalé dans le champ les notices du *Répertoire*.

Dans la base de données, les différents types de documents ont été rattachés à cinq catégories génériques : écrit, audiovisuel et son, iconographie, objets d'art, décor, costumes et accessoires de scène. Or, certains documents se rapportent à deux catégories : c'est le cas des affiches, qui peuvent être ou non illustrées, ce que les questionnaires ne précisent pas toujours. Les proportions qui suivent sont donc légèrement faussées en faveur des documents écrits et iconographiques, les affiches étant comptées deux fois. Mais nous avons préféré les garder tels quels plutôt que de les corriger arbitrairement.

Le statistiques montrent que les documents écrits, manuscrits ou imprimés, sont présents dans 39 % des notices ; viennent ensuite l'iconographie (35 %), les costumes, décors et accessoires de scène (10 %), puis l'audiovisuel (9 %), enfin les objets d'art (7 %)[8]. Eu égard à la très forte représentation des musées dans la base, la faible proportion d'objets d'art n'est guère surprenante. Elle confirme la forte présence de l'iconographie, des costumes, des décors et des accessoires de scène dans les musées, ainsi que leur vocation à collecter ce genre de documents. Sans doute certains musées conservent-ils également une part non négligeable des documents écrits recensés dans la base : on

---

[7] Voir, dans ce chapitre, Annexes 6 et 7.

[8] Voir, dans ce chapitre, Annexe 8.

pense naturellement aux maisons d'écrivains, qui rassemblent des objets personnels et des œuvres d'art, mais aussi de la correspondance, des livres, des manuscrits, des périodiques.

Une étude plus poussée du contenu du *Répertoire* reste à faire sur la répartition des types de documents en fonction des établissements, et notamment celle des documents écrits et iconographiques. Malheureusement, ce travail, qui serait très intéressant, n'a pu être mené dans le cadre de cette présentation parce que la structure de la base de données ne permet pas d'obtenir ce genre de statistiques très facilement.

Parmi les documents écrits, ce sont les documents de diffusion (programmes, affiches...) qui sont le plus fréquemment mentionnés (26 %). Imprimés, périodiques, presse, textes de pièces, manuscrits, correspondance, partitions, documents de mise en scène et documents administratifs se répartissent de façon à peu près égale[9]. Pour l'iconographie, ce sont les photographies (33 %), les dessins et les estampes (29 %) qui semblent prédominer[10].

Perspectives d'avenir

Le *Répertoire* a été conçu comme un outil s'adressant avant tout au monde de la recherche et aux professionnels du spectacle. Maintenant que la saisie est en voie d'achèvement et que sa nouvelle interface le rend plus efficace et plus convivial, il semble répondre à ce besoin. Nous espérons que ceux qui le consulteront nous feront part de leurs remarques éventuelles, afin que nous puissions l'améliorer.

À la faveur des liens qui ont été tissés lors de l'enquête, nous espérons inciter les établissements qui figurent dans la base à nous faire part des mises à jour les concernant et à entreprendre des actions de valorisation de leurs collections. La prochaine étape du *Répertoire* leur offrira la possibilité de le faire. En effet, il est prévu d'illustrer les notices de la base à l'aide de reproductions de documents se rapportant aux collections décrites. Ce travail sera probablement long et difficile, en raison des problèmes de droits qu'il pose. Des contacts ont été pris dans ce sens avec quelques grands musées et bibliothèques qui accepteraient de nous communiquer des images déjà numérisées. Nous espérons ensuite inciter les autres établissements signalés dans le *Répertoire*, notamment les plus modestes, à nous aider à mettre en œuvre ce projet, peut-être dans le cadre d'un partenariat entre le ministère de la Culture et les régions.

---

[9]   Voir, dans ce chapitre, Annexe 9.

[10]   Voir, dans ce chapitre, Annexe 10.

Annexe 1. Les établissements du RASP : répartition par type

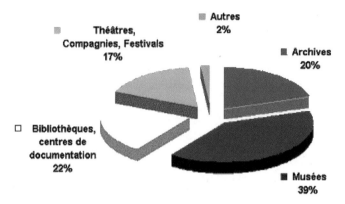

Annexe 2. Les fonds du RASP : répartition par type d'établissement

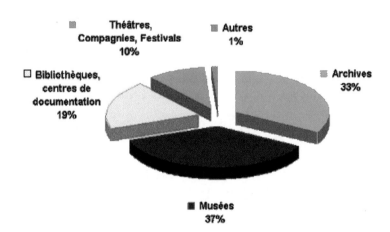

Annexe 3. Nombre de notices par établissement

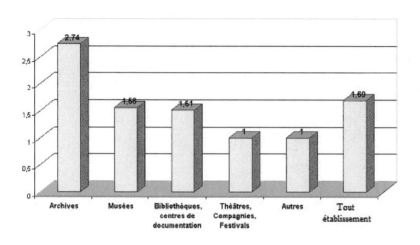

Annexe 4. Répartition géographique des établissements et des fonds

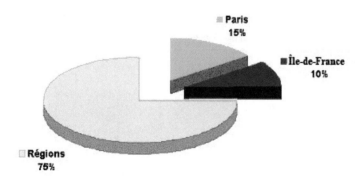

Annexe 5. Répartition régionale des fonds du RASP

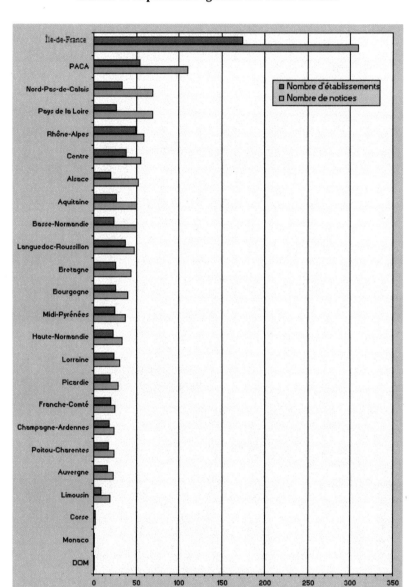

Annexe 6. Répartition des établissements (villes)

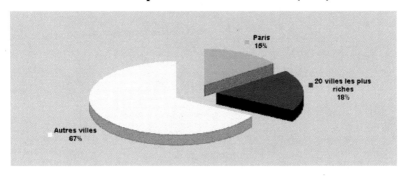

Annexe 7. Répartition des fonds (villes)

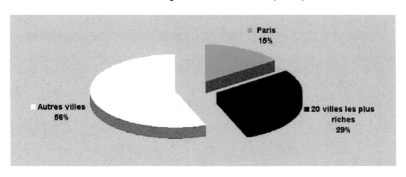

Annexe 8. Typologie et répartition des documents

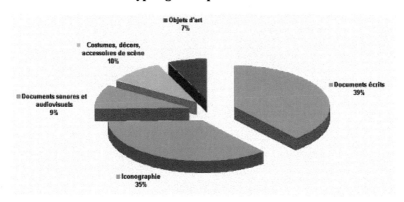

Annexe 9. Typologie et répartition des documents écrits

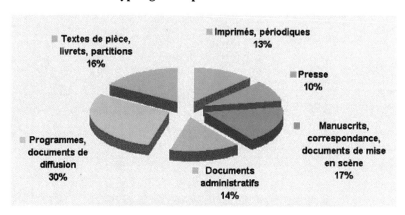

Annexe 10. Typologie et répartition des documents iconographiques

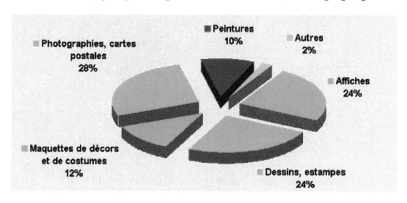

Backstage

Discovering Performing Arts Resources

Claire HUDSON

Theatre Museum (London – United Kingdom)

The Current Information Environment

We live in a rapidly developing information environment. Although we probably did not think so at the time, the impact of automation on libraries and archives was relatively slow and sedate to begin with. The computerised catalogues and circulation systems of the 1970's now seem simple in the extreme. They helped the user to a certain degree; they also greatly eased the workloads of cataloguers and other library staff. But in many ways they simply translated what we had done manually into an electronic form.

It has been the arrival of the Internet and the new opportunities for sharing data which is now really revolutionising the information world. Standards are even more important than ever before because they are enabling this worldwide sharing of records and documents to happen.

The Backstage project is an example of a project which has been enabled by the development of new standards, by a favourable funding environment and by current trends within the UK library, archive and museum sectors.

These current trends can be defined as:

- Increased emphasis on the needs of users, especially researchers in the Higher Education sector (i.e. universities). Now that users have experienced the first wave of computerised catalogues they are vocalising their needs more clearly. They want user friendly catalogues, access to all types of materials (not just published books and journals) and of course they ultimately want delivery of full text documents and images to their desktops.

- Resource discovery and mapping projects. Earlier automation projects tended to focus on cataloguing monographs and periodicals. Let's face it – they are easy to catalogue because they have title pages, blurbs and contents pages which tell the cataloguer almost all they need to know; they also offer libraries economies because they only need to catalogue an item once, and the record will be reusable by other libraries with the same item to catalogue. But now we are increasingly conscious that a wealth of non-published material – archives, ephemera and artworks – exists in our heritage collections. They have the potential to be of even greater value to research than published material but their cataloguing is much more difficult. Standards have usually not been used to catalogue them in the past, and catalogue records often exist outside the electronic world, if at all. The use of standardised cataloguing rules and formats has been far less common in archives and museums than in libraries. Converting or creating electronically exchangeable data for this material is likely to be slow and expensive, especially as much of it is unique, and so the potential for sharing the work of creating the records is limited. For this reason, there is a drive, at least in the UK, to start at the top level, by making the whole collection the subject of description, not the individual items in it. Collection level description offers a more rapid solution to the problem of dealing with uncatalogued collections (uncatalogued in the sense of not having standardised, electronic records). It also overcomes the problem which we are now encountering in the electronic world – of searches throwing up too many hits. By giving them the option of searching at the broader, collection level rather than the individual item, researchers can identify the important caches of material as a starting point, before homing in on individual items. They can deal later with the individual stray items dispersed around other organisations' collections. And for the managers of collections – librarians, curators and archivists, and the bureaucrats who fund them of course, the use of collection level description allows them to see a map of the national coverage of subject areas. It indicates where duplication may be occurring and also where there is potential for collaborative projects or a more complementary approach to subject coverage. The assigning of responsibility for collection development and user access to designated organisations is likely to be a major development in the UK information world in the next 5 years.

- Merging of the divisions between library, archive and museum domains. As I've already stated, researchers are hungry for access to material and, as long as it is relevant to their subject, they don't much mind what physical format it is in. The somewhat artificial boundaries between library, archive and museum collections are beginning to be questioned. In the performing arts subject area in particular this questioning is particularly relevant. Documenting the subject requires an organisation to collect from all three domains, and many performing arts "libraries" collect works of art, costumes and other 3-dimensional objects, and material such as company and personal archives.

- Stronger collaboration between publicly funded organisations. Organisations are being encouraged to collaborate, not just as a cost saving exercise but also as a means of encouraging them to look outside their own organisations and detect possible duplication and overlaps for themselves. Organisations from different sectors can provide complementary assets, as we found with our project.

These current developments are causing us to ask three fundamental questions: What are we doing? Who is it for? Who else is providing similar or complementary services?

The Aims of the Backstage Project

Like many developments today, the Backstage Project was initiated by a funding opportunity. In 1998, a scheme was set up for the higher education sector and was given £30 million (45 million Euros) to allocate to university libraries with special collections which needed development. This was the Research Support Libraries Programme. The University of Kent, in common with every other eligible university set about identifying suitable uses for this funding. At an early stage it very wisely began involving possible partner universities in discussing a project which would improve researchers' access to unpublished performing arts material. It also spoke to the Theatre Museum, which holds the UK's national collections of library, archive and museum objects relating to the performing arts.

The planned project had the following aims:

1. The overarching aim: to provide a single point of entry for finding and searching performing arts collections in the UK. It was aimed at the research community, plus anyone with an interest in the performing arts.

2. To convert the *Directory of Performing Arts Resources* into a database. This was a traditionally published directory, researched and compiled by SIBMAS member Francesca Franchi, and jointly published in 1998 by the Theatre Museum and the Society for Theatre Research.

3. To supplement the information available in the Directory by creating Collection Level Descriptions for all the special collections held by an organisation.

4. To create item level records for many thousands of playbills, posters and other specialised items held by the partner organisations. The project would also allow for records to be imported into the database from a wide range of cataloguing systems and formats, so it would not be a matter of creating records especially for this project.

The one rather major obstacle to collaboration was that the funding available to the universities was not available to the Theatre Museum. This was, to say the least, a very great frustration to us. An exercise designed to create a map of subject coverage, which omitted the national collection, did not make sense to us. Eventually, the Museum was successful in applying for funding from the British Library, under a scheme partly designed to resolve such inconsistencies of funding. However, the amount of money available was on a far smaller scale but it has covered the costs of creating collection level descriptions for the Theatre Museum's 300 collections.

The main participants were the universities of Kent and Bristol, the Theatre Museum and the Institute for Learning & Research Technology.

But other organisations, including the British Library, the Bodleian Library, and many other university libraries were active partners in the project too.

Collection Level Descriptions are also being created by, or for, the several hundred further institutions with relevant performing arts materials listed in the printed version of the *Directory of Performing Arts Resources* which this gateway replaces.

At an early stage, the project contracted in the services of the Institute for Learning & Research Technology (ILRT), based at the University of Bristol. They have taken responsibility for building the database and Website and finding solutions to all the technical problems.

Implementation Period

Work began in Summer 2000. From the start, all meetings of the Project Board and the Steering Committee were held at the Theatre Museum which was a constant reminder of the co-operative nature of the project.

One of the first tasks to be tackled was the application of the newly developed schema for collection level description, developed by the UK Office for Library Networking.

Late in 2000 Backstage and the Theatre Museum sent out a circular to all the institutions in the printed *Directory of Performing Arts Resources* asking them to update their entries. They were also asked to provide Collection Level Descriptions of significant collections they held. Both directory entries and collection level descriptions could be returned using printed forms enclosed with the mailout, or by entering them directly on Web forms on the Backstage Website, the prototype for which had by then been developed.

As the first year of the project unfolded it became clear that the work on Collection Level Descriptions was becoming a far more significant part of the project than we had originally envisaged. ILRT found that they were spending much more time than they had expected on developing the software to allow searching of the data which was entered on a template based on the UKOLN Collection Level Description schema. Collection descriptions had suddenly become the flavour of the year in projects of all kinds.

So as we entered the second year of the project the prototype Website was up and running with a growing list of directory entries and collection level descriptions, and with Web forms for the online entry of information. In parallel to this work, not yet reflected on the Website, was the gradual creation of electronic records for individual items by the partner universities. This work was not using any one agreed software package or format. Instead, institutions would submit their records from their home cataloguing systems, in the format favoured by their institutions. This meant that a wide variety would be submitted, from systems including CALM, Idealist, MODES and Access, in formats including variants of ISAD(G) (International Standard for Archival Description) and MARC. One of our first questions to ILRT at the start of the project bid had been: can you take electronic records in a variety of formats and convert them to a single searchable format in a separate database? As the whole project was based on their answer being "Yes" – the actual achievement of this conversion was, and is crucial to the success of the project overall.

Another major issue the project is tackling is that of name authority in the performing arts, for terms such as personal names, names of theatres, companies, and so on. As Backstage was not dictating forms of name used in the directory, in collection level or in item level records, and did not intend to centrally edit all the records produced, another mechanism had to be devised. ILRT therefore developed a set of Web forms which allowed for the linking of all the different forms of name used to a single preferred heading (based on Library of Congress and British Library authority wherever possible) with all the forms being retrievable at the point of search. This will constitute a significant body of work with potentially far reaching benefits beyond the lifetime of this one project.

Outcomes

The project is due for completion in October 2002. By then, the Backstage project will have achieved the following:

- Entries for around 400 UK libraries, archives and other collections which hold theatrical material;
- Over 100,000 item level records;
- Around 1,000 Collection Level records, including over 300 from the Theatre Museum.

Demonstration at www.backstage.ac.uk

Future Collaboration

The next step is to look at digitising material and adding it to the collection and item level descriptions. We are awaiting a decision, due in November, on a funding bid for a further stage, this time called "On Stage", whose objectives are to:

- Develop a thesaurus/authority file of personal and corporate names in the performing arts;
- Add 6,000 digital images to the Backstage databases;
- Continue to add to the Collection Level Description and Directory databases;
- Continue to add item level collections when they become available.

But regardless of the outcome of the bid, the project has proved the benefits of collaborating with partners. We have pooled complementary skills and specialisms, and have learned much more about one another in the process. We will also continue to maintain Backstage as the joint responsibility of the Theatre Museum and the Universities of Kent and Bristol, thus forming a permanent working relationship, and providing, we hope, a valuable research and management tool which will continue to grow and develop.

AusStage

Recording Performing Arts Events in Australia

Richard STONE

Performing Arts Special Interest Group (PASIG), Museums (Australia)

AusStage is the latest major development in performing arts information and resources in Australia. In what is believed to be a world first, a national online index to a wide range of performing arts events in Australia has been developed.

Australia has seen the increasing availability of online catalogues of collections, of finding aids and directories of collections. One such directory, the *Australian Dance Collection*, is a particularly successful guide to key resources in various formats on Australia's rich dance history.

However, until now, there has been no comprehensive, national index to Australian performing arts events. The initiative for such an index did *not* come from the library or museum sector. Rather, the initiative came from the academic world, from university departments teaching drama and theatre studies.

The genesis *of AusStage lies* in a printed publication now ceased – *ANZTR: Australian and New Zealand Theatre Record* which was published by the Australian Theatre Studies Centre at the University of New South Wales in Sydney between 1987 and 1996. *ANZTR* was basically a monthly compilation of reviews of performances in Australia and New Zealand. It was sourced from the major capital city daily newspapers, selected journals and periodicals and some regional newspapers. It was well indexed, including an annual cumulative index, and had a monthly theatre news digest, illustrations etc. It was a very useful publication not only for academic researchers and students, but also libraries and information centres.

The academics, who had nurtured and used *ANZTR*, were determined to find a replacement, but one which would use online technology. They found a large part of the answer at the Adelaide Festival Centre which is a large performing arts complex comprising several venues. To keep track of what was appearing in each of the venues the Centre developed TED - The Event Database. This is essentially an internal management system. After its initial success, the coverage of the TED database had been extended beyond the confines of the Adelaide Festival Centre to include performing arts events elsewhere in the city of Adelaide and in the state of South Australia through indexing newspaper advertisements and reviews.

Joh Hartog, from the Drama Studies department at Flinders University in Adelaide, had worked on the development of TED and saw its potential for further development on a national basis. The challenge was to combine the type of information in *ANZTR*, with the underlying concept of events information from TED, in order to construct a database which would allow theatre data to be included in sociological, political and cultural research. Theatre data can be a barometer of society's concerns and how well it is functioning at any given time. At the moment this is something that is not part of the research paradigm.

A development project was established three years ago funded partially by a grant from the Australian Research Council (ARC) and by contributions from eight universities with departments of theatre and drama studies. This development of Phase One (the prototype) is virtually complete. A submission has been made to the Australia Research Council to advance the fully-fledged application of the system in Phase Two. This will include a vastly increased number of records, as well an increase in the breadth of data collected on each record.

The project is managed by a board representing the eight universities as well as representatives from the theatre industry, from the Australia Council which is the major federal government arts agency, and the performing arts resources sector in the person of the Chairman of PASIG (Performing Arts Special Interest Group). The computer base of the project and the daily management is at Flinders University in Adelaide, South Australia.

There are two components to AusStage:
- the Index of performing arts events;
- a Directory of performing arts resources.

I will deal briefly with the Directory first. It is still in the early stages of creation. It has been important to establish realistic guidelines in the context of existing directories and catalogues. Care has been taken to identify the types of performing arts collections to be included in the Directory with the result that three major categories of information have been identified:

- information on the archives of performing arts companies which is an area that has been virtually ignored in other directories;
- performing arts resources in libraries, museums and archives which are *not* already described in an online form;
- providing online links to performing arts resources which already exist in online catalogues and collection descriptions.

In the creation of the Directory the first two categories will be targeted initially, i.e. the archives of theatre companies, and the collections in large institutions which are relatively unknown.

The AusStage Index

The priority of the AusStage project so far has been developing and refining the Index of performing arts events. The exercise has not been without its problems as might be expected with such a trailblazing effort to capture ephemeral information from a diverse range of sources.

It should be remembered that it is *not* a bibliographic database although there are elements in it of library concepts of cataloguing.

What is the coverage of the Index? At the beginning all performing arts were included which was a very ambitious brief. It was soon decided to exclude music events such as recitals and concerts whether they were classical, jazz or rock. The sheer number of such events is overwhelming and introduces a major problem for indexers dealing with musical terminology outside their expertise. It was agreed therefore that only live events with a dramatic component would be included. Therefore, opera and musical theatre are included.

There are two input streams to the AusStage Index – current events (January 2001+), and retrospective events prior to January 2001.

The indexing of current events from January 2001 has been based primarily on newspaper advertisements, on reviews in newspapers and selected magazines, and finally on programmes for performances and events.

Information about such events tends to pass quickly, especially for small-scale events whose publicity resources are limited. The AusStage index is meant to preserve a snapshot of society that would otherwise be lost forever. Thus, the basic requirement is for limited information, on as many events as possible, in a form which is easily gathered, stored and retrieved.

Indexers are employed on a part-time contract basis, in academic terms as "research assistants". There are six indexers located in five cities and between them an extensive coverage of current performing arts events around the capital cities of Australia is being achieved. The question of identifying and indexing events in regional centres outside the capital cities is being addressed.

As at the end of June 2002 there are over 10,000 records for current and past events on the database.

Indexing of retrospective events prior to 2001 is based on the following sources:

- programmes and printed ephemera;
- data from the publication mentioned earlier, ANZTR: the *Australian and New Zealand theatre record.*

There are three indexers employed on retrospective events, one on the ANZTR data and two using programmes in the rich collections of the National Library of Australia and the Dennis Wolanski collection in the University of New South Wales Library.

Given the diverse range of ephemeral sources, the amount and the reliability of information in the Index is variable. For example, the entries for retrospective events are naturally richer and more extensive because the sources are primarily programs. And, whilst minimal records are created based on newspaper advertisements, these can be upgraded and amended when more information is subsequently found in other sources, such as a programme. Whatever the source the basic aim of the AusStage Index remains – to record a performance event.

With the data entry format established and indexing proceeding, attention is now concentrating on developing search mechanisms. Testing of the database in 2002 by academic users and others is taking place. A Website is now available as a prototype to a public audience.

The curtain has gone up on AusStage[1]!

---

[1]   For the latest news on AusStage and to use the database see: www.ausstage.edu.au (Editor's note).

QUATRIÈME PARTIE

LES COLLECTIONS NUMÉRISÉES

FOURTH PART

DIGITAL COLLECTIONS

Sveriges Teatermuseum

The Combined Databases and a New Project: "Documentation of Performing Arts on DVD"

Inga LEWENHAUPT

Sveriges Teatermuseum (Sweden)

A Short Presentation of Sveriges Teatermuseum[1]

Sveriges Teatermuseum was founded in 1922 in connection with the public reopening of Drottningholms Slottsteater, built in 1766, after more than a hundred years of "beauty sleep". Since 1945 it belongs to a foundation with support from the Swedish government. For the last 80 years it has been known under the misleading name "Drottningholms Teatermuseum". In early 2002 the name was changed when the public library and the main part of the collections moved to a new building at Gäddviken, Nacka, just outside Stockholm City, where also the workshops of The Royal Opera and The Royal Dramatic Theatre, the office of the Swedish ITI, TeaterAlliansen, an agency for actors and the ateliers of some scenographers, are located.

Museum Collection

Unfortunately the museum has very limited possibilities for exhibitions. At the Drottningholm Castle, close to the Court Theatre, the museum disposes of a pavilion with a permanent summer exhibition (May-Sept.) of paintings, models, engravings, decoration set pieces and costumes mainly from the 17th and 18th centuries from Swedish and European court theatres. In the new building at Gäddviken we have very few possibilities to show our other large museum collections covering items from the Middle Ages until today. Temporary exhibition work is

---

[1] For more information see our Website: www.sverigesteatermuseum.dtm.se (Editor's note: current (2011) Website address: http://www.teatermuseet.se/).

carried on in the form of loans to and in co-operation with other museums.

Library and Archives

The large public theatre library (with more than 70,000 registered printed books) and the archives of personal documents, manuscripts, press cuttings etc., are open for five hours on all week days, and researchers can work up to eight hours per day in a special room.

Phototek

At the moment we have over one million photos and with expected collections from Gothenburg and The Royal Opera in Stockholm we will soon have over two million photos, in addition to photos of museum items.

Repertoire Registration/Continuous Theatre Documentation

A register of the total Swedish performing arts events concerning opera, spoken theatre, mime, puppet theatre, dance etc. is currently being set up. It is based on information from theatres, programmes etc. and also gives information about existing press cuttings and other preserved material connected to the performances. The theatres with government support are since 1977 obliged to send their material (including photos) to us; the other theatres do it of free will by recommendation of the Swedish Theatre Union.

The Prehistory of the Choice of Digital System

Parallel to efforts of using the TANDEM system (from 1978) and the IBT (International Bibliography of Theatre) we continued with older card systems until 1994 when we finally entered the "digitalized" world.

In order to be able to give information about our books on the Internet, it was decided in 1995 that the library should start entering titles in the Swedish National Library database for research libraries and special libraries. The database is called LIBRIS.

But – as LIBRIS, which is an all-embracing database, does not include too detailed references on terms, names and performance titles, we, like most research libraries, had to find a local programme. Into this local programme we then could import entries from LIBRIS and in our own programme add a more specific classification. This daily transmission is free, but the software for transference and all the necessary modifications meant extra costs for us.

A special database for the repertoire (TMA) had been used at the museum since 1994, but it became slower as more repertoire information was entered. The TMA database was built from the needs of only one theatre. Now we saw an opportunity to build a new programme, which could manage all our departments: Museum collections, Phototek, Library, Archives and Repertoire.

In 1996 we looked for a programme which both had different modules for library, museum and archives and at the same time could communicate with LIBRIS mainframe for import and also was available at a reasonable price. Our initial costs, ca 50,000 €, were paid by one of the Wallenberg foundations.

In 1996 there was not very much to choose from but in England we found the ADLIB information programme (www.uk.adlibsoft.com), just introducing a version made for museums with integrated library and archives. The inventors, among them Chris Turner who came from a theatre family, were very helpful and even willing to enlarge their programme with a module for repertoire according to our requirements and also promised to import our earlier records from TMA.

The ADLIB Information System Developing since 1997

Thus we have split up the ADLIB Information System in four parts:
- ADLIB for the library
- ADMUSE for the museum
- ADARCH for the archives
- ADREP for the repertoire

All four modules share the same name register, and ADMUSE, ADLIB and ADARCH share the same performance database. ADREP is separated since it is exclusive for performances given in Sweden, while the other modules could refer to non-Swedish performances as well. We want to keep ADREP an exclusive Swedish database.

I would explain more explicitly what can be recorded in the four modules.

To ADLIB we import all our books earlier registered in LIBRIS. In our system ADLIB we also register different small prints and manuscripts from the theatres and index important articles from non-theatre related periodicals and useful articles from theatre programmes. We register:
- author, title, shelf reference;
- publisher, publication year and pagination etc.;

- classification numbers, subject terms, subject names, subject titles (connected to performance database) and (for play scripts) how many male, female and total parts.

ADMUSE is meant for all objects of the museum collection: decorations, set pieces, sketches, engravings, paintings, scene models, costumes, technical advises etc. Photos of the objects will be recorded together with the registration of the objects. In ADMUSE we also intend to register photos from the Phototek, which will start in the autumn of 2002. We register:

- administrative name, object name and object number;
- acquisition information, home location, condition and number of negative photos;
- maker, creator, production country & date, material, technique, physical description;
- references to portrayed actor, part, user, place and stage title (connected to performance/repertoire database);
- related information and references to other sources. Object movement, exhibitions, loans, preservation etc.

ADARCH: Here we intend to register all united archives (now over 200). It has not yet started, but will include references to the actor or institution, part, user, place and stage title (connected to the performance database).

ADREP is a central database for all performing arts of Sweden. Here we register the repertoire of all Swedish theatres; about 1,100 performing arts events are given per year, with cast and information about existing material within the different collections at Sveriges Teatermuseum. We register:

- titles, theatre/company, first performance date, genre, place, city, creators, language, copyrights, related materials (press cuttings, photos, programmes etc.);
- artists, actors and their parts, extras, dancers, musicians and how many males, females, children (and total) included in the performance;
- statistics, amount of performances, audiences etc.

The aim is that only one authorised form of name and original title should be used all over the collections.

For names of persons as well as for institutions there is a zoom-screen where related names, "used for" (instead for) forms and equivalent names are connected. Thus if a person changes the family name, both names will give the same records.

For visitors we will offer a clean Web-interface where you could select the database or bases you want to investigate:

Museum	Library	Archives	Repertory	All together
A query form will be added:				
Title		Title of printed material		List of titles to choose from
		Stage title		
Personal name		Author, creator, actor		List of names to choose from
		As subject		List of names to choose from
Institutions		Organisations, theatres		List of names to choose from
		As subject		List of names to choose from
Place		Publisher's place		
		Of performance		
Year		Of publication		
		Of first performance		
Names of parts				List of names to choose from
Subject terms				List of terms to choose from, with related, broader or narrower terms suggestions
Classification numbers				
Language				List of languages to choose from
ISBN				
Amount of parts		Female Male Children		Total in play texts or performances

Every field could be truncated or not truncated, and duplicated and applied to Boolean searching (and/or/not). In this way one can search for:

- two different actors in the same performance;
- which plays of a certain author has been staged by a certain director;
- what sketches of an artist do we have from plays given in a certain place, etc.

The "amount of parts" is for searching plays with for instance four parts, or only two parts that also are female.

We now understand that in many ways it would have been better not to start with all the modules at once but it gave us a good opportunity to discuss terms and get on with our thesaurus work. After more than five years experience of developing and using the programme the tempo has not become what was expected in 1996 due to the continuously diminishing number of staff. With the present staff, we will have our books searchable on the Internet in 222 years from now!!! And a new problem has come up with the digitalization of photos, which we get from the theatres. It is expensive and it requires more people in the archives to preserve these photos on discs. And how long will the discs last? Some say only up to 20-50 years depending on storage. Our glass negatives are perfect, and they are over a hundred years old.

What really have developed are the costs! The service for computers, network and help desk of the software have increased in the same tempo as our funds have decreased.

The government wants to see all collections funded by the state to be accessible on the Internet as soon as possible. Accordingly our goal is to get the Web interface included in our Website on Internet. But with the present lack of funds I am afraid we have a long, long way to go.

A New Project: Documentation of Performing Arts on DVD

Finally I would like to present a first example of media documentation, made as a start of a new project to find a method for digital documentation of stage performances[2].

The project aims to:

1) invent what kind of media documentations is being done in Sweden today;

2) work out a methodology for media documentation of performances especially with regard to the requirements of research and education;

3) work out a handbook for documentation of performances;

4) make some twenty documentations on DVD from performances within various genres;

5) give recommendations for a programme for future preservation of stage performances.

There will be a test period of two years with a long-term goal, and – as far as we know – it will be internationally unique in its presentation. An important task to deal with is the legal one. There are several regulations concerning printed material but in the field of media there are still many grey zones. Thus we have a lawyer connected to the project, which will be carried out in co-operation with the Department of Theatre Research at Stockholm University, the Dramatic Institute and The National Archive of Recorded Sound and Moving Images.

---

[2]   This lecture included a demonstration of the DVD-record from a production of *Asis e Galatée* in 2001 by the baroque opera group "Nya utomjordiska" in Gothenburg.

We are very keen on co-operating with members of SIBMAS on this pilot project, which will start in 2003 and is financed by The Bank of Sweden Tercentenary Foundation.

Theatre Iconography and
the Challenge of Digitalization

An Account of a Pilot Project Carried out
in the Library of the University of Amsterdam

Willem RODENHUIS

University of Amsterdam (Netherlands)

As we all are aware, as curators and librarians active in the field of the performing arts, theatre research is largely depending on *related sources*, as the performance of a given play is characterised by its *hic et nunc* occurrence. We, who foster the collections we are responsible for, and the researchers are one in this basic conviction that a performance is the very object of our skills and ambitions. In a performance several elements (playtext, interpretation, scenery, diction, costumes…) are merged to a single piece of art, appreciated by an audience in a unique setting, enclosed by the mutual presence of both actors and audience in time and space.

By tradition performing arts researchers have used, among other sources, paintings, drawings, books and pamphlets, programmes, posters, scrapbooks, diaries, costume designs, elements of scenery and props and all kinds of related *realia*. These sources have added over the decades to a more profound understanding of the medium, despite the fact that the *real thing, i.e. the performance* by definition could not be included in the process of description of what had really happened on stage. Archives, museum collections and libraries have been active in collecting these items during decades. Most of them dating back to the second half of the 19th century when *fans*, whether professionals or mere lovers of the theatre, began to collect memorabilia related to the world of the theatre.

Once the collections had been established several initiatives have been developed, directed at a better access to the holdings by researchers. Apart from cataloguing, one could think of the thematic series as published by *Chadwyck-Healy* since the 17th of the 20th century, containing a series of slides in combination with a book on a particular subject. Microfilm has been an important tool for research as well, like single issues of photo books, dia-series, films and later video registrations on performances. However, the researcher was still the one to manage this kind of information, its arrangement and presentation. Collection management did not allow a pro-active attitude when presenting material in storage, hampered by the limits of what card catalogues and even computers could achieve. Research material was kept *in loco*, waiting for a particular researcher, putting forward his, or hers, need for information. The boundaries of what technology could facilitate were tight, and it is only since a decade that we really have seen that progress can be made, thanks to stronger and faster machines, content linking, standardisation of communication processes and the like. This being the situation we are in, a new impulse could be given to a longer living wish among theatre researchers, namely the building of a database, fit to support research in the field of theatre iconography.

Our partner organisation FIRT already recognised the new horizons by installing a task group dedicating itself to the development of a methodology for an applied theatre iconography. Among others it were Robert Erenstein, Thomas Heck, Christopher Balme and Cesare Molinari who have taken the initiative. Until now professor Molinari has managed to give shape to his pictorial research in his *Dionysos*-project at the University of Florence, leading in the year 2000 to two CD-ROM discs as a concrete result.

In my introduction I'll to go into the question of the building of a database, fit to meet the needs of theatre iconographical research. In Amsterdam we have begun a pilot project, directed at the description of 18th century illustrations, depicting scenes from plays. We have formulated our objective as: "The pilot project should provide an inventory, classification and description of all the visual (non-textual) material as present in the holdings of the Library of the University of Amsterdam and allow digital access to these sources."

Against this background we have begun to study existing methods for the description of pictorial material like ICONCLASS, which has proven to be highly effective and has been accepted widely in the field of art history. The digital world has made considerable progress by adopting last year's September Dublin Core as a standard for the description of digital sources or so-called *metadata*. By merging these two standards, and by looking closely to the achievement Professor Molinari has made, we have made a framework, which includes all the data needed for the input in the database. We also made use of the existing analysis of the theatrical communication as formulated by for instance Tadeusz Kowzan (1975), and in later years adjusted and extended by Erika Fischer-Lichte (1983) and Patrice Pavis (1996).

This led to the following questions that we answer when putting the data into a database.

The questions asked are spread over four sections, each of which containing a specific field of interest.

Section 1: Historic Data of the Picture

- Maker of the picture
- Title
- Technique applied
- Function of the picture
- Size
- Place or country of the making of the picture
- Date of the making of the picture
- Present location/collection where the picture can be found
- Database number

Section 2: Iconography

- Place and date of the depicted play and/or scene
- What is depicted?
- Is the picture performance- or text related?
- When Text: style, genre
- When Performance:
    a. actor related expression: text, diction, facial, gesture, movement, make-up, hair, costume
    b. non-actor related expression: prop, scenery, lighting, music, sound
    c. other elements: auditorium, audience, and text reference in the picture.

Section 3: Elements of Dramaturgy in the Depicted Work

- Playwright/librettist
- Adaptor/translator
- Genre
- Title of the play depicted/scene indication

- Country/language of origin
- Playtext publication date
- Original title
- Place of performance
- Acting company/roles
- Theatre venue
- Other context related sources: posters

Section 4: Notices and Commentaries

- Short description of the depicted scene
- Commentary by the iconographer
- Literature, related to the picture

Since early spring of this year we have made an effort to secure an input in the database when following the questions of the framework above, making use of several kinds of sources: pictures alongside with playtexts, portraits of actors when in action or when posing as a "private" individual, etchings of scenery or/and auditoria, paintings of exteriors. All these pictures have one uniting principle: they date back to the 18th century and belong to the collection of the University of Amsterdam.

Let me introduce to you three examples of how we have applied the above designed framework to the pictorial material that we have researched. The pictures I have chosen represent three categories of different ways to deal with sources where theatre-related subjects are at stake. In the first place I chose a picture of an actor related, performed scene. Facial expressions are depicted, gesture and attitude as in action, together with a plausible outline of the costumes and scenery. Secondly I chose a picture of a non-actor related situation. However, the scene is full of information for researchers as one can clearly see what the theatre looked like, its scenery, its lighting, the costumes, the auditorium, the actors and the musicians. Thirdly I chose a picture depicting a scene without a direct link to the actual performance, but a mere result of fantasy of the artist, who made the engraving.

I

Collection Bibliotheek Universiteit van Amsterdam.

Section 1: Historic Data of the Picture

Maker: C. Bogaerts, after P. Wagenaar Jr.

Title: *Macbeth*

Technique applied: Copper engraving

Function of the picture: Depicting of a scene

Size: 14 x 8 cm

Place or country of the making of the picture:
Amsterdam, the Netherlands

Date of the making of the picture: 1780
Present location: UBA-125 6.KB
Database number: xxxx

Section 2: Iconography

Place and date of the depicted play or scene:
Amsterdam, 18th century
What is depicted: The dagger scene in Shakespeare's *Macbeth*
Text, or performance related?: Performance related, making use of the following fields of expression:

    a. actor related: mimic, gesture, movement, hair, costume

    b. non-actor related: prop, scenery, and lighting

    c. other elements: text reference in the picture

Section 3: Elements of Dramaturgy in the Depicted Work

Playwright/librettist: William Shakespeare
Adaptor/translator: N.N.
Genre: Tragedy
Title of the play depicted: *Macbeth*, II, 5
Country/language of origin: England, English
Playtext original publication date: 1605/06
Original title: *Macbeth*
Place of performance: ?
Acting company/roles: ?
Theatre venue: ?
Other context related sources: ?

Section 4: Notices and Commentaries

Short description of the depicted scene:

The dagger scene. Left Macbeth, horrified, refuses to put the daggers near Duncan's corpse (just visible in the bed in the background), while Lady Macbeth holds her hand on the dagger that is in Macbeth's fist.

By the scarce artificial lighting the spooky atmosphere is well evoked. The engraving most probably is a result of the maker's fantasy, as no records are known of a performance of the play in the Netherlands before 1780. The engraving may have been inspired by existing contemporary English material, with David Garrick as Macbeth.

Commentary by the iconographer: None

Literature related to the picture: None

II

Collection Bibliotheek Universiteit van Amsterdam.

Section 1: Historic Data of the Picture

Maker: S. Fokke, after S. Fokke

Title: *Afbeelding der eerst uitslaande Vlamme in den Amsterdamschen Schouwburg, op maandag den 11 May 1772 des Avonds even over half negen Uuren*

Technique applied: Copper engraving

Function of the picture: Book illustration (unfolding)

Size: 19 x 26 cm

Place or country of the making of the picture: Amsterdam, the Netherlands

Date of the making of the picture: 1772

Present location: UBA-125 3.KB

Database number: xxxx

Section 2: Iconography

Place and date of the depicted play or scene:
Amsterdam, 18th century

What is depicted: The outbreak of the fire on May 11 1772
that ruined the Amsterdam City Theatre

Text or Performance related?: No, depicted are: Actors, costumes,
props, scenery, lighting, auditorium, audience, musicians

Section 3: Elements of Dramaturgy in the Depicted Work

Not applied

Section 4: Notices and Commentaries

An eyewitness account is given of the moment that the first flames
burst out during the prison scene in the opera *The Deserter* by
Monsigny and Sedaine, performed by the company of Neyts. Audience and musicians are on the run. Panic among audience, musicians
and actors. Front left shows two actors who dash to the stage.

This picture exists in many versions and copies, in combination with
a wide range of formats.

III

Collection Bibliotheek Universiteit van Amsterdam.

Section 1: Historic Data of the Picture

Maker of the picture: J. Punt (*inventit et fecit*), after J. Punt

Title: *Ferdinand Cortez*

Technique applied: Copper engraving

Function of the picture: Title page of a printed playtext

Size: 14 x 8,5 cm

Place or country of the making of the picture:
Amsterdam, the Netherlands

Date of the making of the picture: 1764

143

Present location: UBA-125 16.KB
Database number: xxxx

Section 2: Iconography

Place and date of the depicted scene: ?
What is depicted: The final scene of the play
Text/performance related? Performance related:
Actor related: mimic, gesture, hair, costume
Non-actor related: props, scenery
Other elements: none

Section 3: Elements of Dramaturgy in the Depicted Work

Playwright/librettist: Alexis Piron
Adaptor/translator: Joannes Nomsz
Genre: Tragedy
Title of the play depicted/ scene: Ferdinand Cortez;
Overwinnaar van Mexico - V,5
Country/language of origin: France, French
Playtext publication date: ?
Original title: ?
Place of performance: Amsterdam
Acting company/roles: Gezelschap van de Amsterdamsche
Schouwburg
Theatre venue: Schouwburgh aan de Keizersgracht
Other context related sources: None

Section 4: Short Description of the Depicted Scene

In a pompous entourage the final scene of the play is depicted. Left
the dying Montezuma who, supported by two natives, hands over his
kingdom and sovereignty to Cortez, who is on the right together with
Elvira, daughter of Pedro. Middle front, seen on his back as "pous-
soir", is Don Pedro, who accepts Cortez as his son-in-law.

Mutes.

The engraving is a depiction of the text, with no reference to the
factual stage size of the 18th century Amsterdam City Theatre.

Literature: None

Our initial focus was to have a set ready for presentation before the summer of 2002. Unfortunately, this objective could not be met. For the time being I'll spend some time on the perspective the pilot project offers when taking into full account the needs of nowadays researchers and the state of affairs in the realm of (digital) technology.

First some technological implications, and then, as a conclusion to my introduction, an outlook on a strategy directed at a continuation in the year to come.

When taking into consideration the technological implications of the project, it is obvious that the storage of pictorial data, allowing cross links between the elements secured, and in a later stage the (free) exchange of findings between collections, will be the first thing to realize.

In this respect the application of the Z 39.50 protocol is an important tool. Moreover, the tendency towards *portal directed research*, whether or not in combination with bibliographical digital tools like ENDNOTE, would imply an important improvement too.

Much of the energy, when developing the digitisation of library and museum collections, is these days put in the perfection of the principle called *streaming*, implying that separate collections seek digital permanent connections, allowing researchers who are active in a particular collection may use all of the information that can be provided by the partners thus connected. Indeed, this increases the possibilities for research considerably. Moreover, the input in available databases of non-text material, inclusive moving images like film and digital video, will add to the further growth of research potential. One could think of not only academic users of collections, but even more of an increasing appeal for researchers for (documentary) films, book production and television production. Those who are working in these realms get an easier access. Our often still too much hidden collections will get the attention that they deserve by a wider circle of those who have a professional interest in the world of the performing arts.

We intend to continue our work in Amsterdam. I hope that our initiative inspires you to think about the possibilities you have when analysing your situation with respect to this. Exchanging views and experiences will stay one of the vital aspects of our fraternal work within SIBMAS. I hope that our Congress will serve as a kick off for new projects, additions, more perfection and a true *streaming* of our skills and know how to each other and our clients.

De la mémoire vivante au fonds documentaire

Jocelyne PHILIPPEKIN, Alain BERT

Centre d'information et de documentation
Théâtre de la Maison du Spectacle (Bruxelles – Belgique)

Le Centre de documentation Théâtre a été créé au sein du CATFT (Centre d'aide technique et de formation théâtrale) en 1983, pour répondre à deux besoins de types différents : l'information et la documentation.

- L'information : les jeunes issus des écoles de théâtre et les nouvelles compagnies qui s'engageaient dans la profession ignoraient, et ignorent encore trop souvent, comment obtenir un soutien financier ou matériel, comment constituer un dossier, où et à qui l'adresser, où trouver un lieu de représentation, comment payer les artistes...

- La documentation : fréquemment, étudiants, journalistes, représentants d'organismes culturels cherchaient où consulter des revues théâtrales, des dossiers de presse, des programmes de théâtre...

En mai 1988, La Maison du Spectacle La Bellone a accueilli le CID, devenu aujourd'hui le Centre d'information et de documentation Théâtre de la Maison du Spectacle.

La fonction principale d'un centre de documentation sur le théâtre vivant est de cerner au mieux l'attente de ses différents publics (professionnels, étudiants ou simples amateurs). Les questions sont donc complexes, mais également spécifiques.

La demande d'un metteur en scène est souvent liée à la recherche d'un texte, d'un auteur, de multiples expériences d'autres professionnels de la scène, de l'élaboration de sa distribution. Celle d'un scénographe s'exprimera par la recherche de documents iconographiques, d'analyses dramaturgiques, l'étudiant quant à lui sollicitera l'accès au dossier de presse, articles critiques, photos.

Ces exemples illustrent parfaitement la difficulté extrême de concevoir une base de données documentaire capable de répondre à de multiples clés d'interrogation.

Avec l'émergence du multimédia, il s'est avéré indispensable de développer un nouveau programme capable de gérer à la fois le système préexistant mais aussi des supports nouveaux, tels que la numérisation de textes, d'images et la mise en ligne de différents catalogues.

Comment décrire, analyser, rendre accessibles les documents, les images ?

Comment rassembler, renforcer les liens entre des notices catalographiques différentes ?

Nous avons réalisé parmi la masse énorme de nos documents, une distinction entre un ensemble « primaire », ayant un lien direct avec la création théâtrale (programme, communiqué de presse, articles de presse, photos, affiches, etc.) et un autre « secondaire » correspondant, lui, à la littérature générale du champ théâtral (écrits sur le théâtre, répertoires et revues spécialisées).

Le premier groupe de documents a été hiérarchisé en prenant l'événement en tant que tel comme fiche dominante, c'est-à-dire les spectacles. Par ailleurs, l'évolution des arts de la scène nous a conduits à créer de multiples fiches-mères pour chacune des formes de l'évènement (théâtre au sens traditionnel, théâtre musical, théâtre de mouvement, théâtre multidisciplinaire...). Les champs de ces différentes fiches varient donc en conséquence.

De là découle la suite, le spectacle prenant place forcément dans un lieu. Un fichier lieu a été constitué et subdivisées en : théâtre, autres lieux de spectacles, associations culturelles.

De même les personnes participant à cet univers font l'objet d'un fichier personnalité descriptif (biographie, spécialité(s), etc.).

Ces trois fichiers permettent d'associer les documents variés rassemblés et liés aux spectacles que l'on peut consulter au CID.

Le second ensemble de documents est structuré en trois sous-ensembles :

- le répertoire constitué d'ouvrages ou de revues diffusant ces textes (accessible sur le site) ;
- les écrits sur le théâtre (rangés selon un plan de classement mais aussi décrits par des mots-clés) ;
- les revues spécialisées dont chaque article fait l'objet d'une fiche et d'une description par mots-clés.

Ces mots-clés sont potentiellement utilisables aussi pour les fiches-spectacles, personnalités et lieux. Dans la pratique, il est possible d'ajouter à un spectacle un mot-clé tel que « Prix théâtre » pour signaler que cette pièce a été récompensée lors de la remise de ce prix équivalent aux Molières en Belgique francophone.

Sur un autre axe, celui de la communication, notre base de données sert à générer automatiquement tant pour la mise en ligne que pour l'édition papier, l'agenda théâtral *j'yCours* annonçant tous les spectacles professionnels adultes joués en Communauté Wallonie-Bruxelles. Cet automatisme se retrouve aussi au niveau du fichier d'adresses et permet la publication de notre guide d'adresses utiles : le *Souffleur*.

On obtiendra également en ligne des renseignements sur les stages, les archives, les ouvrages et textes de répertoire.

En plus d'une nouvelle méthode de travail, l'informatisation a surtout permis une plus grande ouverture vers le public.

Grâce au site Internet, l'utilisateur peut désormais obtenir une série d'informations pour lesquelles il devait auparavant se déplacer.

Une nouvelle orientation est née, exprimant davantage notre volonté de diffusion, de communication et de partage de l'information.

The Petrolini Collection:
a Project of Multimedia Archive

Maria Teresa IOVINELLI

Biblioteca e Museo Teatrale SIAE del Burcardo (Rome – Italy)

Introduction

Digitalization may appear as the ideal solution for the problems related to the management of large performing arts collections. If we were able to digitalize all the materials our institutions have been collecting for decades, our worries about the lack of stack spaces would find some ease. If the digital copies were available to our users, there would be no need to keep the originals within reach; they could be stored out of the way, at reduced costs. Preservation would be easier too: the original documents would be no longer touched if not for special needs; they could be eventually stored in appropriate spaces, at the best climatic conditions, instead of being stacked in some inappropriate, residual space of our historical buildings.

If we were able to digitalize everything, there would be unquestionable benefits for researchers. Linking our databases to the digital copies of the documents would be quite easy, and researchers would certainly appreciate the possibility of accessing the documents directly from a database record, without waiting and without any mediator.

For most institutions collecting performing arts documentation, however, this is still a dream, and it is very unlikely to become true in the next future. Especially when dealing with large collections, we generally cannot afford the tremendous costs of an extensive digitalization. Therefore, we are forced to make choices. We have to select the materials to be digitalized according to a list of priorities we often have to draw ourselves.

As I have often seen, the first step we often take when deciding to start a digitalization campaign is trying to convince our administrators that digital images can be easily sold, and increase our profits. Yet, in my experience, I have realised that this is not such a realistic approach, as we are unlikely to sell so many copies of digital documents to cover the costs of digitalization. Therefore, selecting the materials to be digitalized according to their selling appeal does not seem to be the best choice.

The thematic approach is much more convincing, though, of course, we can hardly foresee what the subject of future researches will be. Currently, some libraries and museums have started digitalization projects dealing with theatre iconography. This is certainly one of the major fields of investigation for theatre researchers. We have started a selection of the iconographic materials about the *commedia dell'arte* in our collections, and this selection will be probably the object of one of our next digitalization campaigns. Another interesting field of research in our collections is the iconography of Italian actresses and actors. This is one of my priorities, in the next future.

At present, we have chosen a different approach. We have decided to start the digitalization of a relative small, closed collection, the Petrolini Collection. We have made this decision while preparing an exhibition. Linking the different documents together, we have realised this collection is unique because of its consistency. All documents are related to Petrolini's life, to his characters and plays, to his performances and tours. This peculiarity makes the Petrolini collection the ideal object for digitalization.

The Petrolini Collection

Ettore Petrolini was at the same time an actor and a playwright. His personality is very representative of the history of the Italian variety theatre during the first decades of the 20th century, but his innovative writing and acting influenced the comic theatre of the following decades. At the beginning of the century, he created his famous *macchiette*, parodies and nonsense sketches whose irreverence and acrobatic language arouse the Futurists' enthusiasm.

During the years 1915-1920 Petrolini cooperated with the Futurist movement: he produced Luciano Folgore's play *Zero meno zero* (1915), which included some of the most popular characters created by Petrolini; he organised some Futurist shows (the controversial *serate futuriste*) and eventually wrote a one-act play together with Francesco Cangiullo, *Radioscopia di un duetto* (1918)[1], which simultaneously presented the actor on stage and in the backstage.

---

[1] In 1919, Mario Bonnard directed a film, *Mentre il pubblico ride*, whose screenplay was adapted from *Radioscopia di un duetto*. The film featured Ettore Petrolini and Nini Dinelli as leading actors.

Under the Fascism, when the political censorship became more attentive, less tolerant with improvisation and hostile to the free exchange of jokes between the actor and the audience, Petrolini's repertory turned to more complex plays, and to playwrights like Molière and Pirandello. During his last years, he wrote some challenging plays (*Gastone, Benedetto fra le donne, Chicchignola*) and turned again to the cinema (*Nerone* and *Cortile*, directed by Alessandro Blasetti; *Il medico per forza* directed by Carlo Campogalliani).

Petrolini collected a large documentation about himself, with great carefulness and long-sightedness, probably because of his fear of being forgotten, a fear he clearly expressed in his last book, *Un po' per celia, un po' per non morir...*, published just before his death in 1936[2]. He used many documents for his books[3] that he regarded as a guarantee of immortality, more reliable than the sheer recollections of an affectionate public.

After his death, his heirs came into possession of an important archive, containing an extensive documentation about the variety theatre of the first decades of the 20th century. Petrolini's archive proved to be a valuable source of information: variety theatre was considered as a "minor" genre, and only a few documents were left to researchers.

In June 2001, the Petrolini Association donated the archives to the Burcardo Library. It was an important acquisition, completing the small collection two of Petrolini's heirs had already donated in the Thirties.

The Petrolini Collection is made of all kinds of documents. It counts more than 700 photos; a comprehensive collection of contracts, playbills, posters and press clippings; drawings, paintings and caricatures; manuscripts of plays and musical scores; sound recordings; letters Petrolini exchanged with actors, writers, journalists and politicians; costumes, accessories and props; medals, plates and other signs of honours.

The Database

We have built a relational database specifically for the Petrolini Collection using Microsoft ACCESS. It is a model database we intend to use for similar collections.

---

[2] Ettore Petrolini, *Un po' per celia un po' per non morir...* Roma, Signorelli, 1936.

[3] Ettore Petrolini, *Abbasso Petrolini*, Siena, Tip. Cooperativa, 1922. A collection of press reviews about Petrolini's productions.
Ettore Petrolini, *Modestia a parte*, Bologna, Cappelli, 1931. Mostly autobiographical.
Ettore Petrolini, *Io e il film sonoro*, Roma, Tip. Viminale, 1931. A collection of press reviews about Petrolini's films.

The first difficulty we encountered was making the information about different material consistent. Besides, we wanted the database record to give the most possible information about any item, avoiding redundancy. The following table shows the database structure.

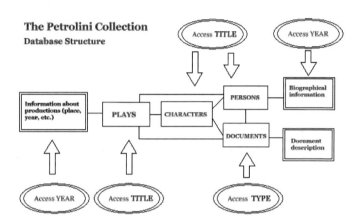

There are four different ways of accessing the documents: by year, by title, by name of person and by document type. Fig. 1-4 presents some examples of records.

There are two different levels of description for each document, a generic one containing the most important information, and a specialised one containing full details about format, content etc. Fig. 5 and 6 show examples of two records for the same document.

We are now developing simplified HTML interfaces for our intranet. Microsoft ACCESS databases allow the users to build data access pages, Web pages designed for viewing and working with data from an Internet or intranet. The page is a separate file that is stored outside Microsoft Access. When users display the data access page in Internet Explorer (5 or up), they are viewing their own copy of the page (Fig. 7). Only librarians work with the ACCESS database, but the data are available to all users on every workstation of our intranet.

The Digital Copies

The digital copies of the documents are stored in our LAN server as high-resolution images. Low-resolution copies are linked to the database records for a fast display via browser.

One of our priorities was the digitalization of all sound recordings. The Petrolini archive includes a collection of about fifty 78-rpm records. It is now forty years since 78-rpm records were discontinued and it is becoming increasingly difficult to find equipment to play them. Besides, these fragile items need a special care to avoid further damages. All records have been digitalized, and the audio files are accessible to the users in our reading room. The digital copies cannot be used differently, because of copyright restrictions.

At present, only sound recordings and bi-dimensional documents have been digitalized. The photo archive has been totally digitalized, and we are working on the other materials. On the contrary, we are still investigating the best way of dealing with three-dimensional objects which need to be observed from different points of view, like costumes, props and sculptures.

Fig. 1 - Access by Year

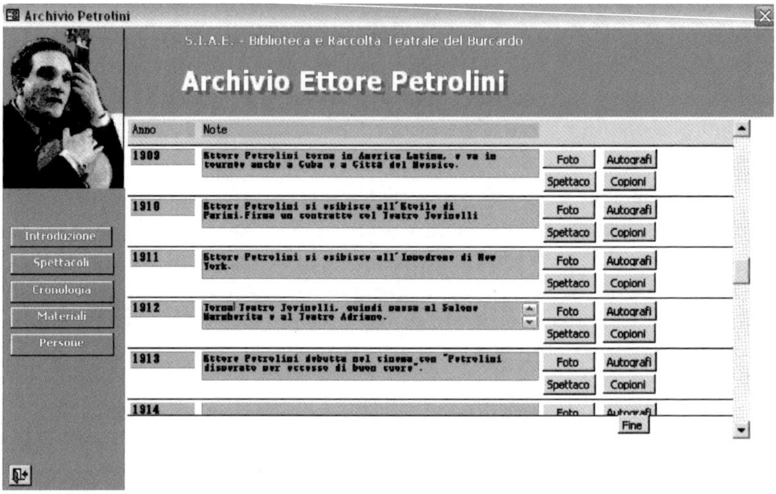

Fig. 2 - Access by Title

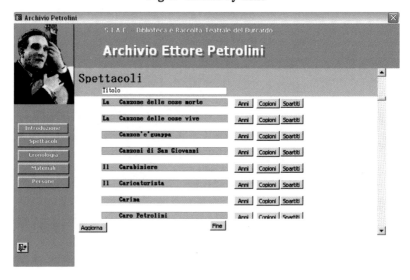

Fig. 3 - Access by Name of Person

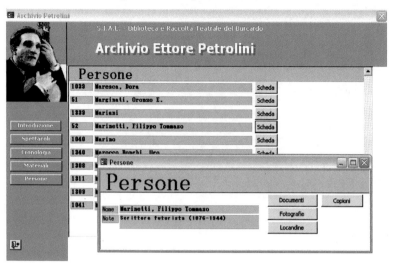

Fig. 4 - Access by Type of Material

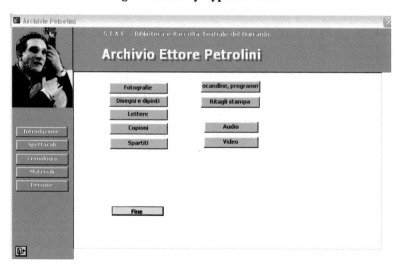

Fig. 5

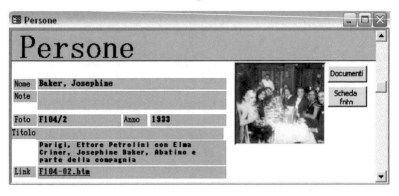

Fig. 6

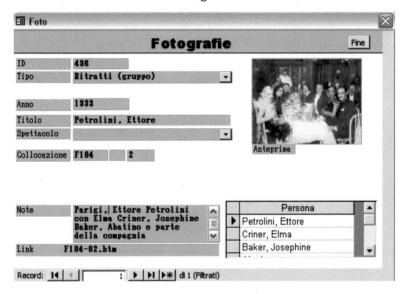

Fig. 7

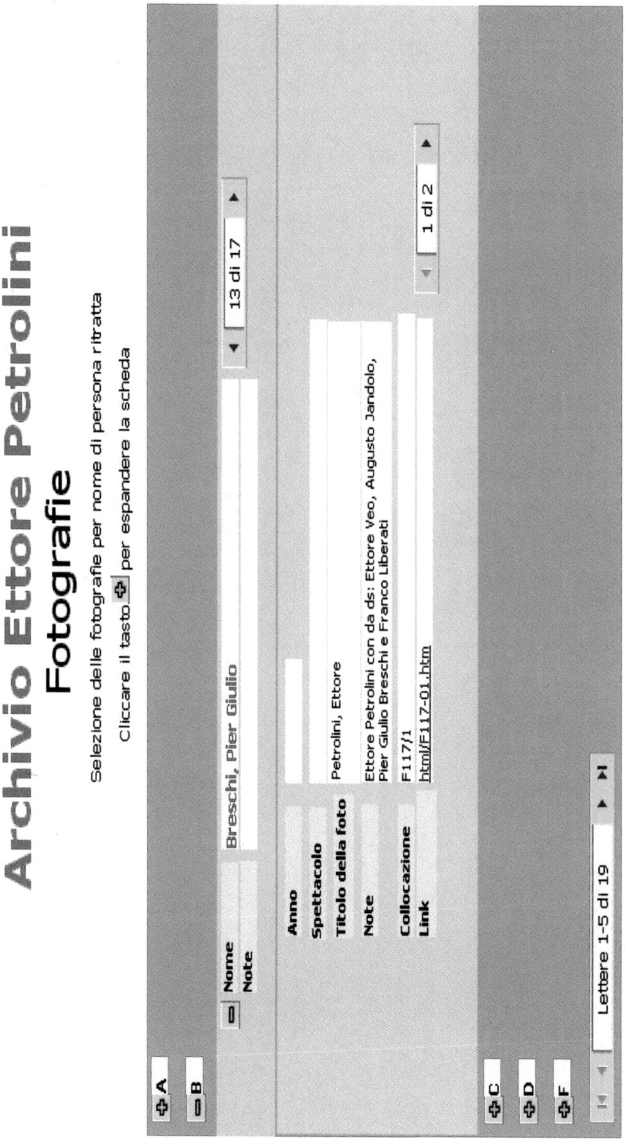
Archivio Ettore Petrolini
Fotografie
Selezione delle fotografie per nome di persona ritratta
Cliccare il tasto per espandere la scheda
A
B
Nome
Breschi, Pier Giulio
Note
13 di 17
Anno
Spettacolo
Titolo della foto
Petrolini, Ettore
Note
Ettore Petrolini con da ds: Ettore Veo, Augusto Jandolo, Pier Giulio Breschi e Franco Liberati
Collocazione
F117/1
Link
html/F117-01.htm
1 di 2
C
D
F
Lettere 1-5 di 19

C.a.r.m.e.n.[1]: a Virtual Access to the Archives of La Monnaie

Jan VAN GOETHEM

Théâtre de La Monnaie (Brussel – Belgium)

La Monnaie:
Synopsis of the History of the Belgian National Opera

The history of the Royal Theatre La Monnaie spans over 300 years!

Plans for founding the theatre were outlined in 1695 and the inauguration of the first theatre took place in the year 1700.

The theatre was at the very centre of the 1830 revolution that led to the declaration of independence of the country – and survived various Belgian political regimes and governments. It saw different types of management and changed owners: from private directors-entrepreneurs to the City of Brussels (after 1830) and – since 1963 – the Belgian government.

Various events have taken place at the theatre: both dramatic and lyric art events and dance performances. It was the venue also for other festive events such as balls, masked balls, circus evenings and other events. Foreign groups and the greatest artists from around the world have performed at the theatre by invitation, while the theatre itself has travelled with its productions in innumerable tours and has participated in numerous co-productions.

Its scenes, costumes and entire stage settings have continuously evolved, in line with the different artistic movements of different epochs. The archives of its spectacles are, however, in a sorry state. An archiving service was nonexistent until 1995: as a result, some archives were lost or destroyed; others have become dispersed over various public and private funds.

---

[1] Acronym of "Computerised archival retrieval in Multimedia Enhanced Networking".

C.a.r.m.e.n.: the Project

Therefore, a scientific committee initiated a project for the development of a centralised, multimedia archiving system – at the occasion of the tercentenary of the Theatre in 1995. They decided that the system would base on state-of-the-art computer technologies, allowing some recuperation of the past and upgrading of the present, in order to save these data and to make them accessible to both specialists and the larger public by means of telecommunication technology.

The project received support by way of a federal programme for the "promotion and distribution of telecommunications" and was then further developed by a consortium. The consortium's main partners were *La Monnaie*, the *Université Libre de Bruxelles* and the *Limburgs Universitair Centrum*.

C.a.r.m.e.n.: a Profile

A preliminary analysis, preceding the development of the system, based on a series of enquiries – as much with internal services of *La Monnaie* as with other national and foreign institutions. As a result, the structure of a relational-database was retained – in which each information item would need to be introduced just once and could then be linked to different other items to which it was related. The database was customised to deal in detail with data regarding opera productions, especially all information relating to:

- programming (titles, cuttings, casting and other elements of the performed works);
- individuals and groups involved in either the creation of a work (composers, authors of librettos, poets) or in the stage settings (directors, set designers, costume designers) and in the performing of the work (singers, musicians);
- situating the various events in time and place (dates, venues);
- documents made before, during or after the staging of the spectacles.

Concept

Other characteristics of the application are:

- multilingualism: as well on the input level as on the consultation level all data are presented in their original language or in both French and Dutch;
- control of part of the data by means of a multilingual thesaurus; this thesaurus not only covers specific domains in the field of performance arts (such as e.g. musical types, theatre types, musical instruments) but also iconographic objects, parts of costumes, materials or even general linguistic and geographical information;
- digital rendering of text documents, images, sounds and videos – giving the tool its multimedia quality, amply illustrating the patrimony of *La Monnaie*.

Database Structure

The application is Oracle-based and resides on a central server. In this way multiple users can access it via a network.

Users

C.a.r.m.e.n. was designed for both internal and external users of *La Monnaie*.

In fact, different data are entered by the different services of the organisation and more data input could be allocated even to other, external sites – depending on the location of the data sources.

Fig. 1: Database Structure

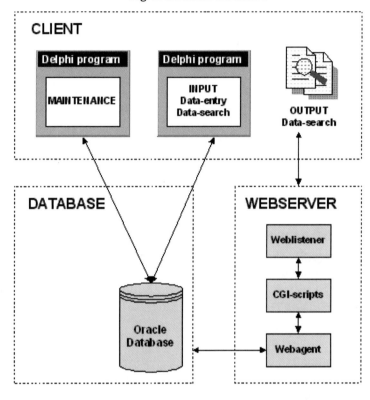

At the same time, the easy access to production data and documents (such as programmes, photos, biographies) improve the work and communication flow between the members of *La Monnaie*. This also meets with research needs of various other types of users: publishers, students, researchers, art amateurs, collectors, and so on.

Document Management in C.a.r.m.e.n.

The documents that make up the archives of *La Monnaie* can be classified into three major categories:

- text (programmes, letters, poems, press articles);
- iconographs (posters, costumes and scene models, photographs);
- audiovisual records.

Inputting of these data into C.a.r.m.e.n. based on the AFNOR and ISBD norms so as to allow for the exporting of standardised lists. Inputting of data runs along a standard general procedure including the following steps:

- a general per-category description, mainly including the title, the statement of responsibility, the language, the publisher's imprint, the collation, the standard identification number, a free zone for notes and, finally, descriptive parameters from the thesaurus. Obviously, not all of these data fields are obligatory for all the different types of documents;
- the physical identification and localisation of copies, so that it is clear whether e.g. they belong to the fund of *La Monnaie* or to external collections;
- a link to a digital representation of the document;
- the establishment of a relationship with one of the other database elements directly related to the same document. For example, models of scenes or posters will be linked to the production for which they have been created; a poem will be linked to the melody that puts it into music; a photograph will be linked to the name of the person represented in the photograph. In this way, each document is represented in its own context so that its origin will be clear to the user.

Search Options in C.a.r.m.e.n.

C.a.r.m.e.n. features two complementary search modes: one mode was designed to produce a more detailed search result than the other.

1. Internet Searches via http://carmen.lamonnaie.be.

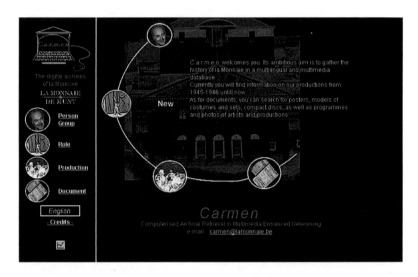

Starting from the C.a.r.m.e.n. Internet-search page, users can search:
- by persons or groups – on the basis of a name, a function or a combination of both criteria;
- by role – on the basis of the name of a character;
- by production – on the basis of a title, a type (opera, dance, concert), a performance date or a combination of these criteria;
- by document – on the basis of a title, a category, a name of an author, a keyword or a combination of these criteria.

In this way, it is possible to find, for example:
- all individuals having occupied a certain function at *La Monnaie* (e.g. all set designers);
- a set of documents:
  o created by one person, or
  o relating to one production (per category, or all categories mixed), or
  o relating to one single category and to one performance (regardless of the different stage settings at different performance dates), or
  o identified by the search term – as it has been defined in the thesaurus.

Today, search results will include data relative to productions realised in or after 1946, as well as documents such as:

- posters, photographs of productions and individuals;
- costume and set designs, engravings, busts;
- programmes, press articles, magazines, books, biographies, synopses, music scores and librettos;
- audiovisual materials (not digitised).

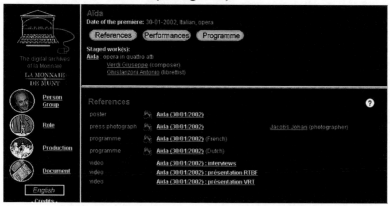

In this type of search, information is fragmented: different results can be accessed via links, one by one, page by page.

2. Search Reports Module

A second search mode is available only at the interface level, where inputs take place and it is reserved for internal users only.

It can generate complete inventories of all data contained in different forms – possibly filtered by search criteria. By means of this tool, indexed catalogues with bibliographical notes can be reviewed by editing all of the related information in one go.

Aïda (30/01/2002) [press photograph] / Johan Jacobs (photographer). - 115 prints
Copy :
16103. - Archives of La Monnaie, IPPX 5/17. - 50 x 65 cm. - 12 colour prints
16219. - Archives of La Monnaie, IPPP 30/3. - 18 x 26 cm. - 25 colour prints
16220. - Archives of La Monnaie, IPPP 30/4. - 18 x 26 cm. - 25 colour prints
16221. - Archives of La Monnaie, IPPP 30/5. - 18 x 26 cm. - 25 colour prints
16222. - Archives of La Monnaie, IPPP 30/6. - 18 x 26 cm. - 23 colour prints
16225. - Archives of La Monnaie, IPPS 72/7. - 18 x 27 cm. - 5 colour prints

C.a.r.m.e.n.: the Future

Because of the scope and the normalisation of the information which the system can register and the fact that it is a multilingual system, C.a.r.m.e.n. has become a product, which can be easily adapted for use by other organisations, artistic houses, museums or archives/libraries.

Access to the Illustrative Graphic Arts Material of the Russian State Arts Library: CD *The Russian Service Uniform*

Ada KOLGANOVA

Russian State Arts Library (Moscow – Russia)

The aim of the project is to provide access to the unique illustrative graphic arts material with the guaranteed search system and printout from the Russian State Arts library.

The CD given presents the peculiarities of the service uniform of the epoch of Tsar Nicholas I.

While reproducing historical scenes painters, publishers, researchers and stage and film directors often encounter problems of recreating uniforms and their history in detail which can be especially difficult.

The purpose of this CD is to make the library stocks accessible to as many users as possible. Moreover, the condition of some illustrative materials forces us to withdraw them from free access.

The Russian State Arts Library holds the collection of Russian service uniforms from a wide variety of its history, periods, branches of the service, etc. The Library gained considerable experience working with production designers, costume designers, illustrators, stage and film directors, consulting and taking part in the production of home and foreign performances and films on historical plots.

The Library holds comprehensive material on the Russian service uniform of the period 1550-1995. The rich subject card catalogue, kept for tens of years, includes information on the peculiarities and comparative characteristics of home and foreign uniforms.

Information on the uniforms, together with detailed images, is a valuable source of information illustrating an esthetical, historical and economic picture of a society and can serve as an illustration of a concrete epoch.

While working on films and performances, production designers and directors use it as a necessary reference source. The following are the examples of the several last years: the opera *Jugin Onegin* staged by Jugin Kolobov; film *The Siberian barber* produced by Nikita Mikhalkov; film *The Russian Rebellion* and TV serial *M. Lomonosov* produced by A. Proshkin.

The authenticity and accuracy of the works, created on the base of libraries, depends on the quality of the information, including illustrative material, distinguished by the careful detailing of the uniform elements. Such a thorough study is necessary because of complicated particular enquiries of specialists, who creating visual aids of films, telecasts, books, meet great difficulties in the reconstruction of the uniform.

The whole illustrative material on the CD is presented by the works of the painters P. Rudakov, G. Verne, L. Belouhsov and of the painters' group, joined by A. Viskovatov.

While preparing the material for the CD, we classified the uniform so as to display its evolution. The painters' works representing the uniform were put into the CD according to its epochs, periods and decades.

All the images in the CD are presented in separate JPEG files with a resolution of 300 dpi. The format given was used to save the quality of the scanned images maximally with the minimum capacity of the space on the CD.

The library computer system IRBIS developed by the State Public Research Technical Library was used.

The record structure includes the indication of the service unit, the years of the introduction of a certain uniform and the years up to which it was used in the Army. In the notes there are some details such as ranks of servicemen, use of a uniform (a full dress, field dress, winter uniform, etc.), and drill exercises.

Any CD gives the opportunity to use the material most completely. Our CD provides the search of uniform images by their service units and years. Thanks to the facilities set in the structure, having selected a certain service unit one can review the whole period of the epoch, all the graphic arts materials, ranks of servicemen, seasons (winter, summer), changes in the uniform.

The disk will be useful to producers, actors, historians, painters, designers, librarians, teachers, students of different institutes and military colleges, pupils and those who are interested in history.

CINQUIÈME PARTIE

LE CATALOGAGE DES COLLECTIONS

FIFTH PART

CATALOGUING THE COLLECTIONS

Does TANDEM Still Exist?

Claudia BALK, Petra KRAUS

Deutsches Theatermuseum (München – Germany)

What Remains of TANDEM in the New Developed Database Management of Archives? Introducing the Background from the Beginning of Electronic Archiving to a New Status Quo

Those who have been members of SIBMAS for a long time and have frequently attended its congresses will perhaps still remember the TANDEM project, which was conceived at the German Theatre Museum at the end of the 1970s. This was accompanied by the vision that as many theatre collections as possible should catalogue their objects with an identical database structure, so that one day a homogeneous and interchangeable data pool could be made available. This idea was just as captivating as the basic idea for the data structure, which gave the project its name: to link two databases by means of references for recording data on productions and the objects relating to them. All information relating specifically to the production was to be entered into the production data file, and linked to this the relevant information relating specifically to objects was to be entered into the other database. If, for example, three costume designs and 20 photographs were available for a production, the information on the production would not have to also be incorporated into each document on these materials referred to, but could be called up via the relational link. Although this basic idea is plausible, for financial and technical reasons it has only recently been possible to translate it into reality at the German Theatre Museum.

The TANDEM concept has not only been demonstrated or presented – to my knowledge several times – at SIBMAS congresses, but several other collections have also begun recording data on the basis of this structure. The German Theatre Museum itself began cataloguing by means of EDP in the mid-1980s. After the departure of the inventor of TANDEM, Dr. Huesmann, the Theatre Museum's staff started to eliminate several categories which were felt not to be practicable, while several other categories were added; in the case of the latter, cataloguing additional material such as videos or sound carriers became necessary. However, the fact is that with the exception of the library, which develops its data stocks online in cooperation with other libraries, cataloguing at the German Theatre Museum is now also still undertaken accurately on the basis of TANDEM.

Since last autumn the German Theatre Museum has been building up a retrieval database structure using newly acquired software called FAUST, into which the older data stocks of all previous formats can be transported. To present this software, which we have since updated, I should now like to hand over to Petra Kraus:

FAUST – Retrieval Picture Database

Advantages in Programming and Screen Design

Technical Application Data

The search for a referential data processing model has occupied us at the German Theatre Museum ever since electronic data processing was first heralded in the 1980s. Now, at last, new database systems can fulfil the referencing requirements of the archivists. In this connection, instead of the large commercial databases such as Oracle or Access, we have opted for a German product, FAUST 3 from the Land-Software Company, which for 15 years has specialised in the needs of text and picture archives. Fortunately, FAUST users also include many related institutions, for example the Dance Archive in Cologne, with which we cooperate. FAUST additionally offers a wide range of application possibilities; it works together with various operating systems, including Windows, Macintosh (announced for this summer) and Linux, and can be operated in various networks, such as, in our case, Novell.

Adaptable for Different Types of Databases

With importing from older data stocks – we have in the meantime been working with LARS, a binary recording model offering a full text or index search and multiple input separated by stop signs, e.g. for several persons in one biography or in one photograph – there are no relevant problems via ASCII files.

Although reference is made here to the FAUST documentation software selected by us, this presentation relates in very general terms to our experience with a referentially operating database system.

The program includes as many databases as desired, to which up to 250 sub-databases, each with a data mask, can be subordinated. Thus a sub-database can easily also illustrate the contents of an entire archive, provided all objects can be recorded in the same data mask. We are attempting to simplify our archive in this way because benefits for wide-ranging research are thereby produced.

Input via Self-Designed Interface

I will now present to you in sequence examples of design possibilities for the mask, input, research and options for printing. Firstly two input masks:

1. Example: Input Interface

2. Example: Input Interface with Macro Application

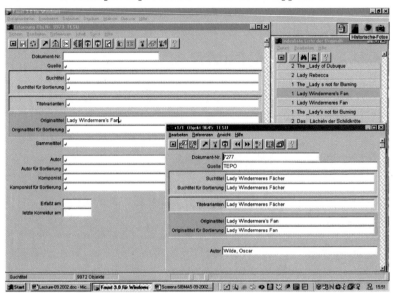

Recording can be undertaken in a network equipped with an Ethernet server structure, simultaneously by all members of staff for all types of objects in the documentation. The numbering of the objects is automatically determined according to the relevant time of storage of a fully recorded document. At the German Theatre Museum documents on individual holdings of the Museum are, for example, recorded by one department in the form of a picture and picture title, and then supplemented or provided with references by the next department. A division of work according to specialist areas is thereby logically put into effect.

Between the databases we can therefore produce links in the form of reference fields, which form a subject-matter bridge to a retrievable linked file.

3. Example: Reference File

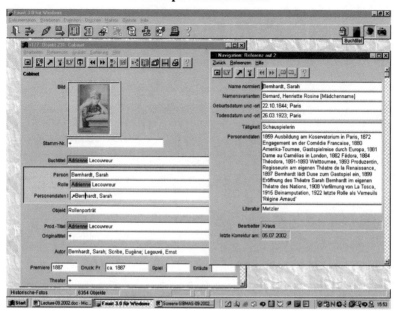

Extended Possibilities of Research and Returns Storage

Central Research in All Databases

Research is possible in all databases opened at the workstation in succession. The user interface is based on icons, from which one can switch from one opened database to another. The results can be brought together in a user-friendly way into a final result. The search items in the research can be linked as desired.

Simplified Work with Indices

The indices can be used both for research and for controlling the entries. For each relevant data field, or a group of similar data fields, a common index is specified. For example, within a document this may be people who are listed in the document masks as different artists and authors. Here I present as an example Sarah Bernhardt, who I am searching for in the "person" and "role" fields either as Adrienne Lecouvreur or Théodora.

4. Example: Linked Research

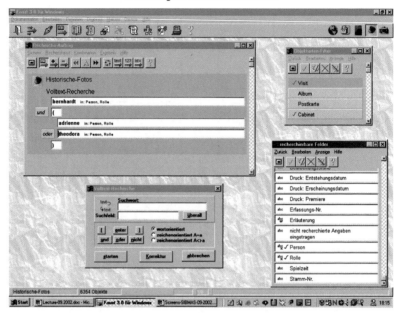

Our documentation of historical photography, in the cabinet format, lists as artist the actress but also the author of the play in whose role she is illustrated. To this second artist's name, from our present perspective as archivists the name of the photographer of the studio scene portrayed is added. All three persons are grouped together in an index and can be searched for through an index search.

5. Example: Result of this Research

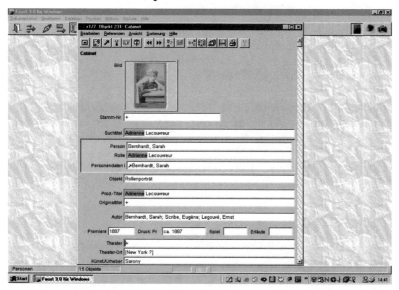

6. Example: Index "Artists"

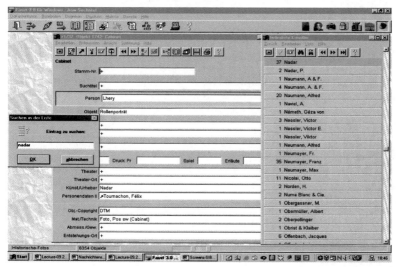

Data Entry: Pictures, Descriptions and References between the Objects

The example of the stage artist of the 19th century leads us to an additional point on which the documentalists have to process a surplus of information: the recording of artists' names and pseudonyms, often as a result of several marriages, maiden names and also different spellings. This produced a call for standardised spelling, which as a search word optimises the user's hit quota. In addition to the possibility of bringing together the index, which has already been dealt with, at the German Theatre Museum all information relating to persons is summarised in a particular "persons" document, which can be added to any other documentation as a reference file. Here are a few examples, which once again emphasise the curious element of the intended identification of an artist using his name:

7. Example: Reference File "Artist Pseudonyms"

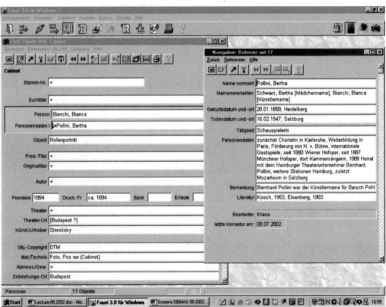

It is apparent that the pseudonym also plays a part with regard to male colleagues, particularly whenever it also becomes established as the married name on marriage, like here Pollini, or for example Félix Tournachon's pseudonym Nadar passes to the son Paul Nadar as a new "surname". There is also a similar case with the photographer Erika Bieber and her son Emil Bieber, who both sign as E. Bieber.

The reference system: taking the example of a project for an exhibition on theatre directors: no clearly definable characteristics of objects.

The example of the well-known theatre director Claus Peymann, whose work often involves new productions of the same plays at different theatres, makes clear to us the advantages of the FAUST reference system. Since it is not always a case of pure repeat productions, we need to make these plays distinguishable from each other in linked files with additional information and further references to accompanying pictorial objects.

8. Example: Reference File: Peymann – New Productions of the Same Play

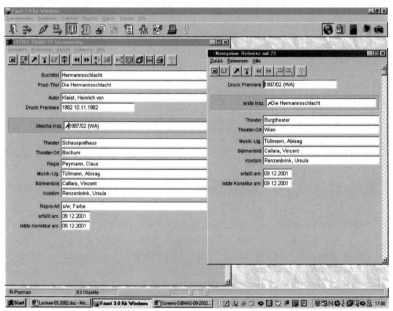

Post-operation, Adapting Features, Data Masks

For the documentalist, and the recorder of data for the collective areas of a museum or archive whom the documentalist instructs in the system-supported data processing, the most important initial steps consist of the systematic conception of the data records. However, the following questions also quickly arise: Who does this serve? What comfort does electronic processing offer? What role does the end user of the data play, i.e. the researcher, in the architecture of a database of knowledge? In archives, data have to be capable of being presented to outsiders as a usable printout, and in view of the LARS abbreviations this printout must at least also be legible.

9. Example: Marie Taglioni Print Format

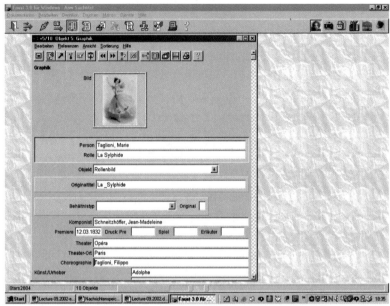

In the museum there is the additional element of the conception of exhibitions: with FAUST the selected data record can be exported both for catalogue planning in Word as an already completed print format, as well as for designing object boards. Across the range of documentation a large number of storable print formats can be produced. And now as a final example, the same object prepared simply as an exhibition text board.

10. Example: Print View for Exhibition Text Board

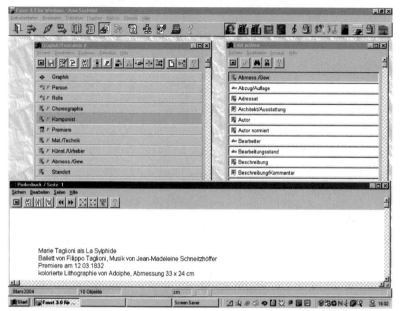

FAUST – an Expanding Model? On Availability and Application of FAUST in Theatre Archive Situations

We are on the best path towards translating our expectations of FAUST into reality. We use FAUST for temporary databases in preparation for exhibitions, in which we collect objects located both in our archives as well as outside the museum. The objective is always to feed back the newly acquired data into our basis documentation.

Of course, a great deal of learning is necessary for all members of staff at the start of a software changeover. Nevertheless, training by suppliers, in-house support and above all a good initial conception and architecture of the databases, with the software managers cooperating closely with the scientific team, create within a few months the possibility of carrying out efficient data recording and evaluation in the new system. Since we are looking back on a long tradition of EDP recording, our main objective is to transfer the architecture of our databases, which has grown over time, to the new software and where possible to simplify its structure. An additional objective is also to make our data stocks useful for external researchers without the direct participation of our personnel.

Barry Russell:
CÉSAR's Standard-bearer[1]

Anastassia SAKHNOVSKAIA, Mark BANNISTER

CÉSAR Project (United Kingdom)

Although he came relatively late in life to an academic career, Barry Russell set out to make his mark in his research. The subject-area he chose for his doctorate was the fairground theatre of 17th and 18th centuries France, an area that had received less attention than the classic theatre of the established playhouses and which was consequently considered marginal in some quarters. By making a slow and painstaking search of the old hand-written card-index of the *Catalogue des Anonymes* at the Bibliothèque nationale in Paris, Russell unearthed a considerable number of hitherto unpublished and largely unknown texts of fairground plays which he transcribed and stored in electronic form.

For a variety of reasons, a break of several years occurred in his research, during which time he became aware of the opportunities offered by the rapidly developing Internet. In particular, thanks to Tim Berners-Lee, the World Wide Web was making it possible for the interconnected servers of the Internet to provide easily accessible information of all kinds in hypertext format. Russell was impressed by the potential of the WWW for the presentation of academic research in a new way. At the same time, he discovered his own potential for mastering and developing the tools of the new medium. The result was a Website (http://foires.net) which allowed access to his research findings on the fairground theatre in an entirely new way. Unlike the classic monograph, in which the data are necessarily "frozen" at the moment of publication, hypertext allows the information to be added to or modified

---

[1] During the Fifth Session of the Conference, Barry Russell gave an electronic demonstration of the CÉSAR database. Sadly, he died on 10 February 2003, and no written record of what he would have produced for the Conference proceedings was left. Therefore, Anastassia Sakhnovskaia and Mark Bannister felt it was more appropriate to give an outline of his contribution to the development of CÉSAR which could also serve as something of a memorial to him.

indefinitely. It lends itself to an exercise in genuine collaboration, since, rather than waiting for the "definitive" work to appear, scholars can carry on a discussion as to future developments, offer alternative interpretations and make their own contributions to the data. Moreover, whereas a book is necessarily linear in its presentation, hypertext imposes no required order on the material. The user is free to follow his or her own interests through the various layers of data and commentary.

In 1996, Russell joined the staff of Oxford Brookes University and in 1997 was awarded an Institutional Fellowship by the British Academy to enable him to develop his work on the Foires Website. As well as adding more results from his own research, he took the opportunity to make available searchable hypertext versions of some of the standard scholarly reference works on the fairground theatre and set up a discussion list for all those interested in this area of work. While continuing with the Foires venture, he turned his mind to a more ambitious project which had preoccupied him for some time. Russell had his own database of details on 17th and 18th-century plays and was in contact with other theatre-specialists who had built up their own specialised databases. In collaboration with two of them, Professor Jeff Ravel of the Massachusetts Institute of Technology and Professor David Trott of Toronto University, he set up CÉSAR (Calendrier Électronique des Spectacles sous l'Ancien Régime), a database designed to cover all aspects of the French theatre between 1600 and 1800. The data provided by the three founders amounted to 90,000 items but other specialists have since made available further datasets concerning their own areas of interest.

Russell himself designed the structure for the database, using MySQL to organise the data into tables that have a well-defined relationship to each other. Although CÉSAR largely follows a classic relational database model, it contains an element that allows it to be considerably more flexible, namely, the use of unique object identifiers (UOID) whereby objects or records created within the database are assigned an identifier which is unique not only across their own table but across the whole database as well. The use of PHP to generate pages on the server in response to queries ensures the most rapid and dynamic interaction between the user's computer and the database.

In 2001, the British Arts and Humanities Research Board provided funding over three years for the development of CÉSAR under their Resource Enhancement Scheme. This has allowed the appointment of a team of researchers and technical staff to complete the first phase of the project. In accordance with Russell's original plan, the aim of CÉSAR is to store detailed data on all aspects of the French theatre 1600-1800, whether it be people (authors, actors, performers of all sorts, directors, etc.), places (theatres, private performance areas, etc.), titles of published or unpublished works, or dates. Each page provides a menu offering a rapid link to the appropriate point from which the user wishes to start (People, Troupes, Places, Titles, Dates, Publications, Publishers, Libraries). Each section provides the opportunity to carry out a refined search by the use of checkboxes to specify the particular categories in which the user is interested. So, for example, under "People", use of the checkboxes for skills, male/female and dates can produce a list of all female theatre writers alive in France between 1750 and 1800, or all male dancers alive in the year 1762. From any such list, the full record for any individual can then be recovered.

In addition to items of data, CÉSAR also offers access to digitised versions of key reference works, many of them published in the 18th and 19th centuries and not generally available outside the main research libraries, e.g. Parfaict, Laporte, Soleinne, Maupoint. By the end of the AHRB-funded period, seven or eight such works will have been put on line, each of them searchable and cross-referenced to the entries in the database.

CÉSAR is built around the principle adopted by Russell for all his online enterprises, that those with an interest in the Website should be invited to join in its development and, where appropriate, contribute actively to it. That means that users who register with CÉSAR are invited to suggest corrections, additions or modifications to the data. Those who are recognised as specialists in Ancien Régime theatre can be given direct internal access to the database in order to add their own data and so bring in as wide a range of expertise as possible. Already several eminent scholars are contributing directly in this way and it is anticipated that more will offer their knowledge and skill in the future.

The present funding by the AHRB will come to an end in 2004, but CÉSAR will continue. Although the hosting of the database will remain with Oxford Brookes, it is intended to set up an International Steering Group consisting of recognised theatre scholars, whose remit will be to ensure that any proposed developments are in accordance with the original aims of the founders. Possible areas for development are theatre iconography, music in theatrical performances and texts of plays.

Sadly, Barry Russell did not live to see the fulfilment of his vision, for he died in 2003 after a short illness. The team who have inherited his project, however, are totally committed to carrying through his aims and ensuring that CÉSAR is established across the worldwide academic community as a model of how rigorous scholarship can be allied dynamically to the latest IT methods to produce a tool of value to all those, scholars and students alike, who work in the area of Ancien Régime theatre. Barry Russell's memorial can be found at http://www.cesar.org.uk[2].

---

[2]   Addendum (2011): CÉSAR has gone from strength to strength, with many academics and theatre-lovers contributing to the database. It is now recognised as an indispensable resource in the world of French theatre studies. In 2004, I obtained a second major grant (£238,704) from the uk Arts & Humanities Research Council for the creation of an imagebank containing images published between 1600 and 1800, supported by descriptive material enabling historians of the theatre, costume, stage-design and theatre construction as well as theatre-lovers of all kinds to gain access rapidly to the images that interest them. The imagebank contains over 3,500 images and can be found at http://www.cesar.org.uk/cesar2/imgs/index.php. This part of the project would not have been possible without the generosity of some of the major academic libraries and museums (notably the Taylor Institution Library, Oxford; the Bibliothèque Historique de la Ville de Paris; the Library of Trinity College, Dublin; the Harvard Theatre Collection; the Ashmolean Museum, Oxford; the Victoria & Albert Theatre Museum, London; the John Rylands Library, Manchester and the Library of the University of Montreal) which allowed us to put online digital copies of engravings in their collections, some of them rare. We are immensely grateful to them.

Performing Art Libraries in Düsseldorf

Their Role in the Field of Introducing Computer-based Information and the Management within the Theatre Museum and the Film Museum

Margret SCHILD

Theatre Museum Düsseldorf (Germany)

Düsseldorf is the capital of North Rhine-Westphalia, the state with the highest number of inhabitants in Germany. The city has a rich cultural history. The theatre history started in 1485 (the festivities in the context of a princely marriage at Düsseldorf). Theatre historiography marks three great periods for Düsseldorf (Immermann, 1834-1837; Dumont-Lindemann, 1905-1933; Gründgens, 1947-1955). The city has a long history of involvement with film, too. For instance the first German film journal *Der Kinematograph* began publishing here in 1907. After 1945, Düsseldorf became a distribution centre and served for decades as site of all major German and foreign distributors' headquarters. It still offers a lot of cultural events: performing arts in different forms (theatre at the Düsseldorfer Schauspielhaus, musicals at the Capitol, opera and ballet at the German Opera Düsseldorf-Duisburg, dance at the Tanzhaus (Dance House) North Rhine-Westphalia, free and independent theatre groups, private theatres, cinema, media, museums, cultural institutions, representing other countries like France, Poland...

The Institutions: Theatre Museum and Film Museum

A part of these cultural offers and events is funded by the City of Düsseldorf. The Theatre Museum and the Film Museum belong to these institutions. The Theatre Museum[1] started in 1947 as donation of Gustav

---

[1] Winrich Meiszies: "A theatre museum for the citizen: local theatre-historiography as socio-cultural research and documentation", in *Collecting and recording the Performing Arts: Why and How?*, Antwerp, SIBMAS, 1995, p. 34-36. [Proceedings of

Lindemann. Louise Dumont (1862-1932) and Gustav Lindemann (1872-1960) founded and ran, between 1905 and 1933, the private Schauspielhaus Düsseldorf. They tried to reconcile their ambitious artistic aims with the economic necessities of a private theatre. Gustaf Gründgens (1899-1963), student of Dumont/Lindemann, ran the Städtische Bühnen from 1947 and from 1951 the Düsseldorfer Schauspielhaus in the difficult post-war times. He was the first actor of his theatre and impressed a generation of spectators. At the beginning the scope of the archive (Dumont-Lindemann-Archiv) was restricted to the history of one theatre (Schauspielhaus Düsseldorf). At the end of the 1970s the collection profile and tasks were extended to the theatre history of the city and the region. Exhibitions became a focal point of the activities, because the archive had for the first time its own exhibition rooms. The term Theatermuseum was added to the name. Because the scope was extended and the names of Dumont and Lindemann faded away and out of the public consciousness, the name Theatermuseum was chosen instead of Dumont-Lindemann-Archiv. Since 1988 the Theatre Museum has been situated in the Hofgarten (park in the city centre) and a new permanent exhibition "Schauplätze in der Stadt" ("Locations in the city") was developed on occasion of the 40th anniversary, The subject can be characterised as follows: theatre scenes (location and architecture of the theatre buildings; theatre management), theatre works (literature and theatre; directing and acting; theatre techniques and scenography) – local theatre historiography as socio-cultural research and documentation. In addition the museum organizes and presents lectures, concerts and other performances with regard to the permanent and temporary exhibition programme as well as to educational activities. Since the 2000-2001 seasons the museum cooperates with the Düsseldorfer Schauspielhaus – one room (70 seats) is used for performances, needing a minimal stage design and few actors. In the future, the Theatre Museum will cooperate with other theatres, situated at Düsseldorf and in the region: the German Opera at the Rhine (Deutsche Oper am Rhein Düsseldorf-Duisburg) will use the room regularly in the next season. The museum tries to establish and maintain contacts to independent groups, to artists and regularly receives inquiries for the use of the room for performances.

The Film Museum[2] has two starting points: in 1956 city school officials established the Düsseldorf Cinematograph of Culture and Youth in

---

the 20th International Congress of the International Association of Libraries and Museums of the Performing Arts, 4-7 September 1994 in Antwerp]

[2] Sabine Lenk, "Visiting the Düsseldorf Film Museum = Visite au Musée du cinéma de Düsseldorf", in *Cinémathèque / Cinémathèque française*, Paris, n°21, 2002, p. 135-151.

order to use film in school and for educational purposes. A bunker was built to store flammable prints. Within the ciné-club movement in 1970s the Film Forum, Department of the Volkshochschule (adult college), started holding film forums, and movie buffs flocked to them. Founded in 1972 it was transformed in 1979 to the Film Institute because of the great success. This Institute had four areas of activities: training, the Filmwerkstatt (film production and equipment), screenings (cinema Black Box) and collection (archives) management. In the late 1980s, the Institute began the planning for a permanent exhibition of items from the collection. The museum was opened in 1993 in a new building, funded by the state North Rhine-Westphalia and the City. The Filmwerkstatt went independent as a non-profit association. Renamed into "Film Museum" it had to respond to financial problems of the municipal administration. The cinema Black Box had to be rent to an independent exhibitor. The museum retained to functions: the running of the museum (permanent exhibition, education programs, temporary exhibitions) and the archive maintenance. Screening films had to be reduced to five to ten per month (previously up to two films every evening) with the help of volunteers and the collaboration of other institutions such as the French Institute, the state literature house (Literaturbüro), the municipal history workshop (Geschichtswerkstatt) and foreign consulates. The museum still successfully organises school screenings and presentations of films out of its own archive to the Friends of the Museum and on special occasions, events such as the Long Night of the Museums.

The Libraries within the Museums

I represent the libraries of both museums. They each have between 15,000 and 25,000 items (monographs, journals and serials, grey litera-ture). Each year between 500 and 1,000 new items arrive in the libraries by acquisition, publication exchange and donation. The collection profile and the acquisition policy orient on the profiles of the museums. In the case of the Theatre Museum we collect, archive and present German theatre history by the example of Düsseldorf and the region. We mainly try to acquire reference works, monographs and journals con-cerning the theatre history of German cities and regions, concerning persons (actors, actresses, costume and stage designers, directors), theatre management and buildings as well as materials from the current plays presented in Düsseldorf theatres, especially at the Düsseldorfer Schauspielhaus and the Deutsche Oper am Rhein.

In the case of the Film Museum we acquire reference works as well as literature dedicated to the history of film (especially the precursor and early history – international), national filmographies, film in Düsseldorf and North Rhine-Westphalia, people on film, restoration and preservation of film, educational use of film, subjects of exhibitions, the workshops and other events, organised and supported by the museum.

The libraries offer their service to the staff of the museums and to the public. The librarian has to manage all kinds of librarianship work: acquisition, cataloguing (alphabetical cataloguing and subject indexing, classification), information retrieval and consulting, support of exhibition and publication projects. The libraries offer monthly information about new acquisitions and regularly provide user guidance. Computer based services play an important role in this context.

The Union Catalogue of Düsseldorf's Cultural Institutions (UCD)[1]

At the end of the 1970s, the City of Düsseldorf established the Bibliotheksstelle in order to form a union catalogue of their library inventories. This intention was only to be achieved by using automatic data processing. The use of data processing offered a much deeper access than conventional cataloguing – for instance in listing artists in exhibition catalogues or in listing participating persons and institutions. Until 1992, the Bibliotheksstellei's central editorship guaranteed a continuous and consistent indexing style according to the *Rules of Alphabetical Cataloguing* and the acquisition of experience and expertise in the field of computer-based recording and the delivery of the catalogue via microfiche (4 issues/year) and as database (DIANA: Düsseldorf's Institutions Art Network Application). During the years the participant libraries recorded their new acquisitions and to a large extend the existing stocks. Participant institutions are: Heinrich Heine Institute, Theatre Museum, Foundation Museum Art Palace (formerly Art Museum), City Museum, City Archive, Goethe Museum, Film Museum, Hetjens Museum (Museum of German Ceramics). Associated institutions are: the Library of the Academy of Arts, the Library of the Art Collection North Rhine-Westphalia, and literature concerning the arts of the French Institute (until 1992).

The Theatre Museum's library stocks are completely catalogued. The Film Museum Library's monographs, journals, scripts have also been catalogued. Now we are on the way to record materials about film festivals and gifts (acquired in the last years) in addition to the recent new acquisitions. One librarian is specially occupied with retrospective cataloguing and not charged with other tasks. This librarian will leave the Film Museum, when the retrospective cataloguing project is finished, and will continue his work in the library of another cultural institution.

The subjects of the UCD focus on the stocks of the participating libraries: i.e. the arts (aesthetics, fine arts, arts and crafts, architecture, graphic arts, design and didactic arts), performing arts, film, history (of the city and the region), and literature (18th and 19th centuries, Goethe / Heine). Special emphasis was added to the listing of "unconventional literature" (exhibition and museum catalogues, folders, leaflets) and the acquisition of international literature, especially via exchange of publications. The information access points take the needs of the potential users into consideration: the activities of the museums themselves and their staff are documented in detail. Up to 25 participating people and institutions – in the case of group exhibitions and itinerant exhibitions – can be listed and every title is documented – under factual, geographical and temporal aspects – by subject indexing.

In December 1992 the Bibliotheksstelle was closed: one librarian, charged with the management of the project, went to the Public Library of Düsseldorf; one librarian is still occupied with retrospective cataloguing (still in the Film Museum Library); two librarians each became responsible for two participating libraries, which had no continuous professional staff – I became responsible for the libraries of the Theatre Museum and the Film Museum. As a consequence, the libraries of these cultural institutions had to be equipped with computers and connected to the LAN of the City. In the case of the Theatre Museum and the Film Museum this transition period took some years: at the Theatre Museum I had a real "personal" computer since the summer of 1999, the implementation of the server and the LAN followed one year later, in the summer of 2000. At the Film Museum the computers and the LAN were implemented in February 2000. Before, I had to share a computer with other colleagues or had to take the books or the title records on paper to the City Library, where I entered the bibliographical records one day a week.

With the decentralisation of the work, and with regard to changing professional standards, the cataloguing practice changed, too. Instead of keywords in the original language of the title we used German keywords, according to the German authority file for subject headings (*Schlagwortnormdatei* – SWD) of academic libraries, established in the meanwhile[3]. We had to carry over about 210,000 titles (in December 1999) from the old fashioned software BASIS-K (library software for public libraries, developed by the City Library of Bochum) into a Y2000

---

[3]   Margret Schild, "Zwischen den Stühlen: Verbale Sacherschliessung zwischen lokaler und nationaler Normung", in *AKMB-news*, Weimar, Year 5, 1999, H. 2, p. 13-16. [Subject indexing between local and national standardisation — report about the practice of subject indexing within the UCD from the point of view of the libraries of the Theatre Museum and of the Film Museum].

compatible software (BBV, former implemented in the City Library of Düsseldorf). That meant: we had still to record in the old format, we had to test and to become well acquainted with the new data format, basing on the German Exchange Format for Libraries (*Maschinelles Austauschformat für Bibliotheken* – MAB). Last but not least we had to develop conversion rules for the complete transition of the existing electronic bibliographical records. In December 1999 we started cataloguing using the new database (with the new data format) and continued by doing this still the testing of the usability of the new software. Since this point we were able to use the bibliographical data of the German National Library and the bibliographical data of the Public Library Düsseldorf for cataloguing as well as the authority files for personal names (*Personennamendatei* – PND) and institutions (*Gemeinsame Körperschaftsdatei* – GKD). In this context we benefited from our affiliation to the Public Library of Düsseldorf. In April 2001 the transfer of the old bibliographical records was carried out successfully. Meanwhile (between January 2000 and April 2001) we had to take into consideration, that the "old" 210,000 bibliographical records were only available on microfiche for reference purposes but not in the database. Corrections and additions to existing bibliographical records had to be put back until the old data were back in the new database.

The UCD is now online available within the cultural institutions. Client software is implemented on each computer in order to get connected to the BBV (mainframe processing, IMSP). The user has to be registered as user for mainframe processing in general and especially to the BBV procedure. Then the search in the OPAC of the UCD is possible. Beside the UCD, the catalogue of the Public Library Düsseldorf and the bibliographic data of the German National Library are accessible and searchable. Since April 2001 we are still waiting for a Web- OPAC to the UCD. A test version has already been implemented and was tested by the librarians of the City Library and by the librarians of the cultural institutions. The implemented Web OPAC is the condition under what the project UCD can be integrated in other projects – for instance the virtual catalogue of art history (*Virtueller Katalog Kunstgeschichte* – VKK)[4]. Basing on the technology of the KVK (*Karlsruher Virtueller Katalog*)[5] German art and museum libraries make their catalogues searchable through a common search form on the Web. The UCD would be a valuable addition to the other special libraries of the VKK – for instance the Kunst- und Museumsbibliothek Köln (Art and Museums Library at

4   Search form of the VKK (in German):
     http://www.ubka.uni-karlsruhe.de/vk_kunst.html (2002).

5   Search form of the KVK (in English):
     http://www.ubka.uni-karlsruhe.de/hylib/en/kvk.html (2002).

Cologne), the catalogue of art historical libraries at Münich, Florence and Rome, the university libraries at Heidelberg and Dresden.

The Public Library Düsseldorf has already established an OPAC, using the operating system OS2 and implemented only for local use. OS2 is not widespread in opposition to Internet technologies, such as http. The Web OPAC shall be made available within the LAN (the internal information system IRIS) and in the Web. A Web OPAC will simplify the retrieval for the users of the UCD – the users within the cultural instituti- ons as well as external users and is a matter of course for similar libra- ries. In this context the affiliation to the Public Library is our disadvan- tage: we (the librarians of the cultural institutions) were not able to choose a different Y2000 compatible software with Web-Interface, but were able to articulate our special needs and to intersperse the outsour- cing of the transition of the existing data into the new database. Con- cerning the further development of the software we depend on the needs of the Public Library as well as on the capacities and abilities of the Office of Information Technology and Organisation Development (Amt für Informationstechnologie und Organisationsentwicklung), responsible for technical support and maintenance in whole municipal admi- nistration.

Role of the Library in Other Computer-based Projects within the Museums

I share the opinion of Gert-Jan Koot, Director of the research library of the Rijksmuseum in Amsterdam, concerning the changing role of libraries in the information age[6]: Museum libraries should be more than the treasurers of book collections. They are treasurers of knowledge and have new tasks to accomplish in this function. In the case of "my" libraries: the library is an independent section beside the others (mu- seum, archives and collections) within the museums. The library was the first area, using data processing for cataloguing and information re- trieval, and has acquired experience and know-how in this field. This is the reason why the library took over other tasks in the field of computer based information management:

1. In the mid of the 1990s we had some meetings of representatives of the cultural institutions in order to discuss and choose a com- mon software for object documentation. This first attempt failed, because of the insufficient technical and personal equipment.

---

6   Geert-Jan Koot, "Der Museumsbibliothekar als Informationsstratege", in *AKMB-news*, Weimar, Year 7, 2001, H. 2, p. 13-19. [The museum librarian as information strategist – lecture within the working session of the AKMB during the German Librarians' Conference at Bielefeld in April 2001].

Some institutions (Heinrich Heine Institut, Film Museum, Restaurierungszentrum) acquired the software LARS and defined database structures for their special needs. Meanwhile, when the introduction of LARS in all cultural institutions was discussed, this software was sold to another firm, who will not continue to develop the software but guarantees support. A second attempt is made now. One person will be charged with the task to collect the needs of the cultural institutions on one hand, and to prepare a European-wide call for software producers on the other hand. The institutions, which still do not have implemented software for object documentation, have to wait until the end of this decision process, because they are not allowed to acquire software for object management for at least two years and will have to use more conventional recording and documentation. The institutions, using LARS, continue recording, but have to face the fact that they work with quite modern technical equipment and out of date coming software.

2. A second task is the coordination of common access points of information in the different sections (library, archives and collections). Core information categories for all sections have to be defined and used for the recording (conventional and computer-based). In the case of the Theatre Museum archive and library, they use different software but the same (bibliographical) data format and the same rules (Rules for Alphabetical Cataloguing in Scientific Libraries) to record the titles in the library and in the archive (letters and manuscripts). A card catalogue of performances in Düsseldorf is used as an access point of other materials, for example photos, press clippings pp., which are yet not recorded. The maintenance of this catalogue belongs to the tasks of the library. In the case of the Film Museum common rules governing the choice of the main entry for film titles are used as far as common filing rules. The *Schlagwortnormdatei* (authority file of subject headings in German scientific libraries) is used in the library as well as in the film archive in order to index the content of printed material and films through subject headings.

3. A further task of the library is the acquisition and evaluation of electronic reference works and information resources: do we use printed and electronic resources at the same time? Shall electronic resources substitute printed resources? Which advantages / disadvantages have printed / electronic resources? Which new services, for which price, can the library offer?

   a. The library produces and distributes a monthly list of the new acquisitions to the staff.

b. In the area of journals – quite a lot are published in printed and electronic form at the same time. Usually the electronic version is free of charge, but often only the table of contents or parts of the journal are available in the Web and nobody knows how long these journals will remain available free of charge and online.

c. Sometime additional services – for example the access to an online database or an online archive – are charged. Often the number of users (at once) or pay per view is the basis for the costs and has to be paid. It's quite difficult to analyse the calculation of charges. One example: the current issue of the journal *Filmdienst* is earlier available on the Web than in printed form. The archive of the journal is only available to the subscribers of the printed journal (each subscriber one access). The same institution produces, among others, the *Internationales Filmlexikon* (the Dictionary of International Films) and sold this dictionary for two or three years on CD-ROM and in printed form (additional annual supplements). Now a new printed edition will be published in combination with the access to the archive in the Web for one year. In this case I have to analyse the habits of the research work in the different sections of the Film Museum: who needs the up to date archives of the journal *Filmdienst* – for example to acquire material about new films? Who needs rather the access to the reference work, i.e. the dictionary – for instance for checking and recording of materials? With regard to the budget of the library: how many printed copies are useful? How many users (at once) will need the additional online access?

d. Some services are only available online – for example the archives of the West German Festival of Short Films at Oberhausen has been published once and will be updated only in the electronic version. Here I have to decide – as in the case of printed journals and other materials – whether we need this service.

e. Last but not least: which services are accessible only for staff members? Which services shall be made accessible to the public use? At the moment, the only services free of charge are made available to the public.

4. Within the Theatre Museum I'm responsible for the administration of the server and the local net, too. The basic concepts and guidelines for the use of data processing are developed and implemented by the Office of Information Technology and Organi-

zation Development. On the second level each Dezernat (Department) or each Amt (Office) has its own administrator(s) with regard to the special needs and the first level support of users in the LAN. In our case the Kulturdezernat (Department for Cultural Affairs) has three people, competent for about ten cultural institutions. Each cultural institution has at least one person, responsible for questions concerning IT. I participated in courses, concerning the field of IT management / administration: a basic course, advanced courses about special subjects – for example, NovelNetware administration and GroupWise administration. Furthermore, the Administrator is responsible for collecting and forwarding the needs in the field of computer skills training.

Administration and providing of information can be defined as fundamental tasks of libraries and librarians. In the information age and with the widespread use of data processing borders between hitherto separated sections fade away and are substituted by a new definition of tasks and aims. Consistent and detailed recording in order to enable multi-purpose and detailed research and information retrieval shall be the common aim of the library and the other sections in order to meet the inquiries of the users and visitors of the museum.

Networking Strategies

Libraries have a strong tradition in the field of networking. The interlibrary loan and union catalogues are examples for this networking strategy. Networks can be established on different levels (local, regional, national, international) and with regard to different aspects (subjects, document types, organisation types, pp.). The libraries of the Theatre Museum and the Film Museum already take part in different networks:

1. On the local level (Union Catalogue of Düsseldorf's Cultural Institutions) – the function of the UCD has already been described. The participants meet regularly (between two and four times a year) in order to exchange information concerning the IT and the cataloguing practice.

2. Concerning the subject: the Theatre Museum is member of the Association of Libraries and Museums of Performing Arts in Germany and the Library of Working Group of Art and Museum Libraries (Arbeitsgemeinschaft der Kunst- und Museumsbibliotheken (AKMB)). The Film Museum is a member of the FIAF (International Federation of Film Archives) and the Library involved in the Working Group of Film Libraries (*Arbeitskreis Filmbibliotheken*).

a. Bundesverband für Bibliotheken und Museen für Darstellende Künste: Archives, libraries, academic institutions and museums in Germany dedicated to the subject of performing arts work together. Up to 28 members meet once a year to a conference and publish about 3 issues of the *Informationsdienst*, the newsletter of the Bundesverband. Until last year the Bundesverband served as a national centre within the international association of libraries and museums, dedicated to the performing arts – SIBMAS. Now, the members of the Bundesverband have to decide whether or not they become institutional member of SIBMAS since the national centres do not exist anymore. The Bundesverband is on the way to restructure and redefine its work after the election of a new board in March 2002.

b. Arbeitsgemeinschaft der Kunst- und Museumsbibliotheken[7]: Since the beginning of the 1990s, the AKMB combines the interests of institutions and people concerned with librarianship in the arts and humanities. The AKMB organizes annual meetings of its members to support the professional development by lectures and to enable an exchange between the members. Since 1995, specialised groups have been founded to discuss topics of the day-to-day librarianship and to define objects for the further work of the AKMB (data processing, cataloguing, museum libraries). Another result of the work during the first years is the edition of the *AKMB-news*. The news is published three times a year and reflects the activities of the AKMB by publishing relevant articles.

c. International Federation of Film Archives (FIAF)[8]: Film archives and collections from all over the world work together. The Federation runs a bureau in Brussels and edits quite a lot of bibliographies, filmographies and reference works. FIAF has developed a code of ethics, concerning archiving, preservation and accessibility of films. Furthermore they have developed special rules and codes for cataloguing and indexing. Every institution, wanting to become member, has to fill out a questionnaire and is visited and checked by members of the FIAF. The membership can be seen as a criterion of quality and professionalism for the institution's work.

---

[7] Website of AKMB (in German – with some articles in English): http://www.akmb.de.

[8] Website of FIAF (in English, French, Spanish): http://www.fiafnet.org.

d. Arbeitskreis Filmbibliotheken[9]: This working group was founded in 1997 in order to exchange information and to coordinate the work in German film libraries. About 25 institutions (film libraries, film archives, media centres, public libraries, university and college libraries...) meet regularly (once a year) and discuss current problems of day-to-day work. Subjects are cataloguing and indexing, copyright, the usage of authority files, interlibrary loan of videotapes pp.

3. With regard to the tasks within the different museum sections:

a. Group Museum Documentation[10]: This group was founded in 1994 within the German Museums Association (Deutscher Museumsbund). The group serves as forum for the coordination and exchange of information in the field of museum collection management. It is a platform for working groups, developing methods and tools for museum documentation as well the use of data processing in this area. The members meet twice a year: within the context of the annual conference of the German Museums Association in the spring and autumn. The following special groups exist within the working group: comparison of software, collection of rules, education and training, multimedia and electronic publishing, translation of the UK standard for museums SPECTRUM.

b. Kalliope[11]: Kalliope is a member of the European Network MALVINE (Manuscripts and Letters via Integrated Networks in Europe) and enables access to autographs and letters in seven countries. The Staatsbibliothek Preussischer Kulturbesitz serves as national centre in order to record manuscripts and letters as well as to provide access to these materials for education and research. Information about letters from more than 150 institutions and biographical information about more than 200,000 people are available in the online database. 470,000 records represent about 50% of the whole conventional catalogue of manuscripts and letters (Zentralkartei der Autographen – Central Catalogue of Autographs). The Theatre Museum has been funded by the Deutsche Forschungsgemeinschaft in order to record the correspondence and manuscripts of the Schauspielhaus Dumont-

---

[9] Website of AK Filmbibliotheken (in German): http://www.filmbibliotheken.de.

[10] Website of the German Museums Association (in German – with English pages): http://www.museumsbund.de/navigation.

[11] Website of Kalliope (in German): http://kalliope.staatsbibliothek-berlin.de/index_800.html.

Lindemann and to record the material of Karl Heinz Stroux, Director of the Düsseldorfer Schauspielhaus between 1955 and 1972 (after Gründgens). Printed finding aids have been already published. We are on the way to transfer this information from our software TUSTEP into the database of Kalliope – a script for the transfer has to be written by the author of the TUSTEP software at the University of Tübingen. We are still in contact with Kalliope to test direct online recording through the client, delivered by the State Library to the participants. We hope that we do not need special software – as TUSTEP – in the future and that we will benefit from the services of Kalliope.

Though a high degree of networking can be stated, there are deficits concerning the connection to the community of academic libraries (university libraries, college libraries, pp). In the case of Düsseldorf, the relevant partner would be the Hochschulbibliothekszentrum (HBZ) (Online Utility and Service Centre for Academic Libraries in North Rhine-Westphalia)[12], who runs the union catalogue of academic libraries in the region. This network bases on academic libraries, funded by the state, and provides quite a lot of services – for instance the Digitale Bibliothek Nordrhein-Westfalen (Digital Library North Rhine-Westphalia), and document delivery services. Here we have to deal with the problem of different funding structures within the federal system of Germany and with different policies of the headquarters of the different regional union catalogues. There have been talks between the City Library Düsseldorf and the HBZ concerning the participation of the City Library of Düsseldorf in the union catalogue. The bibliographical records of the UCD could be a valuable addition to the catalogue of academic libraries, but was not realised. The HBZ itself was at this time just in the test and conversion phase of its new software ALEPH. The common projects with the Public Library were terminated in the meanwhile. Although there have been already cooperation, the integration of bibliographical data or closer cooperation is still not in sight.

One attempt through the libraries of the Theatre Museum and the Film Museum has been made: the request for the participation in the regional interlibrary loan has been sent to the HBZ. The benefit of the participation would be the fact that the library as institution is able to participate in electronic document delivery services and to benefit from initiatives as the digital library North Rhine-Westphalia.

---

[12] Website of the HBZ (in German – with some pages in English): http://www.hbz-nrw.de.

Summary

After all it is a question of whether other libraries in the field of the performing arts (or museum libraries) have the same strategy: to point out their experience in the field of computer-based recording, to promote the librarian data formats and authority files for consistent recording and to take over an advisory function for information management within the whole museum.

Geert-Jan Koot mentions in his article several examples in the United Kingdom, in the United States and the Netherlands. In Germany, the Bibliotheksservice-Zentrum Baden-Württemberg (BSZ)[13] plays an active role in this field. The BSZ defines itself as "modern service institution providing library-specific data and services mainly for academic libraries". Additionally, the BSZ provides extensive services for everyone with regard to the Internet, literature search, digital library, etc. The BSZ operates the South-West German Cataloguing Union, a cooperation of more than 1,000 union participants from the German states of Baden-Württemberg, Southern Rheinland-Palatinate, Saarland and Saxony. It also runs the Regional Union Catalogue. The BSZ is involved in the project MUSIS (Museum Information System) in order to support the great state museums in the process of introducing a state-wide software for object documentation[14]. In this context the implementation and use of librarian authority files for subject headings, personal and institutional names are discussed as well as the use of other subject oriented authority files – such as the files of the Getty Institute. The project Gemeinsames Internet-Portal für Bibliotheken, Archive und Museen (common Internet gateway for libraries, archives and museums) tries to develop methods in order to make digital resources of libraries, archives and museums available through one common gateway. Beside a metadata format, basing on Dublin Core, digitalized material concerning special subjects are made available. The following levels of information were defined: basic information about the institution, metadata, containing links to online finding aids and catalogues, finding aids and catalogues as online resources, digitised objects[15]. The BSZ is involved in this project, too.

---

[13] Website of the BSZ (in German – with some pages in English): http://www.bsz-bw.de/.

[14] Karin Ludewig, "Musisches aus Baden-Württemberg: das BSZ – bald ein Servicezentrum auch für Museen?", in *AKMB-news*, Weimar, Year 7, 2001, H. 3, p. 35-37. [The Library Service Centre – in the future a service center for museums, too?].

[15] Gerald Maier, "Germeinsames Internet-Portal für Bibliotheken, Archive und Museen: ein Online-Informationssystem", in *AKMB-news*, Weimar, Year 8, 2002, H. 1., p. 7-13. [A Common Internet Gateway for Libraries, Archives and Museums: an online information system].

The Working Group of Art and Museum Libraries AKMB took the initiative in this area because of the inquiries of her members: the AKMB established contacts between libraries, dedicated to the history of arts – for instance the library of the Zentralinstitut für Kunstgeschichte in Munich (Central Institute for the History of Arts) and the German National Library – in order to promote the active participation of special academic libraries in the SWD, the authority file for subject headings. Furthermore, the AKMB established and maintains the contact to the Group of Museum Documentation in German Museums Association in order to reinforce the dialogue between librarians and document specialists, especially in museums. There are still many examples for the cooperation and communication between archivists, librarians and people, working in museums.

In the field of the performing arts in Germany we have quite a few good starting points: the German Association of Libraries and Museums of Performing Arts and the Working Group of Film Libraries bring different institutions – with regard to the same subject – together. The degree of cooperation will depend on the participating institutions and people: do they agree about standards for recording and making information available to the users? The role of the libraries will depend on the degree of their involvement and their experience in the field of cooperation. Several initiatives have been taken – for example the *FIS Kultur* (gateway for cultural information, specially performing arts, television, radio and film)[16] or a thesis as preparation of a Internet gateway for film and media, presented during the last meeting of film libraries in February 2002 at Oldenburg. The future will tell us, which projects will be successful and which projects will fail. Every institution can contribute by the own recording and documenting activities, usable for several purposes at the same time: to get use with the own holdings, to make information available to the users, and to take part in other projects.

---

[16] Website of FIS Kultur (in German): http://www.fis-kultur.net/index.htm.

Theatre Museum Düsseldorf, Entrance to the Museum in the Hofgarten

© Theatre Museum

**Film Museum Düsseldorf,
Pantheon and Parts of the Permanent Exhibition**

© Film Museum

The Matriz Software Implemented to the Collections of the National Theatre Museum of Portugal

José Carlos ALVAREZ

Museu Nacional do Teatro (Lisbon – Portugal)

The National Theatre Museum is the national museum and archive of the performing arts in Portugal. Through its collections, it aims at increasing the understanding of the history and current practice of the performing arts and to preserve, record, research and make accessible its collections.

The Collections

The Museum is located in the Monteiro-Mor Palace, an 18th century building which was restored and adapted specifically for that purpose. Nowadays, the museum's collections, assembled from 1979 onwards, particularly from the numerous donations received, already amount to approximately 300,000 items, dating from the 18th century up to the present time. They encompass various stage costumes and props, stage models, costume designs, drawings, caricatures, programmes, posters, postcards, albums containing newspaper cuttings, manuscripts, pamphlets, copies, records, music scores, paper theatres dating from the 18th to the 20th century, as well as an archive with approximately 120,000 photographs. There is also a specialised library with 35,000 volumes.

The collections of the National Theatre Museum are grouped as follows:

- material relating to personalities linked to the theatre and the art of show business: actors, authors, designers, musicians, dancers, theatrical producers, and technicians;
- material relating to every show that opened in Portugal, from the beginning of the 20th century to the present day;

- material relating to theatre companies or groups, dance and opera, no longer in existence or still active;
- material relating to theatres that functioned in Portugal in the past or that are still active.

This material is divided according to the following collections:

Stage Costumes

The Museum has a textile restoration workshop that performs all the restoration and conservation work on the costumes, supports the organisation of exhibitions in which these costumes are shown and participates in defining what kind of preventive action should be taken in terms of preserving the garments, as well as the time during which each item can be exhibited for without damage. This depends on how well preserved the costumes are and on the conditions of exposure.

Photographs

This collection which contains 120,000 photographs is constituted by three important sections organised by themes:
- photographic portraits of actors, drama writers, directors, technicians and theatre people;
- stage photographs; photographs of performance spaces;
- theatres (interiors and exteriors), audiences, advertising.

Postcards

This collection, containing approximately 3,500 items, is divided into the following sections:
- Portugal/portraits;
- the stage;
- our actors;
- homage to Garrett;
- miscellaneous, always with the theatre as the central theme.

Stage Models

This important collection is composed of over 2,100 items including a collection of 3D scenery models.

Stage and Costume Designs

This is one of the Museum's most important collections, composed of approximately 6,000 items, with valuable works by important Portuguese artists and theatrical designers.

Caricatures and Portraits

Music Scores

A collection composed by printed music score sheets, songs and musical excerpts of Operetta, Revue Theatre and Cinema. The majority have covers designed by important artists.

Posters and Programmes

A vast collection of posters and programmes for different types of shows organised by theatres and/or theatre groups and companies numbering about 50,000 items.

Records, Recordings and Video Collection

There are about 5,000 recordings on vinyl records and magnetic tape recordings and about 120 video films. This collection is not yet available.

Miscellaneous

The remaining material concerns personalities from the world of the theatre and the theatrical arts, outside the range of the large collections mentioned above. It features souvenirs and personal objects, homage tokens, contracts, professional ID cards and material relating to theatres that no longer exist or those that are still open, as for example dressing room tables, plans of theatres, and tickets.

Inventory and Scientific Study of the Collections

As stated by its basic law, the Portuguese Institute of Museum (IPM), through its Department of Inventory Services, is responsible for setting museum documentation standards and making them accessible to all museums, public or private, which may be interested in using them. This responsibility brings with the following tasks:

- inventory, investigation, updating and digitalization of holdings and collections in the Matriz program;
- national photographic inventory: national gathering archiving and inventory of photographs from the cultural heritage;
- computerisation of the IPM's museums and their connections in a network;
- research and carrying out of studies in the area of reflectography and spectrography;

- technical support to outside parties aiming at the safeguarding and protection of the movable cultural heritage (within the establishment of the Portuguese Network of Museums).

Through concerns of museum computerisation of collection information, the IPM has developed, within a partnership with a private company, software for cataloguing and managing information of museum objects (Matriz). The structure of this database was thought after the standard cataloguing form mentioned above, and complies with international standards such as the Getty Standards Programs (Categories for the Description of Works of Art) and the CIDOC Guidelines for Museum Object Information.

Documentation of Collections

Characterise collections

Evaluate description instruments in use:
- manual records / diffuse documentation;
- typological diversity within museums;
- inconsistency of classification criteria;
- several unknown provenances;
- deficit of images.

Development of a standardised catalogue form:
- promote a critical review of object files;
- normalise documentation on collections;
- prepare / promote the digitalization of information on museum collections.

Development and implementation of a computerised system:
- MATRIZ – Software for cataloguing / inventory purposes.

The guidelines reflect:
- museum experience in cataloguing and classifying collections;
- first stage experience in transposing manual files into a computerised system.

Outcome:
- implement standards for documentation of collections;
- conceptualise acquired information;
- improve communication within IPM;
- create working tools consistent with the Matriz system;
- enforce good practices among museums.

MATRIZ Cataloguing and Management of Museum Collections

Software Features:

- client/server architecture;
- MS Windows nt/2000 environment;
- data structure complies with international standards;
- strong query capabilities;
- slide show;
- sound and video storage capacities;
- 16 Thesauri fields;
- access and safety enforcement;
- different levels of data access privileges;
- access to external Thesauri;
- export of data files to other systems;
- statistics computation (text and image).

Evolution

- development of MatrizNet
  Web interface with access to IPM Database: makes available 12,000 of the 120,000 objects already digitalized;
- bilingual site (Portuguese-English);
- near future:
  - o Regular input of new records;
  - o Translation of contents.

MatrizNet Features

Two users profiles:
- general public;
- researcher.

Two different entrances:
- collections (exhaustive inventory files);
- exhibitions (documentation).

Traitement informatique des collections relatives au Festival d'Avignon[1]

Marie-Claude BILLARD

Maison Jean Vilar (Avignon – France)

Historique

Le festival d'Avignon a débuté en 1947 à l'occasion d'une exposition d'art contemporain organisée dans la grande chapelle du Palais des Papes, imposant vestige du siège de la Papauté entre 1309 (Clément V) et 1403 (Benoît XIII). Jean Vilar, sollicité pour présenter un spectacle dans la Cour d'Honneur, fait le pari d'en proposer trois :

- *Richard II* de William Shakespeare
- *Tobie et Sarah* de Paul Claudel
- *La Terrasse de midi* de Maurice Clavel.

Cette série de représentations s'accompagne de concerts. Elle a lieu en septembre et s'intitule *Semaine d'Art en Avignon*.

Avec l'aide de la Ville d'Avignon et d'un comité d'organisation, l'expérience peut se poursuivre les années suivantes. Dès la deuxième année, elle se déroule en juillet et prend le nom de Festival d'art dramatique.

En 1951, lorsque Jean Vilar accepte la direction du Théâtre National Populaire à Paris, Avignon reste une étape obligée de la troupe du TNP après la saison parisienne et entre de nombreuses tournées en France et à l'étranger. Après son départ du TNP en 1963, Jean Vilar conserve la direction artistique du Festival d'Avignon où il invite d'autres créateurs à partir de 1966, dont Maurice Béjart et sa fameuse *Messe pour un temps présent*.

---

[1] Présentation du catalogage informatisé dans la base opaline du Département des Arts du spectacle de la Bibliothèque nationale de France, à partir de l'exemple du Festival d'Avignon.

Après la mort de Vilar en 1971, d'autres directeurs prennent le relais : Paul Puaux, Alain Crombecque, Bernard Faivre d'Arcier. Le Festival se diversifie et devient de plus en plus important. Parallèlement à la programmation officielle de nombreuses troupes se produisent pour se faire connaître et vendre leurs spectacles. Environ 700 spectacles en 2002 et une quarantaine pour le Festival officiel. Ces chiffres n'ont plus rien à voir avec les trois ou quatre spectacles et la vingtaine de représentations du temps du TNP.

Les collections et leur traitement

En ce qui concerne les collections relatives au Festival d'Avignon, il faut distinguer deux périodes :

- l'époque où le Festival était assuré par la seule troupe du TNP ;

- l'après-TNP où de nombreuses compagnies françaises et étrangères sont invitées.

Les collections du Festival du TNP (période historique) ont pu être sauvegardées par l'Association Jean Vilar qui s'est constituée après la mort de Jean Vilar. Le Département des Arts du spectacle de la Bibliothèque nationale de France s'est impliqué dans leur conservation et mise à disposition du public dans la cadre de la Maison Jean Vilar à Avignon.

Ces collections se composent des documents administratifs, des costumes de la troupe, des maquettes de costumes et des dispositifs scéniques lorsqu'ils existent, des photographies, articles de presse, programmes et affiches.

Pour la période post-TNP, les collections se limitent aux photos, vidéos, articles de presse, programmes et affiches.

Depuis l'ouverture de la Maison Jean Vilar en 1979, l'antenne du Département des Arts du spectacle implantée à Avignon se charge de rassembler et de conserver les éléments de la mémoire du Festival. Le traitement informatique des spectacles et des collections afférentes a débuté en 1990.

Cette opération se déroule en deux temps :

1. rédaction de la notice d'identification du spectacle : auteur, titre, metteur en scène décorateur, distribution, lieu, date et nombre de représentations ;

2. description bibliographique et localisation des documents concernant le spectacle identifié. Ces éléments apparaissent comme documents attachés à la fin de la notice d'identification.

La base utilisée est OPALINE, base établie à partir du format MARC pour les Départements spécialisés de la Bibliothèque nationale de France, format spécifique susceptible d'évolution.

Quelques exemples permettront de mieux comprendre le travail effectué, qui combine base de données (les informations sur le spectacle) et base de catalogage (description de documents). Ces exemples ont été choisis à partir de l'œuvre de Victor Hugo dont on fête en 2002 en France le bicentenaire de la naissance. Cinq pièces ou textes de cet auteur ont été présentés au festival d'Avignon entre 1955 et 1985 :

1. *Marie Tudor*, mise en scène de Jean Vilar, 1955 ;

2. *Un contre tous*, d'après les textes politiques de Victor Hugo, mise en scène de Pierre Barrat, musique d'Ivo Malec, 1971 ;

3. *Lucrèce Borgia*, mise en scène de Fabio Pacchioni avec Silvia Monfort, 1975 ;

4. *L'Âne*, mise en scène et interprétation de Jean Gillibert, 1981 ;

5. *Lucrèce Borgia*, mise en scène d'Antoine Vitez avec Nada Strancar, 1985.

Les exemples téléchargés, présentent tous la même suite de zones :

- date de la première représentation à Avignon ;

- titre/auteur (auteur du texte joué mais aussi auteurs du spectacle ainsi que les trois premiers rôles. Tous les noms de cette zone étant indexés pour permettre une recherche) ;

- lieu de la représentation ;

- notes (cette zone non indexée, souvent importante, sert aux compléments d'information : collaborateurs du spectacle, suite de la distribution, production, nombre de représentations).

Ensuite, les noms indexés apparaissent en caractère gras précédés de leur intitulé : auteur, metteur en scène, acteur…

Après les pointillés et la mention document 1, 2… viennent les documents concernant le spectacle : photos et recueils d'articles de presse pour les exemples choisis. Ces documents sont décrits très brièvement, suivis de leur localisation (Avignon en l'occurrence).

Actuellement tous les spectacles du Festival depuis l'origine ont fait l'objet d'une notice d'identification. Elle sera reversée sur OPALINE au fur et à mesure du catalogage rétrospectif des documents. L'opération n'est pas encore terminée et seuls les spectacles des dernières années ont été saisis directement dans OPALINE avec leurs documents.

Adresse du catalogue : www.bnf.fr.

Exemple 1

Catalogues de la BnF
Catalogues de la BnF

BN-OPALINE - Arts du spectacle

AFFICHAGE DE LA NOTICE BIBLIOGRAPHIQUE

date spectacle	Première représentation : 15-07-1955
titre/auteur	Marie Tudor : drame en trois journées / mise en scène de Jean Vilar ; texte de Victor Hugo ; musique de Maurice Jarre ; décor de Léon Gischia ; costumes de Léon Gischia ; lumières de Pierre Saveron ; spectacle du Théâtre national populaire ; avec Maria Casares (Marie), Monique Chaumette (Jane), Jean Deschamps (Gilbert) [et al.]
lieu représent.	France
	Avignon
	Palais des papes, 19550715
note(s)	Création au TNP
	Produit par le Théâtre national populaire
distribution	Interprété aussi par Roger Mollien (Fabiano Fabiani), Philippe Noiret (Simon Renard), Daniel Sorano (Joshua Farnaby), Jean-Paul Moulinot (un juif), Lucien Arnaud (Lord Clinton), Jean-Pierre Darras (Lord Chandos), Jean Topart (Lord Montagu), Georges Riquier (maître Eneas Dulverton), Jean Winckler (Lord Gardiner), Maurice Coussonneau (le geôlier), Georges Lycan (le bourreau), André Schlesser (premier serviteur de scène), Marcel Bonnaud (deuxième serviteur de scène)
note historique	Spectacle présenté dans le cadre du 9e Festival d'Avignon.
Matière	**Festival d'Avignon, 1955, 9**
Auteur du texte	**Hugo, Victor**
Metteur en scèn	**Vilar, Jean**
Compositeur	**Jarre, Maurice, 1924-....**
Décorateur	**Gischia, Léon, 1903-1991**
Costumier	**Gischia, Léon, 1903-1991**
Eclairages	**Saveron, Pierre, 19..-...., éclairagiste**
Acteur	**Casarès, Maria, 1922-1996**
	Marie
Acteur	**Chaumette, Monique, 1927-....**
	Jane
Acteur	**Deschamps, Jean**
	Gilbert
Créateur de spe	**Théâtre national populaire, Villeurbanne, Rhône**
--------------	-- document 1
titre/auteur	Marie Tudor, mise en scène de Jean Vilar : dossier de presse
adresse arch.	Avignon, 1955
collation	1 dossier, 31 cm
--------------	-- localisation
	BNF, MJV, RP FA 55
--------------	-- FIN de la notice

[Accueil BN-Opaline] [Retour liste des notices] [ ] [<<] [>>]

Exemple 2

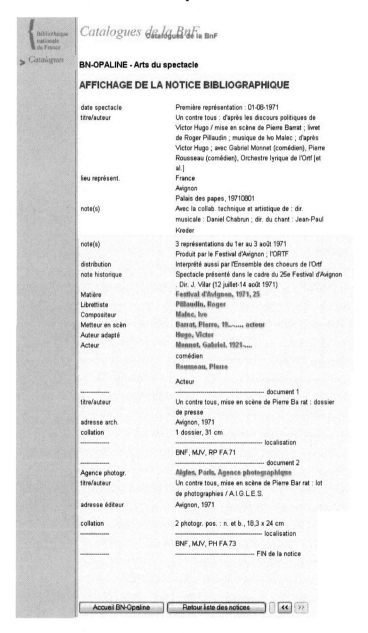

Bibliothèque
nationale
de France

> *Catalogues*

Catalogues de la BnF
Catalogues de la BnF

BN-OPALINE - Arts du spectacle

AFFICHAGE DE LA NOTICE BIBLIOGRAPHIQUE

date spectacle	Première représentation : 01-08-1971
titre/auteur	Un contre tous : d'après les discours politiques de Victor Hugo / mise en scène de Pierre Barrat ; livret de Roger Pillaudin ; musique de Ivo Malec ; d'après Victor Hugo ; avec Gabriel Monnet (comédien), Pierre Rousseau (comédien), Orchestre lyrique de l'Ortf [et al.]
lieu représent.	France
	Avignon
	Palais des papes, 19710801
note(s)	Avec la collab. technique et artistique de : dir. musicale : Daniel Chabrun ; dir. du chant : Jean-Paul Kreder
note(s)	3 représentations du 1er au 3 août 1971
	Produit par le Festival d'Avignon ; l'ORTF
distribution	Interprété aussi par l'Ensemble des choeurs de l'Ortf
note historique	Spectacle présenté dans le cadre du 25e Festival d'Avignon . Dir. J. Vilar (12 juillet-14 août 1971)
Matière	Festival d'Avignon, 1971, 25
Librettiste	Pillaudin, Roger
Compositeur	Malec, Ivo
Metteur en scèn	Barrat, Pierre, 19..-....., acteur
Auteur adapté	Hugo, Victor
Acteur	Monnet, Gabriel, 1921-....
	comédien
	Rousseau, Pierre
	Acteur
------------	-- document 1
titre/auteur	Un contre tous, mise en scène de Pierre Ba rat : dossier de presse
adresse arch.	Avignon, 1971
collation	1 dossier, 31 cm
------------	-- localisation
	BNF, MJV, RP FA 71
------------	-- document 2
Agence photogr.	Aigles, Paris, Agence photographique
titre/auteur	Un contre tous, mise en scène de Pierre Bar rat : lot de photographies / A.I.G.L.E.S.
adresse éditeur	Avignon, 1971
collation	2 photogr. pos. : n. et b., 18,3 x 24 cm
------------	-- localisation
	BNF, MJV, PH FA 73
------------	-- FIN de la notice

[Accueil BN-Opaline] [Retour liste des notices] [««] [»»]

Exemple 3

Bibliothèque
nationale
de France

Catalogues de la BnF

Catalogues de la BnF

Catalogues

BN-OPALINE - Arts du spectacle

AFFICHAGE DE LA NOTICE BIBLIOGRAPHIQUE

date spectacle	Première représentation : 04-08-1975
auteur	**Hugo, Victor**
titre/auteur	Lucrèce Borgia / Victor Hugo ; spectacle de Nouveau Carré ; mise en scène de Fabio Pacchioni ; décors de Jacques Noel ; costumes de Jacques Noel
lieu représent.	France
	Avignon
	Cloître des Carmes au cours de : 29e Festival d'Avignon 1975-08-04
note(s)	Musique : Yoshihisa Taïra
	Mime : Gérard Le Breton
	Eclairage : André Collet
référ. biblio.	Le Figaro, 30.5.75 [festivals] ; 22.7 [phot.1 ; 7.8 [crit.]
	Inf. du soect., n°110
	ATAC Inf., n°69
distribution	Avec : Jean Brassat : Jeppo Liveretto ; Claude Brosset : Maffio Orsini ; Jean-Pol Dubois : Ascanio Petrucci ; Alain Duclos : Astolfo ; Philippe Gauguet : Gennaro ; Marcel Imhoff : Don Alphonse d'Este ; Jean-Pierre Laurent : Oloferno Vitellozzo ; François Maistre : Gubetta ; Gérard Melki : Don Apostolo Gazella ; Silvia Monfort : Dona Lucrezia Borgia ; Christian Peythieu : Rustighello ; Claudine Raffalli : La Princesse Negroni Elèves mimes du Nouveau Carré : Joëlle Brover, Jean-Louis Civade, Chantal de La Haye, Bernard Lepinaux, Morgane,
distribution	Béatrice Reuillard, Christian Rognant, Roger Simonnet
Metteur en scèn	**Pacchioni, Fabio**
Décorateur	**Noël, Jacques, 1924-....**
Costumier	**Noël, Jacques, 1924-....**
Créateur de spe	**Nouveau Carré**
---------------	--
voir	**Représentation 04-11-1975**
---------------	------------------------------------- FIN de la notice

[Accueil BN-Opaline] [Retour liste des notices] [<<] [>>]

Exemple 4

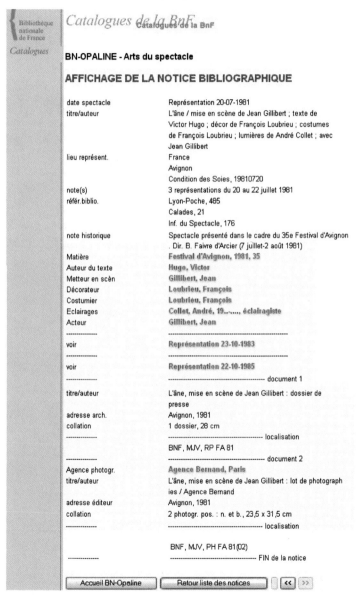

Bibliothèque nationale de France

Catalogues

Catalogues de la BnF

BN-OPALINE - Arts du spectacle

AFFICHAGE DE LA NOTICE BIBLIOGRAPHIQUE

date spectacle	Représentation 20-07-1981
titre/auteur	L'âne / mise en scène de Jean Gillibert ; texte de Victor Hugo ; décor de François Loubrieu ; costumes de François Loubrieu ; lumières de André Collet ; avec Jean Gillibert
lieu représent.	France
	Avignon
	Condition des Soies, 19810720
note(s)	3 représentations du 20 au 22 juillet 1981
référ.biblio.	Lyon-Poche, 485
	Calades, 21
	Inf. du Spectacle, 176
note historique	Spectacle présenté dans le cadre du 35e Festival d'Avignon . Dir. B. Faivre d'Arcier (7 juillet-2 août 1981)
Matière	Festival d'Avignon, 1981, 35
Auteur du texte	Hugo, Victor
Metteur en scèn	Gillibert, Jean
Décorateur	Loubrieu, François
Costumier	Loubrieu, François
Eclairages	Collet, André, 19......., éclairagiste
Acteur	Gillibert, Jean
-------------	--------------------------------------
voir	Représentation 23-10-1983
-------------	--------------------------------------
voir	Représentation 22-10-1985
-------------	------------------------------------- document 1
titre/auteur	L'âne, mise en scène de Jean Gillibert : dossier de presse
adresse arch.	Avignon, 1981
collation	1 dossier, 28 cm
-------------	------------------------------------- localisation
	BNF, MJV, RP FA 81
-------------	------------------------------------- document 2
Agence photogr.	Agence Bernand, Paris
titre/auteur	L'âne, mise en scène de Jean Gillibert : lot de photograph ies / Agence Bernand
adresse éditeur	Avignon, 1981
collation	2 photogr. pos. : n. et b., 23,5 x 31,5 cm
-------------	------------------------------------- localisation
	BNF, MJV, PH FA 81(02)
-------------	------------------------------------- FIN de la notice

[Accueil BN-Opaline]　[Retour liste des notices]　[<<] [>>]

Exemple 5

Catalogues de la BnF Catalogues de la BnF

Bibliothèque nationale de France

Catalogues

BN-OPALINE - Arts du spectacle

AFFICHAGE DE LA NOTICE BIBLIOGRAPHIQUE

date spectacle	Première représentation : 25-07-1985
titre/auteur	Lucrèce Borgia / mise en scène de Antoine Vitez ; texte de Victor Hugo ; chorégraphie de Milko Sparembleck musique de Georges Aperghis ; scénographie de Yannis Kokkos ; décor de Yannis Kokkos ; costumes de Yannis Kokkos ; masques de Robert Nardonne ; maquillage de Robert Nardonne ; régie générale de Michel Ambert régie générale de Alain Pinel ; lumières de Patrice Trottier ; régie lumières de Jean-Paul Mace ; régie son de Joël Simon ; avec Anne Benoit (La Princesse Negroni), Gilles David (Oloferno), Joël Denicourt (Gennaro)...[et al.]
lieu représent.	France
	Avignon
	Palais des papes, 19850725
note(s)	Avec la collab. musicale de Martine Viard ; assistant à la mise en scène : Eloi Recoing ; collab. dramaturgie : Bruno Collet et Muriel Trembleau ; construction décor : Ateliers du Théâtre National de Chaillot, Studio de la Bastille, Alain Bony, Isabelle Clerte, Christian Bony, Michel Fizet ; réalisation des costumes : Atelier mine Barral-Vergez, Monique Dauvergne ; habilleuse : Josette Planet ; accessoires costumes : Maison Denis Poulin, Joachim Fernando Mendes, Gencel, C.t.s. pompei ; dir. artistique : Didier Monfajon, Françoise Peyronnet
	7 représentations du 25 au 31 juillet 1985
	Produit par : la Ville de Venise, le Teatro regionale Toscano, la Ville de Florence, le Teatro di Roma, l'AFAA, le Théâtre National de Chaillot (Paris), le Festival d'Avignon
distribution	Interprété aussi par Françis Frappat (Maffio), Eric Frey (Astolfo/ Le Page/ Montefeltro/ Bautista), Philippe Girard (Apostolo), Jean-Pierre Jorris (Alphonse d'Este), Christophe Odent (Rustighello), Gégoire Oestermann (Jeppo), Christophe Ratandra (Ascanio), Nada Strancar (Lucrèce Borgia), Jean-Marie Winling (Gubetta)
note historique	Spectacle présenté dans le cadre du 39e Festival d'Avignon . Dir. A. Crombecque (6 juillet-31 juillet 1985)
Matière	Festival d'Avignon, 1985, 39
Auteur du texte	Hugo, Victor
Metteur en scèn	Vitez, Antoine
Chorégraphe	Sparembleck, Milko
Compositeur	Aperghis, Georges, 1945-
Costumier	Kokkos, Yannis, 1944-....
Maquillage	Nardonne, Robert
Régisseur	Ambert, Michel
Eclairages	Trottier, Patrice, 19...-...., éclairagiste
Eclairages	Mace, Jean-Paul, 19...-...., éclairagiste
Son	Simon, Joël, 1952-....
Acteur	Benoit, Anne, 19...-...., actrice La Princesse Negroni
Acteur	David, Gilles Oloferno
Acteur	Denicourt, Joël, 19...-.... acteur Gennaro

218

```
--------------                    -------------------------------------------- document 1
titre/auteur                      Lucrèce Borgia, mise en scène d'Antoine Vit ez : dossier
                                  de presse
adresse arch.                     Avignon, 1985
collation                         1 dossier, 28 cm

--------------                    -------------------------------------------- localisation
                                  BNF, MJV, RP FA 85-12
--------------                    -------------------------------------------- document 2
Photographe                       Enguérand, Marc
titre/auteur                      Lucrèce Borgia, mise en scène d'Antoine Vit ez : photograp
                                  hie / Marc Enguérand
adresse éditeur                   Avignon, 1985
collation                         1 photogr. pos. : coul., 23,7 x 31,5 cm
--------------                    -------------------------------------------- localisation
                                  BNF, MJV, PH FA 85(2)

--------------                    -------------------------------------------- document 3
Photographe                       Gafner, Claude, 19..-...., photographe
titre/auteur                      Lucrèce Borgia, mise en scène d'Antoine Vit ez : photograp

                                  hie / Claude Gafner
adresse éditeur                   Avignon, 1985
collation                         1 photogr. pos. : coul, 20,2 x 25,4 cm
--------------                    -------------------------------------------- localisation
                                  BNF, MJV, PH FA 85(2)

--------------                    -------------------------------------------- document 4
Photographe                       Méran, Georges, 19..-...., photographe
titre/auteur                      Lucrèce Borgia, mise en scène d'Antoine Vit ez : lot
                                  de photographies / Georges Méran
adresse éditeur                   Avignon, 1985
collation                         6 photogr. pos. : n. et b., 17,7 x 23,7 cm
--------------                    -------------------------------------------- localisation
                                  BNF, MJV, PH FA 85(2)

--------------                    -------------------------------------------- document 5
Agence photogr.                   Agence Point de Vue, Avignon, Agence photographique
titre/auteur                      Lucrèce Borgia, mise en scène d'Antoine Vit ez : photograp
                                  hie / Agence Point de Vue
adresse éditeur                   Avignon, 1985
collation                         1 photogr. pos. : n. et b., 17,7 x 23,7 cm
--------------                    -------------------------------------------- localisation
                                  BNF, MJV, PH FA 85(2)

--------------                    -------------------------------------------- document 6
Photographe                       Bricage, Claude, 19..-...., photographe
titre/auteur                      Lucrèce Borgia, mise en scène d'Antoine Vit ez : photograp
                                  hie / Claude Bricage
adresse éditeur                   Avignon, 1985

collation                         1 photogr. pos. : coul., 10 x 15 cm
--------------                    -------------------------------------------- localisation
                                  BNF, MJV, PH FA 85(2)
--------------                    -------------------------------------- FIN de la notice
```

[Accueil BN-Opaline] [Retour liste des notices] [<<] [>>]

Les arts du spectacle en Roumanie

Anişoara BURLACU, Camelia SAVU

Institut de Mémoire culturelle (Bucarest – Roumanie)

Le théâtre est-il un art pérenne ? Si le texte dramatique traverse les siècles et les millénaires, en gardant sa valeur et son actualité, le spectacle, lui, s'évanouit au moment où tombe le rideau, où les lumières s'éteignent, où les derniers applaudissements cessent.

Au fil des ans, chaque génération de spectateurs accumule ses impressions et souvenirs de créations scéniques remarquables, qui peuvent faire le sujet de chroniques et d'articles de spécialistes ou qui, au contraire, disparaîtront, remplacés par de nouvelles expériences scéniques.

En tenant compte du fait que chaque spectacle constitue un acte culturel unique, que les témoignages matériels d'un spectacle (affiches, cahiers programmes, chroniques, photographies, captations audiovisuelles) sont répandus dans beaucoup d'institutions culturelles (bibliothèques, musées, théâtres…), que l'inventaire des spectacles est partiel et n'est réalisé qu'en système classique manuel, que les spécialistes, les institutions et le grand public ont besoin d'informations, nous avons considéré qu'une gestion centralisée et automatisée des données concernant les spectacles serait à la fois importante et utile.

C'est la raison pour laquelle l'Institut de Mémoire culturelle basé à Bucarest, en collaboration avec le ministère roumain de la Culture (par sa Direction générale des Institutions des arts du spectacle) a initié un projet d'enregistrement, de stockage et de traitement automatique des informations concernant les spectacles. On a commencé avec le projet STAR, qui concerne les spectacles dramatiques, auxquels se sont ajoutés, depuis quelques années, les spectacles musicaux (opéra, opérette, music-hall) et les spectacles de danse.

Conçue comme un système ouvert, la sphère des informations considérées peut être continuellement élargie grâce au dialogue avec les fournisseurs de données et les utilisateurs de nos archives. Les informations sont stockées dans des bases de données de type FoxPro (pour le répertoire théâtral) et ACCESS (pour le module « Musique & Danse », réalisé au cours des dernières années).

En utilisant un système spécialisé de gestion des données, nous avons abouti à :

- une réduction du temps nécessaire à l'introduction, au traitement et à l'interrogation de la base de données ;
- un accès rapide aux informations comprises ;
- une réduction des coûts ;
- un accès interactif aux informations et un accès en ligne pour les utilisateurs.

Les informations gérées sont de type :

- rétrospectif (historique) ;
- actuel (synchronique) ;
- prospectif (synchronique).

Les entrées du système sont :

- le spectacle ;
- le réalisateur ;
- l'institution ;
- la référence critique.

Chacune d'elles est développée dans des bases de données liées entre elles par le seul code du spectacle (Fig. 1 : Schéma du système).

L'unité principale du système est donc le spectacle.

Pour la définition du spectacle, nous avons déterminé quatre types d'informations qui forment la structure du formulaire de collecte des données :

1. *la zone d'identification du spectacle* qui contient : une cote unique et le titre du spectacle (original et/ou traduit), la saison théâtrale, la date de la première ;

2. *la zone d'identification de l'œuvre* dramatique, musicale, chorégraphique, source d'inspiration du spectacle, qui contient : le titre (original et/ou traduit), un résumé, des informations sur la première absolue ;

3. *la zone d'attribution* de la typologie qui contient : la thématique abordée, le type de spectacle et le genre (dramatique, musical, danse etc.).

4. *la zone du générique* qui contient : l'auteur, le traducteur, l'adaptateur, le metteur en scène, le scénographe, le compositeur, le librettiste, le chef d'orchestre, le chorégraphe, les

acteurs etc. En ce qui concerne le générique, il faut préciser que le nom de chaque acteur est suivi par le nom du rôle interprété.

Les types d'informations définitoires pour le réalisateur (des données biographiques et professionnelles) ont été stockés dans un fichier d'autorité de personnes. La structure adoptée pour ce fichier contient : un code unique, nom, prénom, pseudonyme, autres noms, date de naissance et de mort, études, les principaux domaines d'activités, créations artistiques. Dans les sources d'information, dans la zone du générique, on emploie plusieurs variantes des noms. La création d'un fichier d'autorité qui établit une invariante standardisée pour le nom (celui qui correspond en bibliologie à la rubrique de « vedette ») nous permet de répondre le mieux possible aux exigences des utilisateurs.

Bases de données concernant les spectacles

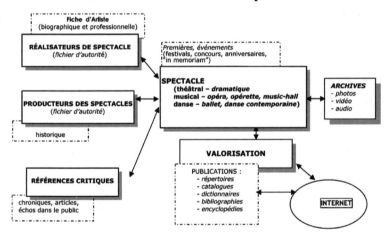

Les types d'informations qui définissent le producteur (institutionnel) de spectacle (histoire, organisation, données techniques sur la salle du spectacle – types, caractéristiques, installations – etc.) sont également organisées dans un fichier d'autorité. La nécessité de ce fichier est liée à l'apparition, depuis 1990, de plusieurs institutions nouvelles – surtout privées –, dans le domaine des arts du spectacle (théâtres, associations, groupes indépendants de danse contemporaine, fondations, groupes multi arts).

La dernière entité – les références critiques – concerne les chroniques, articles, échos dans le public, données statistiques, etc.

Nous avons en outre créé des listes de validation de genres dramatiques, de types de spectacle, de thématique... pour que les données
soient contrôlées au moment de leur enregistrement.

Ce fonds documentaire peut être interrogé selon des critères :

-   thématiques ;
-   chronologiques ;
-   alphabétiques.

Le type de réponses obtenues peut être :

-   le répertoire d'un théâtre, d'un opéra ou d'une compagnie
    (en détail ou résumé) ;
-   la fiche de création d'un ou plusieurs réalisateurs ;
-   des répertoires structurés conformément à une certaine
    thématique, un certain genre, un type de spectacle, une saison,
    etc.

Nous pourrons de la sorte mettre à la disposition des personnes inté-
ressées (critiques, historiens, spécialistes des arts de spectacle, institutions) les instruments nécessaires pour :

-   établir les répertoires conformément aux exigences du public,
    aux disponibilités artistiques et techniques des institutions ;
-   suivre l'audience du public spectateur d'un certain spectacle ;
-   analyser la réceptivité du public envers un certain auteur ou
    créateur de spectacle (dramaturge, metteur en scène,
    chorégraphe, acteur, etc.).

Grâce à la compréhension exacte du but recherché et au profession-
nalisme de ceux qui nous ont fourni les informations – les secrétaires
littéraires et musicaux des institutions concernées – nous possédons
actuellement des données concernant 12 000 créations théâtrales, mises
en scène après 1944 dans les théâtres en Roumanie (base de données qui
s'enrichit chaque année d'une centaine de fiches de premières) ;
200 premières musicales, mises en scène après 1990 ; 215 000 réalisateurs (mais seulement 2 000 fiches d'artistes) ; 200 institutions (d'État
ou privées).

L'accès à Internet a permis de diriger notre attention sur l'ouverture
du système aux utilisateurs, pour une mise en valeur maximale des
informations disponibles. Ainsi, ce système s'impose comme un instrument utile au monde du spectacle.

Un site Web a donc été créé[1] qui présente de façon dynamique les
bases de données « STAR » et contient :

---

[1]   www.cimec.ro/teatre/Star_Home.htm.

- le répertoire du théâtrale national après 1944
  (premièrement la liste des titres de spectacles, puis
  la présentation de la distribution de chaque spectacle) ;
- l'historique des institutions théâtrales dramatiques
  de tout le pays ;
- la présentation des réalisateurs de théâtre du point
  de vue de la création scénique.

Il y a aussi un site Web pour chaque saison théâtrale antérieure, qui contient toutes les premières (distributions et illustrations).

Un autre site Web, http://www.cimec.ro/arte/perf.htm, présente le domaine « Musique & Danse ». On peut y consulter :

- un agenda qui contient institutions (d'État ou privées),
  ensembles, compagnies, associations, groupes ;
- le répertoire national musical après 1990 ;
- les répertoires courants de l'Opéra national et
  du Théâtre national de l'Opérette ;
- les événements musicaux et chorégraphiques
  (base des données on-line, qui peut être consultée
  par année, lieu ou type d'événement) ;
- les sites Internet des musiciens roumains contemporains ;
- la bibliographie des œuvres pour piano.

Cette année est dédiée à Ion Luca Caragiale, l'un des plus grands écrivains et dramaturge classique roumain. À cette occasion, un site Web a été réalisé[2] où l'on peut trouver :

- la liste des manifestations dédiées au jubilé ;
- la biobibliographie de l'écrivain ;
- les textes politiques (publiés pour la première fois en ligne) ;
- le répertoire des spectacles théâtraux et musicaux tirés des écrits
  de Caragiale ou inspirés par son œuvre.

Nous espérons que notre travail contribuera à une meilleure connaissance des arts du spectacle roumains dans le monde entier, et à la libre circulation des informations dans ce domaine.

---

[2] www.cimec.ro/Teatre/Caragiale_pag/caragiale_ferestre.htm.

ANNEXES

André Veinstein (1916-2001)

Noëlle GUIBERT

Bibliothèque nationale de France (Paris – France)

Avec la disparition d'André Veinstein, la SIBMAS perd son fondateur et la recherche théâtrale, une personnalité originale de dimension internationale. Licencié en droit, docteur ès lettres, André Veinstein entre en 1947 au Centre national de la recherche scientifique.

En 1953, l'administrateur général de la Bibliothèque nationale, Julien Cain, le charge de la responsabilité des collections des Arts du spectacle, initialement réunies par le bibliophile et mécène, passionné de théâtre, Auguste Rondel, avec pour mission la préfiguration de ce qui deviendra le Département des Arts du spectacle de la Bibliothèque nationale, réalisant ainsi le vœu des praticiens du spectacle en France.

Tout en travaillant à ce projet, André Veinstein ne cesse d'enrichir les collections en faisant entrer les fonds Edward Gordon Craig, Louis Jouvet, Jacques Copeau, Georges Pitoëff, Gaston Baty, Charles Dullin... en tête de nombreuses autres collections, ainsi que des centaines de maquettes de décors et de costumes, des documents concernant l'ensemble des arts du spectacle, la danse, le mime, le cirque, le cinéma, la radio, le music-hall... Il organise des manifestations dans le cadre de l'association Spectacle-Documentation, qu'il crée dans le but de rapprocher les activités de la Bibliothèque nationale des professionnels du spectacle.

En 1954, André Veinstein fonde la Société internationale des Bibliothèques-Musées des Arts du spectacle, afin d'établir des liens permanents entre les différentes collections qui se développent dans le monde depuis les années 1945. À la même époque, il participe largement à la création de la Fédération internationale de la recherche théâtrale, la FIRT, association sœur, avec laquelle la SIBMAS continue d'entretenir des liens privilégiés.

Multipliant les contacts et les initiatives, il renforce les rapports entre ces associations durant sa présidence et au cours des congrès biennaux organisés par les centres de la SIBMAS, dans le monde.

Il facilite le travail de la recherche et des ressources dans le domaine en faisant publier le répertoire *Bibliothèques-musées des arts du spectacle*, le « Livre bleu », à la rédaction duquel il participe encore dans l'édition de 1992.

Producteur d'émissions radiophoniques, rédacteur en chef des *Cahiers d'études de radiotélévision*, directeur des collections « Bibliothèque d'esthétique », chez Flammarion, et de « Pratique du Théâtre », chez Gallimard, dans lesquelles paraissent des textes référentiels de Jacques Copeau, Louis Jouvet, Edward Gordon Craig, Jean-Louis Barrault, Étienne Decroux, ainsi que les *Registres du Vieux-Colombier* établis par Marie-Hélène Dasté et Suzanne Maistre, il est l'auteur de bibliographies concernant les Films sur le théâtre et l'art du mime, le Théâtre radiophonique et télévisuel, qu'il a réalisées seul ou avec ses collaboratrices – Cécile Giteau, son successeur à la tête des Collections théâtrales et Marie-Françoise Christout –, ainsi que de nombreuses expositions sur le Lieu théâtral, Louis Jouvet, Edward Gordon Craig, Jacques Copeau, Gaston Baty, à la Bibliothèque nationale.

Nommé professeur à l'Université de Paris VIII en 1969, il a largement participé au renouvellement de la conception de la recherche théâtrale grâce à des ouvrages de référence tels que *La Mise en scène théâtrale et sa condition esthétique*[1], ses études sur les revues de théâtre *Du Théâtre libre au Théâtre Louis Jouvet*[2], ou *Le Théâtre expérimental*[3].

Un esprit brillant, l'art de susciter des recherches auprès de ses étudiants, une curiosité mise au service des courants les plus novateurs, l'audace de sa démarche fondatrice, ont profondément imprimé sa marque à l'édification du patrimoine théâtral.

---

[1] André Veinstein, *La Mise en scène théâtrale et sa condition esthétique*, 2ᵉ éd. rev. et augm., Paris, Flammarion, 1955.

[2] André Veinstein, *Du Théâtre libre au Théâtre Louis Jouvet, les théâtres d'art à travers leur périodique, 1887-1934*, Paris, Billaudot, 1955.

[3] André Veinstein, *Le Théâtre expérimental, tendances et propositions*, Paris, La Renaissance du livre, 1968.

Assemblée générale[1]

1. Les comptes rendus des réunions de Paris en 2000 sont adoptés.

2. Rapports

- Claudia Balk, présidente de la SIBMAS fait son rapport annuel et demande que soit observée une minute de silence en mémoire d'André Veinstein, président fondateur de l'association.

- Rosy Runciman fait part aux membres du rapport de Claire Hudson, secrétaire générale de la SIBMAS.

- Rapport du trésorier : Joël Huthwohl commente le tableau qui dresse le bilan financier du compte de la SIBMAS à Paris. Il manque trop d'éléments pour faire le bilan des autres comptes.

3. L'assemblée générale accepte à l'unanimité les nouveaux montants des cotisations :

Membres institutionnels : 35 euros

Membres individuels : 25 euros

Étudiants : 15 euros

4. Élections du Comité exécutif et du Conseil

Le Comité électoral était composé de Helena Hantakova, Margret Schild et Daniela Montemagno.

Ont été élus :

Présidente : Claudia Balk (Deutsches Theatermuseum)

1e vice-présidente : Montserrat Alvarez-Massó
(Institut del Teatre de la Diputació de Barcelona)

2e vice-présidente : Ulrike Dembski
(Österreichisches Theatermuseum)

Secrétaire générale : Maria Teresa Iovinelli
(Biblioteca e Raccolta Teatrale del Burcardo della SIAE)

Trésorier : Joël Huthwohl
(Bibliothèque-Musée de la Comédie-Française)

Autres membres du Comité exécutif :

Martin Dreier (Schweizerische Theatersammlung)

Alan R. Jones (Royal Scottish Academy of Music)

---

[1] Museo di Roma in Trastevere, Rome, 7 septembre 2002.

Rosy Runciman (Cameron Mackintosh Limited)
Jan Van Goethem (Théâtre royal de La Monnaie, Bruxelles)
Autres membres du Conseil :
Helen Adair (The University of Texas at Austin)
Marie-Claude Billard (Maison Jean Vilar, Avignon)
Ada Kolganova (Russian State Art Library)
Inga Lewenhaupt (Sveriges Teatermuseum)
Willem Rodenhuis (Bibliotheek Theaterwetenschap/ Film- en Televisiewetenschap UVA Nieuwe Doelenstraat)
Richard Stone (PASIG Museums Australia)
Paul S. Ulrich

Les membres *ex officio* du Conseil sont : Josette Féral (présidente de la FIRT), Jacques Perot (président de l'ICOM) et Noëlle Guibert (ex-présidente de la SIBMAS).

Compte-rendu par Joël Huthwohl.

Révisé par le Conseil le 5 juillet 2003.

Approuvé par l'assemblée générale le 10 septembre 2004.

General Assembly[2]

1. The minutes of the General Assembly of 2000 in Paris were approved.

2. Reports
   - Claudia Balk, president of SIBMAS, gave her yearly report and asked for a minute of silence in memory of André Veinstein, president and founder of the Association.
   - Rosy Runciman read the report written by Claire Hudson, Secretary General of SIBMAS.
   - Report of the Treasurer: Joël Huthwohl comments on the table representing the statement of SIBMAS accounts in Paris. He lacks too many elements to draw up a balance of the other accounts.

3. The General Assembly unanimously accepted the new fees:
   Institutional Members: 35 euros
   Individual Members: 25 euros
   Students: 15 euros

4. Elections of the Executive Committee and of the Council.
   The members of the Election Commission were Helena Hantakova, Margret Schild and Daniela Montemagno.
   The General Assembly elected:
   President: Claudia Balk (Deutsches Theatermuseum)
   1st Vice-President: Montserrat Alvarez-Massó
   (Institut del Teatre de la Diputació de Barcelona)
   2nd Vice-President: Ulrike Dembski
   (Österreichisches Theatermuseum)
   Secretary General: Maria Teresa Iovinelli
   (Biblioteca e Raccolta Teatrale del Burcardo della SIAE)
   Treasurer: Joël Huthwohl
   (Bibliothèque-Musée de la Comédie-Française)
   Other Executive Committee members:
   Martin Dreier (Schweizerische Theatersammlung)

---

[2] Museo di Roma in Trastevere, Rome, 7 September, 2002.

Alan R. Jones (Royal Scottish Academy of Music)
Rosy Runciman (Cameron Mackintosh Limited)
Jan Van Goethem (Théâtre royal de La Monnaie, Bruxelles)
Other Council members:
Helen Adair (The University of Texas at Austin)
Marie-Claude Billard (Maison Jean Vilar, Avignon)
Ada Kolganova (Russian State Art Library)
Inga Lewenhaupt (Sveriges Teatermuseum)
Willem Rodenhuis (Bibliotheek Theaterwetenschap/
Film- en Televisiewetenschap UvA Nieuwe Doelenstraat)
Richard Stone (PASIG Museums Australia),
Paul S. Ulrich

The *ex officio* members of the Council are the following: Josette Féral (President of FIRT), Jacques Perot (President of ICOM) and Noëlle Guibert (former President of SIBMAS).

Minutes: Joël Huthwohl.
Revised by the Council, 5 July, 2003.
Approved by the General Assembly, 10 September, 2004.

Rapport de la présidente

Claudia BALK

Avant d'aborder mon rapport, premier point de notre agenda, je voudrais rappeler l'histoire de notre organisation. Lors de notre prochain congrès, qui se déroulera en 2004 à Barcelone, nous célébrerons le 50ᵉ anniversaire de la fondation de la SIBMAS. Mon rapport vous en dira un peu plus à ce sujet. Mais je voudrais d'abord vous rappeler que la fondation de la SIBMAS est étroitement liée à une personne, Monsieur André Veinstein. J'ai la tristesse de vous informer qu'André Veinstein est décédé en décembre dernier. Au nom de la SIBMAS, j'ai envoyé des condoléances à sa famille et leur ai dit que nous honorerions sa mémoire lors de ce congrès. Je vous demande donc de vous mettre debout pour une minute de silence.

Merci.

Je voudrais à présent revenir, non sur les 48 années d'existence de la SIBMAS, mais sur ses deux dernières années. Quand j'ai pris la présidence à Paris, la SIBMAS était confrontée à des changements. Depuis lors, l'adoption de nouvelles règles a modifié la structure d'adhésion ; nous avons à présent des membres institutionnels et des membres individuels qui ont droit de vote direct, ce qui renforce la responsabilité individuelle de nos membres, alors que le pouvoir des centres nationaux a baissé de manière significative. En Allemagne tout particulièrement, ceci a conduit à une diminution des membres de la SIBMAS parce que ce centre s'est rendu autonome au niveau national en imposant sa propre cotisation de membre et les institutions les plus petites en particulier, n'ont pas pu, ou pas voulu, être membres des deux associations. En dépit de tous mes efforts, je n'ai pas réussi à prévenir cette diminution, qui était déjà prévisible à Paris. J'ai écrit personnellement à tous les membres allemands et j'ai assisté aux réunions de l'association nationale allemande et me suis totalement engagée dans la promotion de la SIBMAS internationale. Dans son rapport qui va suivre, Georg Geldner, secrétaire des membres, expliquera plus en détails l'évolution de la situation des membres.

Pour recruter des membres, nous devons offrir des « avantages » et notamment, le *Bulletin.* Jusqu'au congrès de Paris, celui-ci était édité par Éric Alexander et Liliana Alexandrescu – en remerciement de leur engagement pendant toutes ces années, le ComEx les a nommés tous deux membres honoraires de la SIBMAS – ce que l'on pourra lire sur notre site. Ils ont transmis la responsabilité de cette publication à Nicole Leclercq, initialement pour la réalisation de trois numéros. Après cette période, Nicole Leclercq nous a fait savoir qu'elle ne pourrait pas poursuivre cette mission, à cause de la surcharge de travail. Depuis lors, conjointement avec la FIRT, nous avons cherché une autre solution et c'est la raison pour laquelle David Whitton, secrétaire général de la FIRT a participé à notre réunion du ComEx en octobre dernier, ici à Rome. La recherche d'une solution s'est avérée longue et difficile, notamment parce que la FIRT s'est fortement engagée dans la réalisation d'un nouveau site Internet, qui semble avoir récemment abouti. À mon initiative, une réunion conjointe des deux comités exécutifs s'est déroulée cet été à Amsterdam à l'occasion du congrès mondial de la FIRT. Nous avons formé un groupe de travail commun, dont il est sorti un « conseil consultatif » commun. Un membre de ce groupe, Willem Rodenhuis, donnera davantage d'informations dans le cadre des rapports de commissions qui vont suivre. Toutefois, mon impression est qu'après une phase difficile et lente, nous sommes maintenant sur la bonne voie.

La situation financière de la SIBMAS sera présentée plus tard par notre trésorier Joël Huthwohl qui a maintenant été complètement mis au courant de ses tâches par son prédécesseur, Georg Geldner. Je tiens à les remercier chaleureusement tous les deux. Je n'ai qu'un commentaire à faire à propos de notre budget. Nous avons dû être prudents dans nos prévisions budgétaires, à cause de l'incertitude sur l'avenir du *Bulletin*. C'est pourquoi il n'a pas été possible de réaliser le projet d'un beau dépliant de la SIBMAS, orné par exemple d'illustrations, une idée que j'ai soutenue et encouragée. J'aurais vraiment voulu présenter un projet à ce congrès car j'ai une idée précise de la forme qu'il devrait prendre mais les moyens financiers de démarrage étaient tout simplement inexistants. Toutefois, si vous m'accordez une fois encore votre confiance à l'occasion de l'élection de ce jour, je poursuivrai ce projet.

Quels sont les autres changements, quelles nouvelles positives pouvons-nous donner ? Pendant ces deux dernières années, j'ai mis l'accent sur les relations avec nos organisations sœurs. À cet égard, je me suis penchée sur la réputation dont devrait jouir la SIBMAS dans les autres milieux et sur les occasions potentielles de récolter quelques membres au sein des organisations voisines. Je me suis personnellement beaucoup impliquée dans les relations avec la FIRT et l'ICOM.

Le renforcement des contacts avec la FIRT a commencé par la lecture, par le secrétaire général David Whitton, de mon allocution au congrès de la FIRT à Sydney. Celle-ci y a été bien accueillie. Ensuite, David

Whitton est venu assister à notre réunion du COMEX ici à Rome en octobre dernier. À cette occasion, ma proposition de tenir une réunion supplémentaire du COMEX à Amsterdam en juillet 2002, en marge du congrès mondial de la FIRT – qui n'a lieu que tous les quatre ans – a été approuvée. Nos statuts prévoient qu'au moins une réunion doit avoir lieu chaque année mais je ne puis que recommander fortement au prochain COMEX de tenir une réunion supplémentaire, tout particulièrement pendant l'année où a lieu le congrès ou en cas de problème. En conséquence, une réunion conjointe des deux COMEX s'est tenue à mon initiative le 29 juillet 2002. Je ne sais pas s'il existe dans l'histoire de nos organisations un exemple d'une réunion de ce type mais dans tous les cas, je suis heureuse d'avoir pu frayer ce chemin et je remercie tous ceux qui se sont impliqués dans cette réalisation.

À l'ouverture du congrès mondial, le 1er juillet, j'ai personnellement profité de l'occasion pour présenter une allocution dans laquelle j'ai insisté sur le renforcement de nos relations. Mon principal lien avec la FIRT a eu un effet pratique au sein du groupe de travail « Iconographie théâtrale » où Christopher Balme et moi-même avons présenté au congrès d'Amsterdam un projet commun d'exposition d'iconographie théâtrale sous le titre de travail actuel de « Images de l'acteur », présentation qui a été suivie d'une discussion stimulante. Ce projet, né il y a deux ans à Paris au sein de la Commission des expositions a été exposé plus en détail hier dans cette même commission. La SIBMAS était présente également d'une autre manière à Amsterdam : Paul Ulrich y a présenté le Répertoire SIBMAS qui compte plus de 8 000 entrées. Comme vous le savez peut-être, le Répertoire est accessible en ligne sur notre site Web depuis mars de cette année et il compte actuellement environ 1 000 visiteurs par semaine. Je voudrais donc remercier vivement Paul pour son grand engagement.

J'ai par ailleurs essayé de renforcer les contacts avec des chercheurs en théâtre de langue allemande : j'ai fait cet appel au début novembre 2000 à l'occasion de la réunion de la Society for Theatre Research qui se déroule tous les deux ans. Cela a débouché sur un projet d'exposition supplémentaire, résultant de la coopération entre l'Université de Hildesheim et le Musée de théâtre allemand et portant sur le thème des Stars et du Culte de la star. Je considère l'interdépendance des collections de théâtre et de la recherche théâtrale comme étant d'une grande importance et elle peut se révéler utile pour chacun de nos collègues impliqués dans les collections théâtrales.

Pendant l'été 2001, l'ICOM a tenu son congrès trisannuel à Barcelone au cours duquel la SIBMAS a, pour la toute première fois, délivré une communication en tant qu'« organisation affiliée » ; nous avons en outre été invités à une table ronde qui portait sur la gestion des musées de théâtre, basée sur le thème du congrès. J'ai une fois de plus pris conscience de l'importance de notre présence en tant qu'institution en remplissant le bulletin d'inscription pour le congrès de l'ICOM : chaque participant devait y cocher les manifestations organisées par les différentes institutions présentes auxquelles il ou elle envisageait de participer. Il était possible de choisir la SIBMAS parmi différentes propositions, même si la SIBMAS n'a pas participé aux autres congrès de l'ICOM. Il n'y a eu que quatre membres du ComEx qui ont participé à cette session de la SIBMAS alors que, pourtant, celle-ci avait été décidée lors de la réunion du ComEx à Paris le 30 septembre 2000.

Ceux qui ont assisté au congrès de Paris auront certainement gardé un très bon souvenir de Jacques Perot, président de l'ICOM, de l'excursion à Compiègne et des collections qu'il gère. Je l'ai rencontré au printemps à Munich, lors d'une conférence de presse pour la Journée internationale des musées où il m'a officiellement félicitée en me souhaitant la bienvenue en tant que nouvelle présidente de la SIBMAS. Nous avons bien sûr eu d'autres conversations à Barcelone, où il était également présent à l'occasion de l'ouverture du Musée du Théâtre.

À Barcelone, j'ai également rencontré le Secrétaire général de l'ICOM, Manus Brinkmann, pour une discussion approfondie sur les relations entre ICOM et SIBMAS et sur leurs situations actuelles.

Toujours à Barcelone, j'ai pu approfondir avec le Secrétaire général de l'ICOM, Manus Brinkmann, la question des relations entre l'ICOM et la SIBMAS et leur état actuel. Dans la foulée, Brinkmann m'a invitée, en décembre dernier, à devenir l'un des dix membres qui constituent le groupe de travail de l'ICOM pour le renouveau des comités internationaux. Suite à notre correspondance par mail, constante ces six derniers mois, nous nous sommes vus le 1er juin 2002 à Paris et nous avons passé la journée à formuler des propositions précises pour le « Comité consultatif », à la réunion duquel (la SIBMAS y a sa voix) j'ai participé deux jours plus tard. Grâce à ma collaboration, les deux parties essayent de renforcer leurs relations, même si cela ne changera pas les statuts de la SIBMAS, lesquels posent un problème en raison de nos modalités d'adhesion. Ainsi, nous ne remplirons jamais la demande de la Charte de l'ICOM, à savoir que 50 %, sinon 100 %, de nos membres soient aussi affiliés à l'ICOM : en effet, nos adhérents comptent également, outre les musées et leur représentants, des bibliothèques et des centres d'archives.

Par ailleurs, que les membres de l'ICOM puissent être également membres de la SIBMAS sans payer de cotisation et sans que l'ICOM ne reverse la moindre contribution financière n'est pas défendable. Cela devra changer à l'avenir. Il en a été question à Paris, d'autant plus que, de leur côté, les « Comités internationaux » vont également demander une cotisation pour leurs adhérents. J'y reviendrai dans un point de notre ordre du jour.

Selon moi, il est essentiel que les archives théâtrales soient représentées dans l'organisation des musées la plus importante au monde : presque 14 000 membres. Ne l'oublions pas : si la SIBMAS jouit d'une bonne réputation dans le monde des musées, cela rejaillira sur chacune des personnes qui travaillent dans nos musées et bibliothèques des arts du spectacle.

Si nous voulons de notre côté faire avancer les choses, nous pourrions peut-être donner l'occasion aux représentants de l'ICOM de faire une présentation détaillée de leur organisation lors de notre prochain congrès. Ce sera d'ailleurs un plus pour nos membres, puisque l'ICOM compte des comités spécialisés dans de multiples domaines, dont la conservation – ce qui intéressera chez nous ceux qui s'occupent des costumes ou des instruments de musique anciens –, les prêts intermuséaux ou la documentation – leur savoir-faire spécifique pourrait être d'une grande aide pour les membres de la SIBMAS, souvent confrontés à une profusion de matériaux et à une carence de personnel pour les traiter.

Il est important de renforcer les relations avec d'autres organisations sœurs, c'est pourquoi j'ai formé un petit groupe de travail lors de la réunion du ComEX en octobre dernier à Rome. Parmi les décisions prises, je citerai, par exemple, le fait que le ComEX a désigné Willem Rodenhuis responsable des contacts avec l'IFLA – dans un premier temps, pour une année – et cela a déjà porté ses fruits : une présentation de la SIBMAS, avec un entretien entre Willem et moi est apparu dans le bulletin de l'IFLA et, il y a quelques semaines, Willem a participé au congrès de l'IFLA à Glasgow, où il a présenté une communication portant sur la SIBMAS. Nicole Leclercq a été choisie pour entretenir les contacts avec l'IIT, et cela aussi a déjà amené à des résultats. Selon moi, un tel réseau constitue une innovation essentielle et je ne peux qu'en recommander la poursuite au futur ComEX.

Maintenant, se profile déjà le 25ᵉ congrès de la SIBMAS à l'occasion duquel l'on célébrera, notamment, ses cinquante ans. Le réseau renforcé comme je l'ai décrit plus haut pourrait déboucher sur des résultats concrets. Barcelone pourrait être le lieu où l'on réunirait les représentants de nos organisations membres les plus importantes pour leur permettre de se présenter.

Parmi les thèmes envisagés pour le 50ᵉ anniversaire de notre organisation, il serait bon de réfléchir à ce que font nos institutions – musées, centres d'archives ou bibliothèques. C'est pourquoi je suis très contente que ce soit Barcelone qui ait été choisi comme hôte, car nous pourrons mieux connaître une institution passionnante, où diffé-

rents organes ont été réunis sous un même toit et ce, depuis l'été 2001 :
le Musée du Théâtre, l'Académie de Théâtre et le Centre d'étude du
Théâtre – en d'autres termes, sous ce toit on peut danser, répéter, étudier, récolter, documenter, exposer... Pour tout son dévouement, qui a
débouché sur cette invitation à Barcelone, je voudrais mille fois remercier Montserrat Alvarez-Massò.

Et c'est sur ces mots que je souhaite clore mon rapport, non sans remercier, chaleureusement, tous les membres du ComEX actuel, ainsi que
les membres du Conseil, pour leur implication, leur aide et leur soutien.
Je répondrai bien sûr à toute question que vous pourriez avoir lors de la
session plénière ou lors de discussions en tête-à-tête – si nous en trou-
vons le temps.

President's Report

Claudia BALK

Before I come to the first item of our agenda, my report, I should like to recall the history of our organisation. At our next congress, which will take place in 2004 in Barcelona, we will be able to celebrate the 50th anniversary of the existence of SIBMAS, about which you will shortly be able to learn more in my report. However, I should firstly like to remind you that the formation of SIBMAS is particularly linked to one person: Monsieur André Veinstein. It is my sad duty to inform you that André Veinstein died last December. On behalf of SIBMAS I have sent our condolences to his family and told them that we will honour his memory with a minute's silence here. So I would like to ask you to now stand for this minute's silence.

Thank you.

I should now like to look back, not at the 48 years of the existence of SIBMAS, but at the past two years. When I took over as President in Paris, SIBMAS was facing several changes. Through the adoption of the new rules the membership structure has since changed; we now have institutional and individual members who have a direct right to vote, which strengthens the personal responsibility of our members, while the power of the national centres has significantly weakened. Particularly in Germany this had led to a loss of SIBMAS members, since this centre has made itself autonomous on a national level by imposing its own membership contribution, and especially the smaller institutions cannot or do not want to be a member of both associations. Despite all efforts, I have been unable to prevent this decrease, which was already foreseeable in Paris: I have written personally to every German member and attended all the meetings of the national German association, and have been fully committed to promoting the international SIBMAS. The Membership Secretary Georg Geldner will explain the development of the membership situation in greater detail in his report to follow later.

In order to recruit members we need "benefits", which also include the *Bulletin*. Up until the Paris Congress this was published by Éric Alexander and Liliana Alexandrescu – for their commitment over a great many years, at the beginning of 2001 ExCom made both of them honorary members of SIBMAS, and this news can also be read on our Website. They have handed over responsibility for publication to Nicole Leclercq – initially for the production of three issues. Nicole Leclercq has had to inform us that after this period she was unable to continue this activity due to excess workload. Together with FIRT we have since been searching for a new solution, and for this reason FIRT's General Secretary, David Whitton, also attended our ExCom meeting last October here in Rome. Finding a joint solution proved to be lengthy and difficult, particularly as FIRT had strongly committed itself to establishing a new Website, which recently seems to have been achieved. For this purpose there was – on my initiative – a joint meeting of both ExComs at FIRT's World Congress in Amsterdam this summer. We formed a joint working group, from which emerged a joint "advisory board". A member of this group, Willem Rodenhuis, will briefly present further details of this following the reports of the "commissions". However, my impression is that after a difficult and slow-moving phase we are now on the right path.

The financial situation of SIBMAS will later be presented by our treasurer Joël Huthwohl, who has since been thoroughly familiarised with his new duties by his predecessor in office, Georg Geldner – for which I should like to thank both of them very much indeed. I only have one comment to make about our budget. Due to the uncertain future of the *Bulletin*, our financial planning has had to be cautious. For this reason, it has also not been possible to translate into reality the idea of a decorative SIBMAS folder, i.e. one filled with pictures – an idea favoured and promoted by me. I would really like to have presented a draft at this Congress, since I already have clear ideas about the form it should take, but the financial start-up funds were simply lacking. However, I will stick to this project if you once again pass a vote of confidence in me in today's election.

What else has changed, what positive news is there to report? Over the past two years I have placed the main emphasis on the relationships with our sister organisations. In this respect I was interested in the reputation SIBMAS ought to enjoy in other circles, and in the potential opportunity of gaining new members in the neighbouring organisations. I was personally very much involved in the relationships with FIRT and ICOM.

Strengthening contact with FIRT began with the reading of my greeting at the FIRT Congress in Sydney by the General Secretary David Whitton, which was well received. This was followed by David Whitton's attendance at our ExCom meeting last October here in Rome. At this meeting there was approval of my proposal that on the fringe of the World Congress of FIRT, which only takes place every four years, an additional ExCom meeting be held in Amsterdam in July 2002. Our rules prescribe that a meeting be held at least once a year, and I can only most strongly recommend to the future ExCom an additional meeting, especially in the year of the congress and if problems should arise. Following this, on my initiative a joint meeting of both ExComs was held on 29th July 2002. I don't know whether there has ever been such a joint meeting in the history of our organisations, but in any event I am pleased that we have been able to blaze this trail and thank all those involved.

To open the World Congress on 1st July I then personally took the opportunity to present a greeting, in which I urged a strengthening of our relationships. My essential link with FIRT is given practical effect through the working group "Theatre Iconography", where Christopher Balme and I presented at the congress in Amsterdam the joint project of an exhibition of theatre iconography with the current working title of "Images of the Actor", followed by a stimulating discussion. This project, which began two years ago in Paris in the Exhibition Commission, was introduced in more detail yesterday in this commission. And SIBMAS was also present in Amsterdam in another way: Paul S. Ulrich presented the SIBMAS Directory with well over 8,000 entries. As you might know, the Directory has been available online on our Website since March this year and now has around 1,000 visitors a week. At this point I should like to thank Paul very much indeed for his great commitment.

I have also tried to strengthen contact with theatre researchers on the German-language level: I made such a plea at the beginning of November 2000 at the meeting of the Society for Theatre Research, which takes place every two years. This resulted in an additional exhibition project, arising from cooperation between the University of Hildesheim and the German Theatre Museum and dealing with the topic of Stars and Star Cult. I regard the interrelationship of theatre collections and theatre research as extremely important, and it may turn out to be useful for every single colleague involved in theatre collections.

In the summer of 2001 in Barcelona ICOM had its congress, which takes place every three years, and at which SIBMAS for the very first time also offered a presentation as an "affiliated organisation": we extended an invitation to a round table, which had as its subject: The management of theatre museums, based on the main theme of the congress. I realised the importance of our presence as an organisation once more by filling out the registration form for the ICOM congress: here every member has to choose which event of which organisation he/she plans to visit. It was possible to select SIBMAS from a number of options, although SIBMAS had not been present at previous ICOM congresses.

Only four ExCom members attended this SIBMAS session, although the meeting had been decided during the ExCom meeting in Paris on September 30th 2000.

Those who attended the Paris Congress will certainly have fond memories of the President of ICOM, Jacques Perot, from the excursion to Compiègne and of the collections he manages. I met him in the spring of 2001 at a press conference for the worldwide Museums Day in Munich, where he officially welcomed me and congratulated me as the new President of SIBMAS. We of course spoke to each other again in Barcelona, where he also took part in the opening of the Theatre Museum there.

In Barcelona I also met the Secretary General of ICOM, Manus Brinkmann, for a detailed discussion on the relationships between ICOM and SIBMAS and their current standing. This contact eventually led to Brinkmann's invitation last December to become a member of the ten-member ICOM taskforce for the renewal of the International Committees. Following very intensive e-mail discussions lasting 6 months, we met on 1st June 2002 in Paris, where we spent another entire day in discussion to draw up specific proposals for the "advisory board", whose meeting – at which SIBMAS is also entitled to vote – I also attended two days later. As a result of my cooperation, both parties are to try and strengthen the relationships, although we will maintain the status of SIBMAS. I recognised the latter as compelling due to our membership structure. We will never fulfil the requirements of the ICOM Charter to have 50 or even 100 percent ICOM members in SIBMAS, since some of our members are not museums or their employees, but also libraries and archives.

The situation whereby ICOM members can be SIBMAS members without paying any fee and without any additional financial support by ICOM is not tenable, and this will change in the future. The possibility of this was discussed in Paris and reinforced by the fact that the "International Committees" will in future also demand their own membership contributions. I will return to this under item of our agenda.

I regard the presence of the theatre collections in the world's largest museum association of almost 14,000 members as extremely important. If SIBMAS enjoys a respectable reputation in the museum world, this will flow back to every single employee in our theatre collections – this should not be forgotten.

To step up activity on our part, I suggest that the representatives of ICOM be given the opportunity to give a full presentation of themselves at our next congress. This seems to me very interesting for our members as well, since ICOM runs specialist committees relating to many areas, such as conservation, matters relating to costumes or old musical instruments, exhibition exchanges or documentation, which with their specialist knowledge could usefully support SIBMAS members, who often have to deal with an enormous wealth of material with insufficient personnel.

To enable relationships with additional sister organisations to be strengthened in a similar way, at the ExCom meeting last October in Rome I formed a kind of taskforce. As a result, for example, ExCom has appointed Willem Rodenhuis as "liaison partner" for IFLA – initially for a period of one year – and this has already borne several fruits. A report on SIBMAS, with an interview between Willem and me, has appeared in the IFLA publications and a few weeks ago Willem attended the IFLA Congress in Glasgow, where he also gave a lecture about SIBMAS. We have appointed Nicole Leclercq as the contact for ITI, which has also already achieved an initial result. I regard this network as a very important innovation and can only recommend it very urgently to the future ExCom.

A future task is the organisation of the 25th SIBMAS Congress, including the celebration of the 50th anniversary of its existence. In this connection the strengthened network described above could take concrete shape, and in Barcelona it should be possible to gather together representatives of all our major affiliated organisations and arrange for them to present their greetings or brief introductions of themselves.

Our planned topic:

On the 50th anniversary of our organisation's existence this means a reconsideration of our own direct tasks in our institutions, comprising museums, archives and libraries. I am very pleased that Barcelona has now been settled upon as a venue, because we will get to know a very interesting institution, where several institutions have been gathered together under one roof since the summer of 2001: Theatre Museum, Theatre Academy and Theatre Research – or in other words, dancing, rehearsals, research, collecting, documenting and exhibiting all take place here. For her great commitment, which has brought about the invitation to Barcelona, I should like to thank Montserrat Alvarez-Massò very much indeed.

And with that I would like to end my report, but not without thanking all members of the current ExCom, as well as the members of the Council, very much indeed for all their cooperation, advice and support. Of course I will be pleased to answer any questions you may have, either at the plenary session or in individual discussions, if we can find time for this.

Rapport de la secrétaire générale

Claire HUDSON

Chers collègues,

Cela a été une joie pour moi de participer aux travaux du Comité exécutif, tout d'abord en tant que vice-présidente puis, depuis le congrès de Paris, en tant que secrétaire générale. Mais aujourd'hui, trop de travail me force à me retirer.

L'on aura vu, ces dernières années, des changements considérables dans les activités de la SIBMAS. La bataille pour maintenir en vie le *Bulletin* aura été difficile pour tous, mais aujourd'hui, nous avons tous accepté qu'il doit évoluer. Nous ne pouvons pas laisser passer l'occasion de le remplacer par un bulletin électronique qui sera vraiment utile. Pour les professionnels de l'information que nous sommes, il va de soi qu'il faut se servir d'Internet pour annoncer les nouveautés qui nous concernent, car les méthodes électroniques ont déjà révolutionné d'autres champs de notre travail quotidien.

Le développement de notre site et de l'annuaire en ligne nous a beaucoup apporté. Cela n'a pu être possible que grâce à l'implication personnelle et au dur labeur d'une petite équipe, et spécialement Paul Ulrich et Maria Teresa Iovinelli.

En fait, mon expérience à l'ExCom m'amène à me demander si les membres qui ne font pas partie du Conseil de la SIBMAS se rendent compte de tout le travail que l'on y fait. À l'occasion d'un autre congrès, peut-être pourrions-nous prévoir une brève session pour expliquer le fonctionnement du Comité et ce que recouvre son travail. Les ordres du jour et les comptes rendus de ses réunions pourraient aussi être insérés dans le site, ce qui permettrait à tous nos membres de connaître les points à débattre et les encouragerait à s'impliquer davantage.

Enfin, je ne peux que faire l'éloge de votre présidente, Claudia Balk, qui a travaillé vraiment dur et qui s'est dévouée pour faire avancer les intérêts de notre organisation. Je souhaite à mon successeur et à tous les membres de la SIBMAS beaucoup de réussite à l'avenir et je me réjouis à l'avance de renforcer les précieux contacts que ce congrès et d'autres comme lui m'auront permis de faire.

Secretary General's Report

Claire HUDSON

Dear Colleagues,

I have enjoyed participating in the work of the executive Committee, first as Vice President and, since the Paris Conference, as Secretary General but now pressure of other work forces me to stand down.

Recent years have seen considerable change in the activities of SIBMAS. The struggle to keep the *Bulletin* alive has been difficult for everyone but now we have accepted that it cannot continue in its traditional form, we can grasp the opportunity to create a really useful electronic resource in its place. As information professionals, it is highly appropriate that we should employ the medium of the Internet to communicate our news because electronic methods have already revolutionised other areas of ours working lives.

The development of our Website and of the online directory has been of huge benefit to us all. This has been achieved only through the personal commitment and hard work of a small number of people, especially Paul Ulrich and Maria Teresa Iovinelli.

In fact, my experience of working on the ExCom makes me wonder whether those members who are not involved with the SIBMAS Council realise how much work it carries out. Perhaps a future conference could include a short session explaining how the committee works and the operations its covers. Agendas and summaries of meetings might also be added to the Website, allowing all members to see what the current issues are, and encouraging their greater involvement.

Finally, I must commend to you your President, Claudia Balk, who is exceptionally hard working and committed to advancing the interests of our organisation. I wish she, my successor, and all the members of SIBMAS success for the future, and I look forward to strengthening the valuable contacts which this conference, and others like it, have enabled me to make.

Réunions des Comités

Rapport sur le *Répertoire international
des collections et institutions des Arts du spectacle*
de la SIBMAS – Commission du site Web

Présidence : Paul S. ULRICH,
Maria Teresa IOVINELLI

Modifications du design du site

Il est nécessaire de modifier le site :
- modifications dans la mise en page : le logo et la liste de navigation devront être placés à la droite de chaque page ;
- l'arborescence placée du côté gauche de la page permettra un meilleur positionnement pour les résultats du moteur de recherche ;
- l'efficacité visuelle sur écran est meilleure dans le cas où il y a plus d'une fenêtre ouverte : les utilisateurs sauront précisément, grâce à l'arborescence, sur quelle page ils sont ;
- l'aperçu à gauche correspond au sens normal de la lecture. C'est donc le bon endroit pour l'affichage des contenus.

Nouveau nom de domaine pour la SIBMAS

Maria Teresa Iovinelli se chargera de déposer un nom de domaine pour la SIBMAS :
- un nom de domaine (même si cela implique un coût) donnerait à la SIBMAS une meilleure visibilité, car le site deviendrait indépendant et ne serait plus un sous-ensemble du site theatrelibrary.org. Ceci faciliterait en outre l'analyse des statistiques de fréquentation ;

- si possible, le nom sera : www.sibmas.org ;
- (remarque parallèle : SIBMAS est également le nom d'un char d'assaut belge).

Mise à jour de la liste des membres de l'ExCom sur le site

La mise à jour est prévue. Maria Teresa Iovinelli effectuera le changement le plus vite possible après le congrès.

L'archivage des actes de congrès antérieurs

- les actes des congrès de la SIBMAS avant 1988 doivent encore être mis sur le site. (Les actes de 1988 à 1994 et ceux depuis 1996 qui sont disponibles s'y trouvent déjà.) Noëlle Guibert enverra une copie des actes manquant à Paul S. Ulrich qui les scannera et les convertira en format HTML pour qu'ils puissent apparaître sur le site. Les textes du congrès de Paris seront mis en ligne plus tard, afin de permettre que les actes publiés soient vendus ;
- tous les participants devront envoyer, dès que possible, leur communication pour le présent congrès à Maria Teresa Iovinelli ;
- l'index des orateurs pour les anciens actes devra être réactualisé.

Le *Répertoire des collections des Arts du spectacle* de la SIBMAS

- la situation actuelle du répertoire de la SIBMAS a été présentée par Paul S. Ulrich dans sa communication au congrès. Il a demandé que les corrections et les compléments lui soient envoyé aussi vite que possible. Les modifications seront introduites dans la semaine qui suivra leur réception ;
- résultat positif de la mise en ligne du répertoire : Paul S. Ulrich a reçu un grand nombre de courriers électroniques pour des corrections à apporter aux listes dans le répertoire ;
- les critères pour introduire une institution dans le répertoire sont discutés. Les différences culturelles qui existent entre institutions rendent difficile de toujours savoir si oui ou non telle ou telle institution devrait être intégrée. Le sentiment général est qu'en cas de doute, une institution

sera insérée jusqu'à ce que des informations plus précises permettent de prendre une décision définitive ;

- les statistiques montrent que la partie la plus consultée du Répertoire est l'index des collections. L'on déploiera à l'avenir encore plus d'énergie pour inclure même les petites collections dans le répertoire ;

- la question est soulevée de savoir si les institutions qui n'ont que peu de matériel concernant les arts de la scène ne risquent pas de s'opposer à ce que leur institution soit listée dans le répertoire. Paul S. Ulrich rétorque que, puisque c'est une bonne publicité pour eux, et qu'il en résultera sans doute un accroissement des visites sur leurs sites, ce serait plutôt l'inverse qui devrait être vrai ;

- puisque tous les membres de la SIBMAS sont identifiés dans le répertoire de la SIBMAS, il est important que l'information soit transmise à Paul S. Ulrich. Joël Huthwohl, en tant que secrétaire des adhérents, enverra à Paul la liste mise à jour des adhérents, de telle sorte que les corrections nécessaires puissent être introduites.

Élargissement structurel du site

- Claudia Balk suggère d'élargir les missions du site Web de la SIBMAS de telle façon qu'il puisse devenir un portail des arts de la scène sur Internet. À la lumière de tous les passionnants projets de base de données qui ont été présentés au congrès, il est suggéré que les bases décrites, et d'autres encore, soient proposées dans un répertoire séparé sur le site de la SIBMAS. En effet, ces données ne s'intègrent pas dans le *Répertoire des collections des Arts du spectacle* de la SIBMAS et donc, elles apparaitront comme un répertoire à part. Si l'on veut que tous ces liens servent à quelque chose, il faut qu'ils portent un nom qui sonne bien. Christelle Cazaux et Paul S. Ulrich se pencheront sur la création d'un tel répertoire. Paul S. Ulrich fournira des liens du *Répertoire des collections des Arts du spectacle* de la SIBMAS pour les bases de données évoquées (par exemple, le Répertoire français et l'English Backstage), afin d'accroître encore leur visibilité ;

- on pourrait également compléter le site avec une liste de toutes les publications (répertoires, annuaires, etc.) où apparaît la SIBMAS. Quiconque aurait entendu parler de ce genre de liste est prié d'envoyer l'information à Maria

Teresa Iovinelli qui, en tant que secrétaire générale de la SIBMAS, aura pour tâche d'en informer les éditeurs de ces publications. Ce serait une bonne façon de mettre en avant les lieux où l'on peut en apprendre plus sur la SIBMAS autant que cela pourrait être un rappel pour les membres sur les lieux où les informations à propos de la SIBMAS doivent être mises à jour ;

- discussion sur le mot « portal » (portail) qui n'est pas universel : en Australie, par exemple, on utilise plutôt le mot *gateway* (passerelle).

Remerciements

Hanna Hantakova exprime ses remerciements pour l'article consacré aux inondations de Prague sur le site de la SIBMAS.

Nouvelle structure du groupe de travail du bulletin de la FIRT-SIBMAS

- les ComEx de la FIRT et de la SIBMAS ont formé un groupe de travail pour mettre en œuvre la migration du bulletin sur Internet. Les membres de ce groupe de travail sont : David Whitton, Peter Eversmann, Martin Dreier, Claudia Balk ;
- les mises à jour s'effectueront plus facilement dans un format électronique, qui fige les informations quatre fois par an (contre trois fois précédemment) dans un format PDF imprimable à la demande (destiné spécialement aux membres de la SIBMAS) gratuit ou payant.

L'annuaire de la SIBMAS

Au congrès de la FIRT à Amsterdam, Erika Fischer Lichte a suggéré que la SIBMAS pourrait éditer un annuaire à la place du bulletin. L'annuaire intégrerait des informations complètes sur le contenu et les activités des bibliothèques, des musées, des centres d'archives, etc., qui travaillent dans le domaine des arts de la scène. Le mode de financement reste par contre assez vague, tout comme d'ailleurs la personne qui pourrait superviser un tel projet.

Rapport de la
Commission des expositions

Présidence : Claudia BALK

Claudia Balk ouvre la réunion en remerciant ceux qui sont présents. Elle explique qu'elle souhaite reprendre la structure qui a déjà fait ses preuves lors de la première réunion en 2000 à Paris. L'on part des trois thèmes principaux suivants : information, organisation et réflexion.

Information

Ce qui compte, ici, c'est le site, d'autant que le *Bulletin* n'existera bientôt plus. L'on s'est mis d'accord à Paris sur l'idée de mettre en ligne des informations sur les expositions sur le site de la SIBMAS, et de les rendre plus attrayantes en les accompagnant d'illustrations. Mais aucun progrès ne vaut d'être signalé à ce propos, étant donné que Maria Teresa Iovinelli, qui avait proposé ses services pour ce travail, n'a pas reçu les informations nécessaires. L'on estime que cela doit évoluer et qu'il serait bon qu'une étroite coopération soit établie avec le bulletin électronique à venir.

Organisation

À mi-chemin entre l'information et l'organisation, il y a la mise en ligne des conditions de prêt sur le site – une idée évoquée à la première réunion, à Paris. L'on estime que ce serait bien, mais que de premiers pas concrets doivent être faits.

Les conditions de prêt du pays hôte sont un sujet évoqué par la Commission des expositions aux congrès de la SIBMAS, aussi bien qu'en Italie. Maria Teresa Iovinelli propose un survol très informatif sur les conditions de prêt dans son pays.

De sa propre expérience, Claudia Balk confirme la relative difficulté d'emprunter des objets à exposer en Italie – cela est dû selon elle aux structures hiérarchiques.

On propose que le rapport détaillé de Maria Teresa Iovinelli soit mis en ligne. Ainsi, ce sera une façon d'avancer dans la mise en ligne des conditions de prêt.

Réflexion

Claudia Balk signale que, pour des raisons financières, il ne serait malheureusement pas possible d'inviter quelqu'un à chaque séance de la Commission des expositions, pour approfondir le point principal du jour, ainsi que l'avait fait Christopher Balme à Paris. Peut-être cela sera-t-il possible de nouveau à Barcelone, si l'on élargit le sujet de la réunion. Claudia Balk songe à une communication sur la façon dont les musées de théâtre approchent l'organisation d'expositions sur la vie des praticiens des arts du spectacle.

Claudia Balk rappelle la communication de Christopher Balme à Paris en 2000 sur l'iconographie théâtrale et signale que ce sujet a débouché sur une collaboration entre l'orateur et elle, avec pour objectif de monter une exposition sur l'iconographie théâtrale. Celle-ci a été conçue comme une exposition itinérante qui pourrait être organisée sous les auspices conjoints de la SIBMAS et de la FIRT. Au congrès mondial de la FIRT à Amsterdam, au début de l'été 2002, Christopher Balme et elle-même ont présenté une communication commune portant sur ce concept d'exposition.

La réunion de la Commission des expositions est close.

Committee Meetings

Report of the SIBMAS *International Directory of Performing Arts Collections and Institutions* (IDPAC) – SIBMAS Website Committee

Chair: Paul S. ULRICH, Maria Teresa IOVINELLI

Change in Website Design

A change in Website is necessary:
- formal change in the layout: logo and navigation list should be placed on the right hand side or each page;
- because content on the left hand side of the page, this results in better placement in the result of search engines;
- better optical results on screens with more than one open window: people should know precisely by content on which page they are;
- the look on the left side is the normal reading direction = the place of content.

New Domain Name of SIBMAS

Maria Teresa Iovinelli will apply for a domain name of SIBMAS:
- although this means running costs it would give SIBMAS more visibility. This would make it clear that SIBMAS is an independent organisation – not just a subset within the Website theatrelibrary.org and it would make the evaluation of Web usage statistics much easier;
- www.sibmas.org if possible;
- (side remark: SIBMAS is also the name of a Belgian tank).

Update of ExCom Member List on the Website

The update has to be organised. Maria Teresa Iovinelli will make the changes shortly after the conference.

Archiving Old Proceedings

- the proceedings of the SIBMAS conferences prior to 1988 have still to be placed on the Website. (The proceedings from 1988 to 1994 and those from 1996 which are available are on the Website.) Noëlle Guibert will have copies of the missing proceedings sent to Paul S. Ulrich, who will scan them and convert them to HTML format so they can be placed on the Website. The texts of the Paris conference will be mounted on the Web at a somewhat later time in order to guarantee, that the published proceedings will be purchased;
- all referents should send in their papers for the current conference to Maria Teresa Iovinelli as soon as possible;
- the index of presenters of papers for the past proceedings needs to be brought up to date.

SIBMAS *Directory of Performing Arts Collections*

- the current status of the SIBMAS directory was presented in a paper by Paul S. Ulrich at the conference. He requested that corrections and additions be sent to him as quickly as possible. Changes will be made within a week of his receiving them;
- the number of emails received by Paul S. Ulrich giving corrections for the listings in the directory was seen as a positive result of having the directory on the Web;
- criteria for inclusion of institutions in the directory were discussed. The cultural differences in the various institutions make it difficult to always know whether or not an institution should be included. The general feeling was that in case of doubt an institution should be included until more specific information is available to make a definite decision on inclusion;
- the statistics show that the most used part of the directory is the collection index. In the future even more work will be done to get even small collections included in the directory;
- the question was raised, whether institutions with only minimal performing arts materials would object to having their institution listed in the directory. Paul S. Ulrich responded, that since this is

good PR for them and would also result in more visits to their Websites, that the opposite would seem to be the case;

- since all members of SIBMAS as identified in the SIBMAS Directory, it is important that this information be passed on to Paul S. Ulrich. Joël Huthwohl, as Membership Secretary will send the current membership list to Paul, so that these corrections can also be made in the directory.

Structural Enlarging of the Website

- Claudia Balk suggested enlarging the scope of the SIBMAS Website so that it would become a portal for performing arts on the Internet. In light of all the interesting database projects presented at the conference, it was suggested that these and other databases be presented in a separate directory on the SIBMAS Website. This material does not fit in with the SIBMAS Directory of Performing Arts Collections and will have to be a separate directory. In order for this collection of links to be successful, it is necessary for it to have a name which would be effective for PR purposes. Christelle Cazaux and Paul S. Ulrich will work on creating this directory. Paul S. Ulrich will provide links from the SIBMAS Directory of Performing Arts Collections to the respective databases (for example the French Répertoire and the English Backstage) in order to make them even more visible;

- another addition to the Website should be a listing of all publications (directories, yearbooks, etc.) where SIBMAS is listed. Anyone knowing of such listings should send information to Maria Teresa Iovinelli, who as Secretary General of SIBMAS will be responsible for providing such information to the editors of these publications. This would be a good way of advertising where information about SIBMAS can be found and also serve as a reminder to the members, where information about SIBMAS needs to be kept current;

- discussion: name portal is not universal: Australia, for example, uses term "gateway" instead of "portal".

Thanks

Hanna Hantakova expressed thanks for the coverage of the flooding in Prague on the SIBMAS Website.

New Structure of the FIRT-SIBMAS Bulletin Task Group

- the ExCom of FIRT and SIBMAS have installed a task group to handle the migration of the bulletin to the Web. Members of the task group are: David Whitton, Peter Eversmann, Martin Dreier, Claudia Balk.
- Updates could be made easier in an electronic form, that freezes four times a year (instead of earlier 3 x) the information as a .PDF /print on demand (especially for the SIBMAS librarians) with, or without costs.

SIBMAS Yearbook

At the FIRT Congress in Amsterdam, Erika Fischer Lichte suggested that SIBMAS produce a yearbook as an alternative to the bulletin. The yearbook could include extensive information about the content and activities of libraries, museums, archives, etc. with material on the performing arts. Unclear is how such a project could be financed. Equally unclear is who would supervise such a project.

Report of the Exhibitions Committee

Chair: Claudia BALK

Claudia Balk opened the meeting and welcomed those present. She explained that she wanted to retain the structure which had already proved successful at the first meeting in 2000 in Paris; these are the three main topics – information, organisation and reflection.

Information

The focal point here is the Website, particularly as the bulletin does not currently exist. It had been agreed in Paris to provide information about exhibitions on the SIBMAS Website, and to also make this information attractive with pictures. There has so far been no progress worth mentioning in this respect, due to the fact that Maria Teresa Iovinelli, who had offered her services in this connection, is not receiving the necessary information. The wish was expressed that this situation be significantly improved and that close cooperation be established with the future electronic Bulletin.

Organisation

Halfway between information and organisation is the topic of the publication of the lending conditions on the Website, which had been proposed at the first meeting in Paris. It was decided that this would be desirable. Initial concrete steps should be taken.

The lending conditions of the host country are a topic for the Exhibition Committee at the SIBMAS congresses, and here in Italy as well. Maria Teresa Iovinelli gave a very informative overview of the lending conditions in her country.

From her own experience, Claudia Balk confirmed the relative complexity of the lending of exhibition items from Italy, which is due to the hierarchical structure.

It was proposed that the detailed report by Maria Teresa Iovinelli be placed on the Website so that a start can be made with the abovementioned publication of lending conditions.

Reflection

Claudia Balk pointed out that for financial reasons it would unfortunately not be possible to invite an external guest to every meeting of the Exhibition Committee, to review this main topic, as Prof. Christopher Balme had done in Paris. Perhaps this would again be possible in Barcelona, if the topic of exhibitions were given a broader scope. Claudia Balk suggested that a paper be written about how theatre museums approach curating exhibitions on the life of individuals in the performing arts.

Claudia Balk recalled Christopher Balme's paper in 2000 in Paris on theatre iconography and reported that this topic had given rise to cooperation between the speaker and her, which had as its objective an exhibition on theatre iconography. This exhibition is conceived as a touring exhibition and could be organised under the joint auspices of SIBMAS and FIRT. At FIRT's world congress in Amsterdam in the early summer of 2002 Christopher Balme and she had presented a joint paper on this exhibition concept. Claudia Balk gave a PowerPoint presentation which summarised this paper which focused in detail on the history of media.

The meeting of the Exhibition Committee was thereby brought to a conclusion.

Liste des participants /
List of Participants

Allemagne / Germany

BALK, Claudia	Deutsches Theatermuseum (Munich)
KRAUS, Petra	Deutsches Theatermuseum (Munich)
PARGNER, Birgit	Deutsches Theatermuseum (Munich)
RIST, Simone	Förderverein Deutsch-französischer Kultur.e.V. (Stuttgart)
SCHILD, Margret	Theatermuseum Düsseldorf (Düsseldorf)
ULRICH, Paul S.	(Berlin)

Australie / Australia

DAVIS, Beryl	Queensland Performing Arts Museum (South Bank)
LEONG, Jenny	University of Sydney (Sydney)
STONE, Richard	Performing Arts Special Interest Group of Museums Australia – PASIG (Hughes, ACT)

Autriche / Austria

DEMBSKI, Ulrike	Österreichisches Theatermuseum (Vienne/Vienna)

Belgique / Belgium

BERTH, Alain	Maison du Spectacle La Bellone (Bruxelles/Brussels)
PHILIPPEKIN, Jocelyne	Maison du Spectacle La Bellone (Bruxelles/Brussels)
RADERMECKER, Vincent	Archives & Musée de la Littérature (Bruxelles/Brussels)
RENNENBERG, Roger	SIBMAS Nationaal Centrum Derne (Anvers/Antwerp)
VAN GOETHEM, Jan	La Monnaie – De Munt (Bruxelles/Brussels)

Espagne / Spain

ALVAREZ-MASSÓ, Montserrat	Centro de Documentación de las Artes Escénicas (Barcelone/Barcelona)

PEREZ DE ARENAZA,   Fondacion Juan March (Madrid)
Carmen

VARGAS-ZUNIGA, Dolores   Centro de Documentación de las Artes Escénicas de
Andalucía (Séville/Seville)

États-Unis / United States

ADAIR, Helen   University of Texas (Austin)

MARINI, Francesca   University of California Los Angeles (Los Angeles)

France

BILLARD, Marie-Claude   Maison Jean Vilar (Avignon)

CAZAUX, Christelle   Bibliothèque nationale de France (Paris)

GUIBERT, Noëlle   Bibliothèque nationale de France (Paris)

HUTHWOHL, Joël   Bibliothèque Musée de La Comédie-Française (Paris)

ROTH, Florence   Bibliothèque de la SACD (Paris)

ROUSIER, Claire   Centre national de la Danse (Paris)

SEBILOTTE, Laurent   Centre national de la Danse (Paris)

Italie / Italy

ALOISI, Giovanna   Biblioteca e Racolta Teatrale del Burcardo; SIAE (Rome)

BALLARIN, Valentino   Biblioteca e Racolta Teatrale del Burcardo, SIAE (Rome)

BARTOLUCCI, Olimpia   Pérouse/Perugia

BIANCHI, Stefano   Civico Museo Teatrale Carlo Schmidl (Trieste)

BIANCINI, Laura   Biblioteca Nazionale Centrale (Rome)

BIGGI, Maria Ida   Fondazione Giorgio Cini (Venise/Venice)

BINI, Annalisa   Accademia di S. Cecilia (Rome)

BRUNETTI, Simona   Fondazione Mantova Capitale Europea dello Spettacolo
(Mantoue/Mantua)

BRUSCHI, Fabio   Archivi del Teatro Contemporaneo – Riccione Teatro
(Riccione)

BUCCI, Moreno   Archivio Maggio Musicale Fiorentino (Florence)

CONTE, Alessandro   Società Italiana degli Autori ed Editori – SIAE (Rome)

CRISLEY, Roberto   Accademia di S. Cecilia (Rome)

CUFFARO, Stefania   Biblioteca e Racolta Teatrale del Burcardo; SIAE (Rome)

GALLERANO, Maria   Rome
Rosaria

BRENZONI, Marianna Gemma	Fondazione AIDA (Vérone/Verona)
GRASSO, Bruna	Teatro Comunale (Ferrare/Ferrara)
IOVINELLI, Maria Teresa	Biblioteca e Racolta Teatrale del Burcardo; SIAE (Rome)
LOCATELLI, Stefano	Milan
MARGARITELLI, Angela	Centro di Documentazione del teatro Stabile dell'Umbria (Pérouse/Perugia)
MONTEMAGNO, Daniela	Biblioteca e Racolta Teatrale del Burcardo; SIAE (Rome)
NARDI, Giuliana	Biblioteca e Racolta Teatrale del Burcardo; SIAE (Rome)
PEJA, Laura	Università Cattolica del Sacro Cuore (Milan)
PETRINI, Annamaria	Biblioteca Nazionale Centrale (Rome)
REGGIANI, Francesco	Teatro dell'Opera (Rome)

Japon / Japan

RADBOURNE, Catherine

Pays-Bas / The Netherlands

RODENHUIS, Willem — Universiteit van Amsterdam (Amsterdam)

Portugal

ALVAREZ, José Carlos — Museo Nacional do teatro (Lisbonne/Lisbon)

République Tchèque / Czech Republic

HANTÁKOVÁ, Helena — Czech SIBMAS Centre (Prague)
SVOBODOVÁ, Jarmila — Czech SIBMAS Centre (Prague)

Roumanie / Romania

BURLACU, Anişoara — Institutul de Memorie Culturală (Bucarest/Bucharest)
SAVU, Camelia — Institutul de Memorie Culturală (Bucarest/Bucharest)

Royaume-Uni / United Kingdom

BENTON, Margaret	Theatre Museum (Londres/London)
HUDSON, Claire	Theatre Museum (Londres/London)
JACKSON JOWERS, Sidney	Canterbury
JONES, Alan	Royal Scottish Academy of Music and Drama (Glasgow)
PRITCHARD, Jane	Rambert Dance Company (Londres/London)

RUNCIMAN, Rosy	Cameron Mackintosh Ltd. (Londres/London)
RUSSELL, Barry	Oxford Brookes University (Oxford)
SAKHNOVSKAIA, Anastassia	Oxford Brookes University (Oxford)

Russie / Russia

| KOLGANOVA, Ida | Russian State Art Library (Moscou/Moscow) |
| VAGANOVA, Inna | Russian State Art Library (Moscou/Moscow) |

Serbie /Serbia

| RADULOVIĆ, Ksenija | Museum of Theatre Art (Belgrade) |

Slovénie / Slovenia

| SLIVNIK, Francka | Slovenski Gledališki Muzej (Ljubljana) |

Notices biographiques / Biographical Notes

Adair, Helen received her Master of Library and Information Science degree from the Graduate School of Library and Information Science at The University of Texas at Austin in 1998. Prior to her appointment as Associate Curator in 2004, she was Processing Archivist for the theater collections at the Harry Ransom Center from 1999 to 2001 and was appointed Performing Arts Librarian in 2001.

Alvarez, José Carlos est directeur du Musée du Théâtre de Lisbonne.

Bannister, Mark is Emeritus Professor of French at Oxford Brookes University. He specialises in the ideological history of the French 17th century and has written widely on the movement of ideas as manifested in prose fiction, popular literature and philosophy, moral treatises, panegyrics and the theatre. From 2003 to 2009 he was Director of the CÉSAR Project.

Balk, Claudia. Studies of Theatre Research, German Literature and History of Art. Since 1983, working in "Deutsches Theatermuseum" in Munich, responsible for the collection of photographs. 1993-2002 Vice-Director of "Deutsches Theatermuseum". Numerous exhibitions and catalogues, for example: *Theaterfotografie*, 1989; *Theatergöttinnen. Inszenierte Weiblichkeit. Clara Ziegler, Sarah Bernhardt, Eleonora Duse*, 1994; (Together with Brygida Ochaim) *Varieté-Tänzerinnen um 1900. Vom Sinnenrausch zur Tanzmoderne*, 1998. From 2000 to 2004, president of SIBMAS.

Bert, Alain est informaticien à la Maison du Spectacle La Bellone (Bruxelles) depuis 1996.

Biggi, Maria Ida enseigne l'Histoire du Spectacle à l'Université Ca'Foscari de Venise et est directrice du Centre d'études pour la recherche documentaire sur le théâtre et le mélodrame européen de la Fondation Giorgio Cini à Venise.

Billard, Marie-Claude a été Conservateur en chef des bibliothèques, chargée du Centre de documentation théâtre cinéma de la bibliothèque interuniversitaire de l'Université Lyon II de 1972 à 1986 et Conservateur de la Maison Jean Vilar à Avignon (Bibliothèque nationale de France, Département des Arts du spectacle) de 1986 à 2010.

Brunetti, Simona is a performing arts lecturer at the University of Verona (Italy), where she teaches Storia del teatro e dello spettacolo. Her main field of research includes Italian stage direction, 19th century Italian and French theatre, and Renaissance and Baroque spectacular activities. After being part of the Herla Project research team of the "Umberto Artioli" Mantova Capitale Europea dello Spettacolo Foundation for many years, since 2009 she has been coordinating it under the scientific direction of Cristina Grazioli, performing arts senior lecturer at the University of Padua (Italy).

Bucci, Moreno. Curator of the Archivio Storico of the Maggio Musicale Fiorentino, the art historian Moreno Bucci graduated from the Università di Firenze. He has published and curated exhibitions in Italy and abroad on the relations between painting and stage design in 20th century Italy, and in particular the work for the stage of Giorgio De Chirico, Gino Carlo Sensani, Mario Sironi, Galileo Chini, and Felice Casorati. He has also written on 19th century Tuscan painting and about contemporary art, the latter most recently in the catalogue Lorenzo Bonechi Pittore di Luce (2005). In 2008 and in 2010, he published the inventory of the correspondence of 1928-1952 of the Maggio Musicale Fiorentino and of the drawings of 1933-1943.

Burlacu, Anişoara, Institut de Mémoire culturelle (Bucarest – Roumanie).

Cazaux, Christelle est archiviste paléographe et docteur en musicologie. Conservateur à la Bibliothèque nationale de France jusqu'en 2008, elle coordonne, de 2001 à 2005, la collecte des fonds de programmes et de presse au Département des arts du spectacle ainsi que la mise en œuvre de la base *Répertoire des arts du spectacle*. Auteur d'un ouvrage et de plusieurs articles sur l'histoire de la musique du Moyen Âge et de la Renaissance, elle est, depuis 2008, maître de conférences à l'Université de Poitiers, responsable du Département de musicologie et chercheur au Centre d'études supérieures de civilisation médiévale.

Guibert, Noëlle a dirigé la bibliothèque-musée de la Comédie-Française puis le département des Arts du spectacle à la Bibliothèque nationale de France jusqu'en 2008, auteur de travaux sur l'iconographie théâtrale, le décor et le costume ; commissaire des expositions sur le Théâtre de l'Odéon, la Comédie-Française, le Vieux-Colombier, le théâtre de l'Athénée, les costumes de scène, la photographie de spectacle, et sur les décorateurs Jean Hugo, Lucien Coutaud, André Barsacq, Jacques Polieri, André Acquart, ainsi que sur le Baron Taylor, Sarah Bernhardt... Elle a été présidente de la Société internationale des bibliothèques et musées des Arts du spectacle de 1996 à 2000.

Hudson, Claire is Head of Collections Management at the Theatre Museum in London, where she has worked since 1987. Her role is to coordinate the intellectual control of the museum's very diverse collections of objects, archives and library materials, and to provide public access services relating to them. She has been involved with SIBMAS throughout her period at the Theatre Museum, and has served on the Executive Committee since 1996, taking on the role of Secretary General between 2000 and 2002.

Iovinelli, Maria Teresa is librarian at the Biblioteca e Raccolta Teatrale del Burcardo (now "Biblioteca Teatrale SIAE" and "Museo Teatrale SIAE del Burcardo") since 1983, she was appointed Head Librarian and Museum Curator in 1999. In addition to management and general organisation, she is directly involved in the theatre iconography, digital collections and new acquisitions departments. Vice-president (1996-2000) and General Secretary (2002-2007) of SIBMAS.

Kolganova, Ada is the Director of the Russian State Art Library. She is a specialist in bibliology, bibliography, library history, Russian literature and theatre. For many years she worked in the Russian State Library as the Head of the scientific sector, since 1991 she works in the Russian State Art Library. She is the long-term President of the Art and Museum Libraries Section of the Russian Library Association. She is an author of three books, editor of many collections of scientific papers, author of more than 250 articles.

Kraus, Petra, M.A., is an art historian working as the exhibition manager for the German Theatre Museum in Munich since 2001.

Leclercq, Nicole est attachée scientifique, assistante aux Archives & Musée de la Littérature et responsable de la section Théâtre. Elle est en outre présidente du Centre belge de la SIBMAS, vice-présidente du Comité exécutif international, secrétaire générale du Centre belge de l'Institut international du théâtre IIT et présidente du Comité international de la communication de l'IIT. Responsable de la publication des actes de plusieurs colloques et congrès, elle est aussi éditrice de la série *Le Monde du théâtre* (P.I.E. Peter Lang).

Lewenhaupt, Inga, Ph.D, was the Museum Director at the Drottningholm Theatre Museum /Sveriges Teatermuseum[1] from 1999 to 2007 after a long career as an assistant professor of Theatre Science and Musicology at the Stockholm University and as a professor of theatre, opera and dance history at The University College of Opera in Stockholm. She is now doing research concerning early acting practice.

Philippekin, Jocelyne, documentaliste-bibliothécaire, est responsable du Centre d'information et de documentation Théâtre de la Maison du Spectacle La Bellone depuis sa fondation en 1983. Elle a été trésorière du Centre SIBMAS Communauté française-Belgique de 1991 à 2000.

Radermecker, Vincent est diplômé de l'Institut des Arts de Diffusion (section théâtre) et de la Faculté de Philosophie et Lettres de l'Université catholique de Louvain-la-Neuve (Département histoire). Il a travaillé comme comédien sous la direction d'Otomar Krejča et de Gérard Lefur. Un temps spécialiste de l'histoire économique et sociale en région bruxelloise, il est actuellement archiviste et scientifique aux Archives & Musée de la Littérature (Bruxelles) où il est notamment en charge de l'édition critique de l'œuvre complète de Jean Louvet.

Radulović, Ksenija. Born in Belgrade in 1969 and graduated from the Faculty of Drama Arts, Department of Dramaturgy (Belgrade) with MA degree and is now finishing her doctoral thesis. Since 2001, she has been the Director of The Museum of Theatre Art of Serbia; the Editor in Chief of *Teatron* (theatre quarterly), and won the Sterija Award for criticism (2000). She has published a great number of essays and articles in most representative Yugoslav and Serbian news and magazines and is the author of *The step ahead of*, a book about contemporary directing (the main subject is leading ex-Yu and Serbian director, Dejan Mijac). Since 2010, she has been the Art Director and Selector of Sterijino pozorje, the leading theatre festival in Serbia.

Rodenhuis, Willem is a theatre historian, active as the subject librarian for the performing arts at the Library of the University of Amsterdam. Moreover he is the library's coordinator of the cluster Geschiedenis, Kunsten en Cultuur (History, Arts and Culture). 1996-2000 he served two terms as Secretary general of SIBMAS.

Sakhnovskaia, Anastassia, CÉSAR Project (United Kingdom).

Savu, Camelia, Institut de Mémoire culturelle (Bucarest – Roumanie).

---

[1] From 1st January, 2010, the Sveriges Teatermuseum and the Music Collections belong to the Swedish government: www.smus.se.

Schild, Margret has her diploma in Documentarianship in 1986. Head of the Libraries of the Theatre Museum and the Film Museum Düsseldorf since 1993; 1995 founding member of the AKMB (treasurer 1995-1999, member of the editorial board of the journal *AKMB-news*); projects and publications in the field of information management in art and museum libraries, cataloguing, indexing and presentation of information concerning cultural heritage.

Stone, Richard, since retiring from the National Library of Australia where he worked for many years, is a consultant in Australian performing arts history and documentation. He has been an Executive member of SIBMAS.

Ulrich, Paul S. is a retired librarian, formerly at the Zentral- und Landesbibliothek in Berlin. Active in SIBMAS since 1988 (1988-2009 editor of SIBMAS International Directory of Performing Arts Collections), he is President of the Gesellschaft für Theatergeschichte; treasurer of and publication editor for *Thalia Germanica*. Extensive publications on German-language theatre in 19th century and on reference topics. Major publications: *Biographical Index for Theatre, Dance and Music* (2 Vol. Berlin 1996, also bi-lingual as CD-ROM) and *Das Jahr 1848. Kultur in Berlin im Spiegel der Vossischen Zeitung* (2 Vol. Berlin 2010, with Lothar Schirmer).

Van Goethem, Jan is the Archivist and Head of Collections of the Théâtre royal de la Monnaie (Brussel). He holds Masters Degrees in both Art History (Musicology) and Information Sciences. He is the author of several articles on Flemish music and on the digitalization of archives.